Ruby—

My Precious Gem!

THE
RUBY MURRAY STORY

A Biography about the 'Heartbeat' Girl with the 'Softly, Softly' Voice!

The Ultimate Truth as Told by Her Ex-Husband

Bernie Burgess
(of The Jones Boys)

In Collaboration With

Frank Bowles
(Author of The Toni Dalli Story)

The Derwent Press
Derbyshire, England

www.derwentpress.com

Ruby—My Precious Gem
By
Bernie Burgess & Frank Bowles

All Rights Reserved.

Copyright 2006 Bernie Burgess & Frank Bowles

All rights reserved. No part of this book may be reproduced, stored in a retrieval system, or transmitted, in any form or by any means, electronic, mechanical, photocopying, recording and/or otherwise without the prior permission of the authors or publishers.

ISBN 1-84667-014-4

Cover design and book design by:
Pam Marin-Kingsley
www.far-angel.com

Published in 2006 by
The Derwent Press
Derbyshire, England
www.derwentpress.com

RUBY—My Precious Gem!

Acknowledgements

I would very much like to thank a number of people without whose help this book could not have been written, firstly:

Frank Bowles. I met Frank when I first came to Spain. Before he left England, a number of years ago, he was neighbour to a pianist and friend of Ruby's and mine, Geoff Sanders. He came to Spain to retire but he has never stopped working. He is editor of the Costa Del Sol Golf News. Recently he wrote a biography of Toni Dalli, an artiste of Italian origin who went to England in the early part of World War II and worked in the coal mines. He eventually started a career as a singer around the clubs. Later he went to the States and then, at the suggestion of Jimmy Tarbuck, he opened an Italian Restaurant in Spain (Marbella area) and it soon blossomed into a very successful venue with Toni himself doing the cabaret. I approached Frank when I was tentatively considering writing this book and his professionalism has guided me all the way. Thank you, Frank.

David Frankish. He was fan club secretary to the Ruby Murray fan club for many, many years. David has been a very close friend to me through the years, including after Ruby passed away, and has supplied me with a constant stream of data. Thank you, David.

Timothy Burleson. I was lucky enough to accidentally discover that a young man living on the west coast of America had set up a website for Ruby, namely—www.rubymurray.org. That young man is Timothy Burleson who is from a younger generation to Ruby. His mother was an ardent fan of Ruby's and was constantly playing her records so 'Timmer', as he is known on the website, was raised on Ruby's music. He searched the internet for data on Ruby and when he couldn't find any he decided to create a website for her. From a small beginning the website has really taken off, now it's one of the most interesting show business websites on the net. For your dedication and generosity, thank you 'Timmer'.

RUBY—My Precious Gem!

Through the website I was fortunate enough to make a number of very good friends. They are all fanatical Ruby Murray fans, even 50 years after her world record. Amongst them: Sandy, John K, the two other Johns, Graham, Martin, Don. Thank you, Amigos.

I cannot go through all the names on the website but I will single out one or two for special praise.

Gerald Lawrence. I have spent many very happy hours with Gerald, reminiscing about Ruby's career and we have delved through a mountain of photographs, press cuttings and memorabilia. He has been wonderful to me and has given his expertise unstintingly. He and his wife Rosemary have provided me with generous hospitality and I am extremely grateful to them both. I look forward to repaying their hospitality when they come to Spain. I have never come across anyone who is keener about Ruby and the website than Gerald and he has been an absolute genius with his technical 'know-how'. For all of that, thank you Gerald (and Rosemary)

Brian Henson. I refer to this 'young man' as the encyclopaedia of music and records. Both he and Gerald between them compiled the list of titles for the 4 C.D. boxed set, —Ruby Murray Anthology—A Golden Anniversary Release. Fortunately E.M.I. accepted their list and I must compliment them on the job that they did. Brian is an amazing wealth of musical knowledge from which I have benefited quite frequently. Thank you, Brian.

And thank you—the readers—for choosing to read this book.

Bernie Burgess & Frank Bowles

Contents

	Page
Prologue	1
Foreword – Joan Regan	5
Foreword – Val Doonican	7
Chapter 1 – 'Fly Me to the Moon'	11
Chapter 2 – 'The Green Green Grass of Home'	15
Chapter 3 – 'Now is the Hour'	24
Chapter 4 – 'There's No Business Like Show Business'	32
Chapter 5 – 'You're a Star'	43
Chapter 6 – 'Love is Just Around the Corner'	52
Chapter 7 – 'You always Hurt the One You Love'	65
Chapter 8 – 'Home, Sweet Home'	77
Chapter 9 – 'Chicago! Chicago!'	81
Chapter 10 – 'Yes Sir! That's my Baby!'	87
Chapter 11 – 'Nice Work if You Can Get It!'	101
Chapter 12 – 'Heigh-Ho, Heigh-Ho, It's Off to Work We Go!'	107
Chapter 13 – 'King of the Jungle!'	115
Chapter 14 – 'Around the World'	124
Chapter 15 – 'My Melancholy Baby!'	134
Chapter 16 – 'Little White Lies!'	142
Chapter 17 – 'Summer Holiday'	146
Chapter 18 – 'That's Entertainment'	150
Chapter 19 – 'One Day at a Time'	155
Chapter 20 – 'Doctor I'm in Trouble'	162
Chapter 21 – 'After You're Gone!'	167
Chapter 22 – 'The Second Time Around!'	176
Chapter 23 – 'Over the Sea to Skye'	183
Chapter 24 – 'Every Time We Say Goodbye'	192
Chapter 25 – 'PS – I Love You'	202
Chapter 26 – 'I Remember You!'	208
Author's Footnote	227
Index of Names	229

RUBY—My Precious Gem!

PROLOGUE

So much has been written over the years about the world record breaking, music history-making singing star RUBY MURRAY and yet nobody has, as yet, come anywhere near the true story.

There have been many attempts made over the years, to tell that story included in book form, in newspaper articles, on stage and radio but all were very wide of the mark. Many differing articles have been written about her, most of which have been so far removed from reality that they bear no resemblance to the real truth!

I would like to put the record straight once and for all. I intend to tell the life story and achievements of a show business personality who was so totally different to all other fellow professionals. She was unique in so many ways. I will tell it how it really was, because nobody could have been closer to her than me. Why? Because I'm very proud to say—Ruby was my wife!

I must emphasise right away, for the sake of her multitude of fans and admirers, that whatever I say in this book it is written WITH LOVE IN MY HEART AND IN NO WAY MEANT TO SLIGHT RUBY, HER NAME OR HER MEMORY. There are several revelations, which could be disturbing to some of her very staunch fans, and some that they might consider being too delicate and unnecessary, but there are genuine reasons for doing so. All that I ask of the fans is that they read it through to the very end. I hasten to add that I dearly loved her and still do to this very day.

Without doubt, Ruby deserved to have a better deal from life, from her family and most of those around her, than she ever experienced. Believe me, that is not the way Ruby would have put it. She could see no wrong in anyone, even when she was on the receiving end of their wrongdoing she would always find an excuse for their behaviour.

Ruby was a gem in every sense of the word. Quite a few writers got that part right about her but I'd like to embellish that statement further by say-

RUBY—My Precious Gem!

ing – she was not just a gem, she was a very precious gem, one that is not likely to be found in the world of entertainment ever again. Her life was a topsy-turvy, roller-coaster ride through happiness and heartbreak, success and failure, laughter and tears, comedy and tragedy. Yet through it all, her achievements were unsurpassed and at the same time she was able to maintain her wonderful sense of humour.

She made musical history in the recording industry by becoming a world record holder. In March 1955, she had no less than five hit singles in the Top Twenty at one and the same time. A quarter of all singles being sold in that period were Ruby's, a world record that has never been beaten by anyone before or since, and all of this before she was 21 years old.

In just about every way, Ruby was refreshingly different to other singing stars in the world of entertainment. She never wanted to be a star, never craved for stardom. All she ever wanted to do was sing and be accepted by her fellow professionals for her God-given ability. She was a perfectly natural person with no temperament and no airs of superiority. She never 'upstaged' anyone in her entire career. There was nothing false about Ruby and no affectation. She was a very gentle lady – a true rarity in show business.

Her singing voice was very different too. It was so very distinctive, instantly recognizable, with a huskiness quite uniquely her own. The 'Velvet Fog' voice description suited Ruby just as much as that great American singer/songwriter Mel Torme. There was a hesitancy that made her fans wonder whether or not she would be able to get through the song in question. Her audiences would worry for her, and this factor became part of her charisma. They would sit on the edge of their seats, as I always did, willing her to make it!

This also applied to her speaking voice, which was soft, as though it was wrapped up in velvet. It gave her a quality that appealed to everyone. Ruby had charm, oodles of it.

Another unique thing about Ruby was her walk. Her entrance from the 'wings' to the centre of stage was fraught with fear. She lived in constant terror of falling over and making a fool of herself in front of the public. Consequently, she appeared to be walking on eggs as she made her way across the stage. Finale walk-downs, especially if it involved descending a staircase, were an absolute nightmare to her.

I can remember an incident that happened many years ago when she was playing the Bristol Hippodrome, a huge theatre with a massive auditorium, which held close to 3000 people. The gallery staircase wound its way down to the pavement where the exit door was adjacent to the star's dressing room window. Ruby was removing her make-up and we were chatting away together when we became aware of footsteps gingerly making their way down the staircase. It sounded to us like two elderly ladies, the last ones out. As they passed the window we heard them talking to one another. One asked: "What do you think of Ruby Murray?" "Oh! I think she's lovely" came the reply "with such a beautiful singing voice. But when she talks I feel like going….ahemmm! ahemmm!" (As if to clear the throat.)

Ruby told that tale all over the world in later years. There are so many wonderful stories about Ruby, her voice and her kindness. Yours truly and my co-author Frank Bowles will reveal them all later in The True Ruby Murray Story.

BERNIE BURGESS
Alicante, Spain
2005

RUBY—My Precious Gem!

FOREWORD BY JOAN REGAN

My very good friend Ruby Murray and I had quite a lot in common.

Ruby was born in Ireland and we both had Irish parents. We were both brought up in a musical family background. When I first met Ruby I immediately felt an affinity to her. We both had success in the television series 'Quite Contrary.' Ruby replaced me when I left to tour the theatre circuit in the UK. We both had hit records following our TV appearances and Keith Devon was also our agent.

I was so thrilled when Ruby became an instant star with her natural charm and sincerity. It came right out of that television screen and what a voice too!

From the word 'go' Ruby and I became close friends. I looked out for her because she always seemed so vulnerable. I felt like I wanted to wrap her up and keep her safe. I continued to feel like that about her for many years.

Her success, as we all know, was phenomenal! She always had that loveable quality, unspoilt and quite funny. Ruby had a wonderful presence when talking to an audience. Her Irish charm was always evident.

It was so much fun when we worked together. We would catch up on all the ordinary things in our lives such as our families and things that happened outside show business. We soon picked up again following a long time apart and could we chat!

RUBY—My Precious Gem!

Ruby was one of those very dear souls with so much to offer as a human being. The Ruby I knew and loved made my world a better place to be. She will always be an important part of my fond memories. Thank you Ruby for being you.

My love always,

Joan Regan.

Orpington, Kent
October 2004

Joan's comments to Bernie Burgess, enclosing her foreword, were as follows:

I have enclosed my letter regarding Ruby. I am honoured that you asked me to put my thoughts on paper. I am not a great letter writer but this was a 'must' for me.

I am so happy that Ruby was with you so much towards the end of her life. I know she was in good hands and you did everything to make her happy during her last few days. Please let me have a copy of your book when it comes out. At least you will do her justice and she will now be able to rest in peace. I will always have a special place in my heart for dear Ruby.

FOREWORD
BY VAL DOONICAN

Hi Bernie,

I've just written the few paragraphs below and hope they will be of help. What an amazing piece of timing! Last night I had a call from Ruby's old friend Father Caden. We've been pals since the early fifties and I had the pleasure of introducing him to Ruby for whom he had a great affection. He's now in his eighties and retired although still living in his parish of Sedgefield (Tony Blair's constituency.) They are good mates and he had the experience of having a private lunch with Blair and Bush when they visited his parish.

He reminded me that when I first rang asking him to keep an eye on Ruby, I said something like: "She's a really lovely unspoiled girl, Father, so don't let her wander about on her own without having a label on her." I have no memory of saying that but a priest wouldn't lie... I'm told! By the way, a short while ago Father John was staying with us, having baptised one of our grandchildren. He was rambling on late into the night about all the interesting people he'd met and I encouraged him to write it all down. He did in fact publish a little book some time later. There's a nice bit on Ruby with a photograph of them both!

Anyway, here goes!

It was back in the early fifties, while touring the British Music Hall circuit, as a member of an Irish vocal quartet that I first met Ruby Murray. She was, at that time, a hugely successful recording star topping the bill at major theatres week after week. If my memory serves me right, that first meeting was at the Alhambra Theatre, Bradford when her supporting artists included comedian Jimmy Wheeler, trumpet player Eddie Calvert and ourselves The Four Ramblers.

RUBY—My Precious Gem!

Night after night Ruby would just wander out and stand in the wings backstage, watching the bits of the action on stage and chatting to all of us. Maybe it was because we shared an Irish upbringing that there was so much to talk about. By the end of that first week we'd become friends. Ruby's mother travelled with her as a kind of companion and chaperone on a couple of occasions inviting me into her dressing room for a cup of tea. However, as is the nature of our profession, the following week we went our separate ways but did keep in touch for many years

Coincidentally, I was to meet my future wife a few years later. Lynnette Rae was a well established singing star and it so happened that her next engagement was an eight week pantomime season at the Empire Theatre Liverpool. The subject was Robin Hood, Lynn playing the title part as Principal Boy and Ruby Murray playing her Maid Marion. They got along really well and I know that Ruby was happy to have Lynn's friendship and support as she took on this new role. They even arranged to share their theatrical 'digs' for that very successful season.

Lynn and myself have now been married for over forty years but we still recall dear Ruby with great affection. We both feel that somehow she was never quite at ease with the pressures and media attention that comes with the kind of stardom that suddenly descended on a quite timid and truly nice young girl.

Val Doonican

Bernie Burgess & Frank Bowles

RUBY—My Precious Gem!

CHAPTER ONE
♪ 'Fly Me To The Moon' ♪

All of us have a dream, a dream that will one day make us deliriously happy. For some it's the thought of winning the lottery and having riches galore. Riches that will enable us to live in luxury for the rest of our lives, to travel the world and to be able to buy whatever we want whenever we want it ... but think! Will these riches put paid to all of our worries and fears? Will it buy health? Will it buy happiness?

One could console oneself with the thought that it must be better to be miserable with wealth and comfort than to be miserable without it! However, beware!

Others have a different dream, a dream of becoming a star, a star on television, a star in films, or a RECORDING star. To the majority of people it appears to be a glamorous world, an enviable life full of success and adulation. From the moment you become a star, everybody adores you and clamours for your autograph or signed photograph. Everybody wants to know you, to be seen alongside you, to be photographed with you. You are their idol, they worship you, but remember, dreams do not always turn out the way you planned them. Not all of them have happy endings.

I can speak from experience, not from personal experience but from living with a delightful human being who, as they say, 'had it all'. The success, the fame, the trophies, the adoration, the wealth .. well .. er .. not quite all the wealth that her fame justly deserved, but nonetheless a comfort zone to be envied.

RUBY—My Precious Gem!

Tragically, and all too soon, I was compelled to stand by and watch helplessly as her life, and consequently our marriage, started to crumble and I found myself powerless to help as that gentle, delicate, vulnerable and very loveable someone gradually became dependent and addicted to alcohol. Watching her slowly and irretrievably spiralling out of control is an experience that no-one should have to endure and it certainly left me with irremovable scars that I carry with me to this day.

So you want to become a star! Well, before you try to take that leap into the unknown, let me reveal just a few of the pitfalls that will lie before you and to warn you to avoid them, at all costs. First and foremost, you need someone with vast experience to give you professional advice, someone you can trust (not many of them around) and someone who can foresee all the 'moves' ahead. That person should always be there to give you advice and words of wisdom concerning financial dealings and guidance on contractual and professional matters. He, or she, should have a wealth of 'know how' that will go towards building your career and your future. It is widely accepted that the world of show business is riddled with parasites and hangers-on who are all too eager to grab any opportunity to fleece you along the road to stardom. Unless you have that experienced and knowledgeable person to assist you then watch out, you are entering a minefield, a veritable nightmare.

Many readers of this book will have personal remembrances of Ruby Murray. She was the singing sensation who charmed millions of television viewers and record enthusiasts with her 'girl next door' appeal and her unmistakable husky voice. Her recording success reigned supreme in the music world throughout the 50s and 60s. She continued her career through the 70s, 80s and 90s whilst she was desperately wrestling with her addiction to a drinking problem.

Let me tell you the real story of her life and career. I am extremely proud of the fact that she was my wife. I loved her right from the early days of getting to know her and still love her deeply and cherish all the abundant memories, even now.

She had so many endearing qualities. She never lost the 'common touch' and was honest and generous to a fault. Her sense of humour was legendary and her ability for comedy and mimicry amazed everyone who was fortunate enough to come into contact with it. Despite everything that she had to endure she was capable of providing laughter for all around her. If she had not had her self confidence so crushingly destroyed in her early childhood, she could have competed with some of the comedy greats that were around at that time, like the great female comedy star Lucille Ball. Believe me, she really was that good. It is so sad that only myself along with a handful of close friends and relatives were fortunate enough to see her when she was in full flow.

Fame and fortune meant very little to Ruby. She never sought after it and spent most of her time trying to come to terms with the consequences of finding it thrust upon her. Recording studios and television cameras terrified her. For several days before a television appearance, or a recording session, she would build up with fear and fill with trepidation about the ordeal that she was about to be confronted with. Ruby paid a terrible price for her stardom. The stresses and strains that she had to endure, both inside and outside of the profession, gradually became all too much for her and she succumbed and sought the kind of relief that eventually would bring about her demise.

Her immediate family could, and should, have been kinder to her but in truth they, like so many others around her, abused her unashamedly. She became the goose who laid the golden eggs and as soon as they were laid they were whisked away! Despite all of this, she didn't ever stop loving her family, very dearly, and quite naturally could see no wrong in anything that they did and, believe me, they were guilty of plenty. That also applied to some of her friends and the business people who were close to her and who had an influence, of one kind or another, on her life and career. Her business acumen was virtually nil so consequently she relied and trusted others to take care of her career and her finances. From the outset, and over a period of many years, this was where her trust was so ruthlessly abused. Ruby became easy prey for quite a few unscrupulous people who were all too willing to take advantage of this beautiful young Irish colleen from the Emerald Isle, this gentle lady.

Later in her life she began to realize some of the mistakes that she had made but by then it was far too late. Irretrievable damage had already been done. In possibly her last heartbreaking and deeply moving appearance in a television documentary, a very ailing and fragile Ruby continued to

RUBY—My Precious Gem!

speak only about the good times in her life and tended to gloss over all the bad ones. In a trembling voice, she spoke of the fact that she had experienced many 'ups' and 'downs' in her life. What a great shame that it was never in balance!

When you have read this story, you must decide whether or not you wish to follow the same path that Ruby trod. It's a very human story, one that contains everything about becoming a star. Yes, Ruby became a star, a big, bright, shining star, yet she never ever yearned to become one. She never dreamt that stardom would come her way. Now I often wonder whether she would have been far happier touring around her native Ireland, without the stresses and strains, the heavy responsibilities, the family feuding, the 'conmen', the ruthless business people and all that went together to form part of her success, her fame and the fortune that she SHOULD have had. In a way it was all thrust upon her, yet she had a very simple outlook on life, she just wanted to sing. That is all, just sing. Her enjoyment came from singing, whether it be at home with her family, or in the bath. Music could deeply move Ruby. Little did she realise that one day she would be standing on the stage of the world famous London Palladium. When that incredible moment arrived she turned to her mother, who had accompanied her, and said: "I don't really want to be here Mummy, I'd rather be back home in Ireland."

In contrast to most singers in show business, Ruby didn't rise from relative obscurity to overnight stardom without first having served a long and extremely worthwhile apprenticeship. From the age of just three years old, her father would place her on a table or, more often than not, on a bar top to get her to sing to his friends.

"Show them how you can sing Ruby" was always his way of displaying his daughter to the world. It was just as though she was a little doll, one that could be taken out of its box, wound up and placed before a crowd of people to perform. Once the performance came to an end, the very fragile doll would be promptly returned to her box, before the applause had faded. From the age of five years old, the table, or bar top, had become a stage, where eventually, after the appreciative applause, there would be some small but gradually increasing amounts of financial reward, but not before the little doll had been put back into her box!

CHAPTER 2
The Family Tree
♪ 'The Green, Green Grass of Home' ♪

The personal characteristics of each of the family members were vividly described to me by Ruby herself, her close personal friends and other family members, both before we were married and throughout the 17 years of our married life. From the moment I became personally connected to the family I became fully aware of how closely each description fitted. During frequent in depth conversations between Ruby and myself, she revealed countless personal stories, many of which were detrimental, yet her love for her family remained unshakeable.

Ruby was born at 84 Moltick Street in Belfast, the capital city of Northern Ireland, on March 29th 1935. She was christened Ruby Florence Campbell Murray, the youngest of four children, being preceded by brother Jack and sisters Patsy and Lilian.

At the time of going to press, Lilian is the only surviving member of the family and is hopefully still residing in Florida. Despite extensive enquiries across the Atlantic, I have been unable to establish whether she is still alive. A shadow hangs over her healthwise, due to the fact that, last heard of, she was desperately struggling with her alcohol addiction, an illness which she suffered from for many years.

Quite recently, a member of the family, who lives in the U.S.A., contacted me via the internet when she came across the Ruby Murray website –www.rubymurray.org. Her name is Tina Pollock. She is a member of Ruby's mother's family, the Connellys, and is a cousin to Ruby. Early exchanges of e-mails with Tina established that quote: "The notorious family feuding is still continuing even now. It's hereditary."

RUBY—My Precious Gem!

Ruby's father was Daniel Murray.

He was known around the bars in Belfast as 'Big Dan'. Born on Sixth Street, just off the Shankill Road in the Orange district of Belfast. His parents originated from Ayrshire in Scotland. 'Big Dan' had four brothers and a sister. During a period of enquiry about her family tree, Ruby unearthed a fascinating story in connection with two of the brothers, John and Billy. Both emigrated to Canada and, according to reports, one of the brothers, John Murray, was actually shot whilst rum running across the Canadian-American border. Before he emigrated, Billy Murray married three times in Ireland. His first wife produced for him 10 children before she died. After her death, Billy married her sister and she also presented him with 10 children before she too died. He wedded wife number three and became a father four more times before becoming a widower for a third time! He eventually went off to Canada to join his brother and got married yet again, this time to an Indian Squaw. He later became an alcoholic.

I was interested to learn from Ruby that 'Big Dan' ran away from home at the age of 16 and borrowed an older friend's identity card to join the army. My own father had done a similar thing when he was only 15, in 1920.

Dan spent 12 years in the Royal Inniskilling Fusiliers and his first posting took him to India. On returning to his native Belfast, he met and married Winifred (Winnie) Connolly and the couple, with their first child, Jack, decided to join Dan's brothers and set sail for Canada. Winnie also had brothers and sisters who had emigrated to the land of the maple leaf. During their stay in Canada, the Murray family increased in numbers, two daughters were born Patsy and Lilian. Dan and Winnie stayed in Canada for a few years before returning to Belfast, apparently under some kind of a cloud (Ruby never did reveal the real reason for their hurried departure from Canada.) Unbelievably they left behind one of the young daughters, Lilian, to be looked after by one of Winnie's sisters, who was also called (Aunt) Lilian. Baby Lilian remained in Canada for most of her life but had a brief spell in England around 1958 but last heard of she was living in Florida. Her short stay in England became hugely problematic for Ruby, the nature of which will be revealed in a later chapter. Ruby herself was well aware that during his life 'Big Dan' developed two serious problems—gambling and drinking, the latter was a major cause of his death. He was eventually diagnosed as having cirrhosis of the liver, which brought about yellow jaundice. At the time he was admitted to the Victoria Hospital in Belfast. Ruby and I flew over to Ireland to see him. He did recover for a while, but some time later he started to vomit blood, due to a burst artery which bled into his stomach and he was rushed to hospital. Despite desperate attempts to repair the artery, the surgeon found that it was impossible due to the excess consumption of alcohol and as a result he died on the operating table.

Ruby's mother was Winnie.

Her maiden name was Connolly and it was widely known that the family nicknamed themselves 'The Fighting Connollys.' I was later to learn, through personal experience, that never a truer word was ever spoken. Her father was Billy Connolly (no relation, as far as I know, to the television star) and her mother was Annie Rooney. They had a family of 12 children but only six survived into adulthood due to the scourge of TB (tuberculosis.) Winnie's eldest sister Lilian, (the sister who took charge of baby Lilian) went into service in Canada and was later joined by brother Sam and another sister, Margaret, known as 'Meg'. The whole family lived in fear of 'Meg.' Her wrath had to be experienced to be believed.

Ruby's brother was Jack.

Ruby was very proud of him. Normally a very quietly spoken man, I got on very well with Jack. He was born in 1929. He joined the RAF when of service age but decided that he wanted to come out of the service when Ruby became a star name. At that time it was possible for a serviceman to be able to buy himself out of the service. Ruby related the whole story to me and, as usual, her generosity came to the fore, when he wanted to terminate his service, she dispatched the appropriate sum of money to obtain his release. She also bought him a general grocery shop retail business, stocked it for him and bought him a car. Unfortunately, Jack didn't take too well to the life of a grocer and unbelievably, and much to Ruby's dismay, he decided to return to the RAF, taking his car with him but leaving the grocery shop business in the hands of 'Big Dan'.

Whilst in 'civvy' street, Jack met and married a Belfast girl whose name was also Ruby. Because she was marrying into the Murray family, she too

RUBY—My Precious Gem!

became Ruby Murray but was to be nicknamed 'Wee' Ruby by the family to avoid confusion. 'Wee' Ruby and husband Jack had two sons, Thomas and Jack Junior. He too was nicknamed 'Wee' Jack, separating him from his father Jack! Both of the boys joined the police force in London in later life.

When Dan became the new owner of the grocery shop, a business that he knew absolutely nothing about, his two major problems of drinking and gambling began to eat into the business in a big way. Profits soon evaporated and debts began to mount, causing the shop to run into serious problems. Adding to the financial debts, Dan made a habit of hiring taxis to drive him around from one bar to another to drink with his pals. Exacerbating the problem still further, he would tell the driver to wait outside each bar until he was ready to travel on to the next hostelry. Of course the taxi's meter was left running and the costs escalated.

Once again, Ruby's cheque book had to come to the rescue to relieve the disastrous financial difficulties that Dan had caused, not only with the running of the shop but the backlog of bills for stock that were left unpaid. Finally, Dan came to the conclusion that the shop business would have to go, but just what happened to the proceeds of the sale of the shop, and the stock, Ruby was never informed and nobody ever discovered.

Ruby's sister was Patsy.

Born in Canada but raised in Belfast, she married a George Smiley and they had four children: George Junior, June, David and Murray. I met them all when on our visits to Belfast. Before the children had fully grown, the marriage ended when Patsy departed for London with a new partner—Henry Adair. Ruby's mother had earlier left her husband, Dan, to come to live in the Stamford district in North London. Mother rang Ruby to inform her that sister Patsy was coming to London and asked Ruby to send Patsy the money for two flight tickets from Belfast to London. Ruby didn't question who the other ticket was for. In preparation for their arrival, Ruby's mother, Winnie, had found Patsy a flat near to her own in North London and, when Patsy arrived to occupy the flat, I drove Ruby from our home in Oxshott to visit her sister.

Bernie Burgess & Frank Bowles

At Ruby's suggestion I waited in the car whilst she visited her sister in their newly acquired flat. When she returned to the car, Ruby broke down in tears, due to the fact that it had dawned upon her that in reality she had financed a separation which affected the lives of four young children. She realised that eventually it would inevitably create problems with Patsy's husband George and perhaps the four children back in Belfast. Later, Patsy and her new partner, Henry Adair, had a son David. Both Patsy and Henry had fiery temperaments and frequently sparks would fly. On one of many visits to our home, when we settled in Northampton, pandemonium broke out after a night of family drinking and fisticuffs came into play in a big way. More on that story later.

Ruby's other sister was Lilian.

Like Patsy, she too was born in Canada and from the age of two was brought up by Winnie's sister Lilian, having been left behind in Canada by her mother and father when they returned to Belfast. Ruby told me the story of how the young Lilian met up with a Canadian singing star by the name of Jack Duffy and they married and had one daughter, Janice. Their marriage was also doomed to fail, possibly due to the fact that Lilian was developing a major drink problem, which was perhaps partially due to the trauma that she suffered as a young child when she became parentless. The fact that she probably became an 'orchestra wife' when husband Jack was touring with various bands across Canada, more than likely contributed to her dependency upon alcohol. Very much to Lilian's credit, she joined A.A. (Alcoholics Anonymous) in an attempt to combat her addiction. After her marriage had fallen apart, and during her membership of A.A., Lilian met up with another 'problem drinker' —Bill Zwicker. They combined their efforts to become 'dry' and fortunately they succeeded. They married and lived happily on a small farm on the outskirts of Toronto and despite the occasional lapse from sobriety, they continued to enjoy a 'dry' life together for many years. Unfortunately it wasn't to last. Bill died in the mid-nineties and left a vulnerable Lilian to fight a lone battle against her addiction, with only her young daughter Janice as a comfort.

RUBY—My Precious Gem!

Fortunately for Lilian, she eventually met another partner and went to live in Florida. Towards the end of her life Ruby flew to Florida to see her sister at a time when she, Ruby, was desperately ill yet she found enough strength to leave the nursing home to go to Florida with her then husband Ray, which utterly amazed not only me but the medical staff at the home.

The visit turned out to be totally disastrous. Both sisters lapsed from sobriety during Ruby's stay and a serious row broke out. It was coming up to Christmas and presents were placed at the foot of the festive tree. Lilian trashed them all!

Adding to the ugly scene, Ruby's new husband Ray, who was not only a heavy drinker but a very heavy smoker, smoked in bed and burned a hole in a brand new quilt. Understandably, Lilian's new partner, who was obviously aware of Lilian's need to stay away from drink, was distraught and none too pleased by the chaotic situation and asked the guests to leave. Ruby contacted friends Sue and Peter Barbour, fellow artistes whom we had toured with in show business and who were then appearing in Disneyland as a specialty act. Peter drove many miles to pick up Ruby and Ray and they stayed with them until they could get a flight back to London, allowing Ruby to return to the nursing home.

Despite the way her family treated her over the years, Ruby still dearly loved them all. Although she endured a great deal of heartache and upheaval, especially from her parents, she remained a devoted daughter. After they had both passed away, she continued to cherish their memories and would only remember the good times. 'Big Dan', like his father before him, was a strict disciplinarian and enjoyed dominating his womenfolk. He had a dictatorial attitude to most things and was a staunch Orangeman to boot. It was common knowledge that he had a strong dislike for Catholics in general and despised the Catholic faith and all it stood for in the world of religion.

Ruby however, did not share her father's bigoted feelings, in fact, her life long best friend, Marie Cunningham, was a Catholic. This caused great consternation in the Murray household and to Dan in particular. He became very alarmed when Marie, who had started booking shows, both in the North and South of Ireland, arranged for Ruby to appear in a few of these shows. The fact that Catholic priests negotiated some of the bookings became abhorrent to Dan. He was afraid that these priests might influence Ruby towards Catholicism. His fears were totally unfounded. Ruby saw no barriers whatsoever in religion.

As Ruby grew older, she came to recognise that 'Big Dan' was not the super being that existed in her childhood imagination and began to realise that he abused the privilege of fatherhood. During his bingeing bouts, which unfortunately were all too frequent, Dan developed a definite personality change. When he had consumed quantities of alcohol, the family problems and his own shortcomings became magnified beyond belief. This is very common amongst 'problem' drinkers and was a very ominous sign that would, much to my dismay, manifest itself in Ruby's life later on with very dramatic consequences. There was a distinctly obvious thread that ran through the Murray family. The list of members who had problems with alcohol included Dan himself, his brother Billy and his two daughters Lilian and Ruby. All of them suffered from this debilitating disease in various degrees of seriousness. They were all struck down with alcoholism at some point in their lives and always with tragic consequences. Each in turn vehemently denied that they had a problem with drink, a very common symptom of the disorder, and they all refused to accept any blame for their behaviour, which in turn badly affected, not just their own lives but those of loved ones around them.

Tragically, and very much to my deep concern, many members of the press, and the media in general, appear to be oblivious to the complexities of 'alcoholism' and how it manifests itself within the sufferers, of which there are sadly large numbers. They don't seem to come to terms with the fact that it is a disease, which eventually became recognised as such in the medical world. If they did understand it, they would be aware that the 'sufferer' lies, cheats and deceives and as a consequence their listening ears believe everything that the sufferer tells them. It is fact that the ones who are blamed for their drinking and their misdemeanours are the ones closest to them and self-blame is not an option. When stories are printed, very much with sales of newspapers in mind, innocent persons have their lives permanently blighted, as I personally have experienced. The press never checks out the accusations that are aimed at the loved ones i.e. "Look what you are making me do" and "I never drank until I met you". The strangest logic of all is "Of course I can stop drinking, that is why I go on". It all makes good reading so, in reality, perhaps they do know exactly what they

RUBY—My Precious Gem!

are doing and they go ahead and print and be damned. In a lot of cases they twist and distort the story when they report it, to suit their own ends, and consequently the end result bears no resemblance to the true facts. It may well tarnish someone's good name or destroy their reputation, even cause immense anguish and distress, but who cares. Let's print it.

As a small child Ruby could sing, and sing well. 'Big Dan' always enjoyed basking in the reflected glory that his child received from all and sundry. As soon as she was able, after passing her apprenticeship singing on tables and bar tops, at just five years of age, her father looked for ways for her to sing in public on platforms and stages. Out of its box came the little doll to be wound up in readiness for the performance. By this time of course, once the performance was over, he could not only soak up the plaudits but there were small but gradual financial gains to be made after the doll had been placed back into the box.

Around this time, Belfast was on the receiving end of Adolph Hitler's bombing raids, especially around the shipyard area of Harland and Wolf. The three Murray children were amongst the many evacuees that were dispatched away from the city to safer areas in the countryside. Jack, Patsy and young Ruby were sent to a farm, near to a place called Newcastle I believe. It was here that Ruby was to suffer extreme trauma at the hands of a farmer and his wife, trauma that would forever haunt her and shatter her self-confidence for all time.

Soon after arriving on the farm, both the farmer and his spouse took an instant dislike to this precocious, self assured child performer and straight away decided that her ways must be changed.

Even if Ruby only mildly misbehaved, they would administer some kind of punishment. Fetching buckets of water was one chore that the small child had to carry out. Each time, she would totter with the weight of the load of water, albeit in a small bucket, and water would spill over her clothes, her legs, her socks and her shoes. No concern was ever shown by the farming couple and frequently Ruby would have to wait for her clothes to dry on her. The worst punishment of all was being shut into a dark, dank, smelly shed with rats scurrying all around her. She would desperately try to blot out the sound of their squeaking and the rustle of the straw as they scampered across the floor of the shed. She would cower into the corner of the shed, terrified and trying to make herself as small as she possibly could, sometimes for hours on end. These vile people were not only responsible for shattering the child's confidence but they also irretrievably changed her previously strong personality into one filled with insecurity.

Another unfortunate incident happened on the farm. Ruby was bitten on the leg by a large flying insect. No treatment was administered and the bite eventually turned septic. When Ruby's parents came for one of their visits to see the children, the infected leg was carefully concealed from them. When they were on their way to the station to return to Belfast they talked about the visit and both felt that something was amiss so they decided to go back to check out their feelings. Ruby was in the bath and so both parents saw the ugly wound on her leg. It became obvious that an ominous red line was travelling up her leg. All three children were immediately taken back to Belfast.

The fear that Ruby suffered in that rat infested, darkened shed haunted her for the rest of her life. When she explained to me how she curled up into the corner, making herself as small as she could, the image stayed in my mind too. I was to personally witness that vision of the cowering child in the corner during the final weeks of Ruby's life. Each time I left her in her room at the nursing home to return to Northampton, I would say my farewells and as I turned to leave the room Ruby would curl up at the head of the bed, which was in a corner. I had to leave, desperately fighting back tears, and losing.

That particular vision will also remain with me for the rest of my life. I am at a complete loss to be able to understand how supposedly grown adults can inflict such cruelty on innocent children, thereby scarring them for the rest of theirs lives.

As in most cities during the war, (1939/45), life carried on regardless of the dangers, and so did entertainment. 'Big Dan' found places for his child to perform and Ruby enjoyed being back to her singing. When hostilities came to an end and life gradually returned to almost being normal, it encouraged more and more people to attend 'live' entertainment venues, like concert halls and theatres and young Ruby became part of the scene.

Chapter 3
♪ 'Now Is The Hour' ♪

Ruby's reputation as a child performer became well known, not only in Belfast but in the surrounding areas outside the city. Television was still in its embryonic stage, but when Ruby was 12 years old she was seen by a television producer named Richard Afton, who also was Irish. So impressed by this young, confident and by now experienced artiste, he decided to take her to the Alexandra Palace Television Studios in London where he was producing a show called 'Mrs Mulligan's Boarding House' which featured a very well known Irish comedian Jimmy O'Dea. Ruby was highly successful on the programme, but her age prevented her from being able to capitalise from her success. There were strict 'juvenile' performance laws which applied to minors. The Lord Chamberlain forbade youngsters from performing after a certain time in the evening, and missing schooling was also very much frowned upon.

In the meantime, Ruby's father 'Big Dan' had formed a working relationship with two local Belfast business men, Sam Kirkwood and Jim Graham and they began promoting small local shows using the name KGM Promotions (Kirkwood/Graham/Murray). Now that Ruby had appeared on television, they were delighted to be able to bill Ruby on their posters as—'Star of BBC Television'—a huge boost to their marketing. Local wannabes were given slots in their shows but of course there was no fee offered to them. It was considered to be an honour for them to be included. Ruby was not on the payroll either. After expenses were paid such as printing, posters, programmes, hire charges etc. the total profit was meagre but it provided Dan with the means of following his pastimes!

The little 'trouper' continued to gain valuable experience, which would stand her in good stead later on in her career. When her schooling days came to an end Ruby gave a sigh of relief. Her credentials on leaving school in no way compared to the accolades she received from her performances on stage. Always ready to admit her academic shortcomings Ruby told me: "Every time examination papers were handed out by my teacher she would say— 'I think you ought to go and make the tea Ruby!' Adding to the story: "One gratifying entry was written in my school leaving report. In the space marked 'Ability in Special Subjects' my music teacher wrote, in bold letters SINGING. That meant a great deal to me"

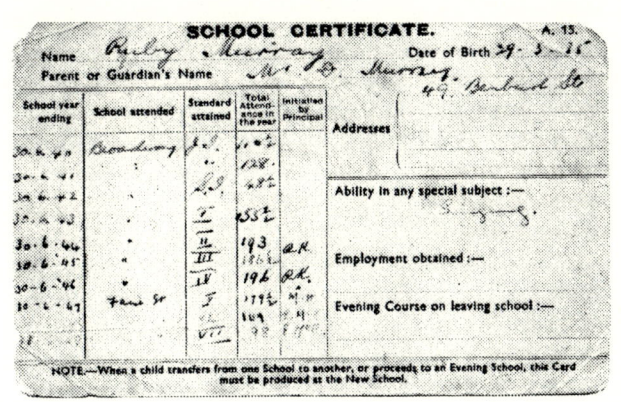

When Ruby reached the age of 14 there was a need to find work. As she related to me: "What could I do? I had no credentials of any kind other than my ability to sing." Of her attempts to find a job she went on to say: "I did start a job in a small sweet shop, but I consumed so much of their stock, by the end of the week, I owed them money!"

Her next application was submitted to the owner of a handkerchief factory making hemstitched hankies. She summed up that situation by saying: "It didn't take me too long to realise that my future was not wrapped up in a handkerchief!"

A jam tart making factory was the next venture Ruby made into the job market.

"It sounded simple enough," she said. "Little did I know what I was letting myself in for."

RUBY—My Precious Gem!

Monday morning came around and on her arrival at the factory she was greeted by a forewoman who was about to accompany her around the site, and eventually to the machine that Ruby would be operating. She explained to Ruby what the operation entailed.

"Your job is to place these pieces of pastry into the machine, which then cuts them out into shapes, crimps the edges and then fills them with jam. Ruby was visibly perplexed, so the forewoman demonstrated the so called simple operation to her.

"It's easy," she said. "Simply place the pieces of pastry in position, like so, wait for the machine to cut out the shapes, crimp the edges, and fill them with jam, then you must remove the filled tarts from the machine and place in more pastry."

Content that she had explained the operation fully, she then invited Ruby to carry out her first trial run which she did .

"That is fine," she confirmed and walked away leaving Ruby to carry on alone. Ruby told me "I watched in utter amazement as this bewildering piece of modern technology carried out the identical cycle with such precision and speed. All that I had to do was follow my leader so I threw myself into the job."

The first few cycles went reasonably smoothly but concentration was the name of the game and soon Ruby suffered a mind lapse.

"Because I was beginning to feel quietly confident, I picked up two pieces of pastry at once and missed taking out the filled tarts," she confessed. "I decided to take a chance and managed to get one of the pieces of pastry into position but by now the cut out shapes had become entangled with the jam filled tarts. It looked a real mess and the machine continued remorselessly on."

Now in a state of sheer panic, a transfixed Ruby could only stare at the pile of oozing, jam filled, misshapen ruined tarts.

"What could I do?" she said. "I had no idea how to stop this monster. Who do I tell? … Where is the switch? … What will they say？ … What will I say to them？… Should I say: 'Can I go home now please？'".

Her stay at the jam tart factory came to a swift end.

"Charlie Chaplin had nothing on me!" Ruby joked. "Besides, I wasn't cut out for it!"

Although Ruby had tried hard to find a day job, her future was being created by working with several fellow artistes, all of whom were striving for success and eventual stardom. A few of the struggling performers went on in later years to be highly successful stars in show business. Amongst them was a close friend of Ruby's, Ronnie Cleghorne. He toured with a show called 'Hollywood Doubles' in which he performed as Nat 'King' Cole. He changed his name to Ronnie Carroll and then rocketed to fame. Also, there was Joe McLaughlin. He enjoyed stardom in the name of Joseph Locke and had a Hollywood film made about his life story. Charlie Sherrard also had a name change. He became Patrick Hagan and enjoyed fame on Irish television. His son made a huge impact on the Eurovision Song Contest and won it more than once. His name was Johnnie Logan. Then there was 'The Singing Sweethearts.' Their daughters did extremely well when they launched themselves in show business as The Nolan Sisters.

Even at an early age, Ruby's voice was quite unique. The husky tones gave her an individualistic sound which was infectious. It had quality and was distinctive, making it unmistakably recognisable from any other female singer. Her voice was always true in pitch. She had the ability of laying back off the beat so far that at times I used to wonder whether she would get back on to it. She always did. She never missed a beat in her entire career. Her visual image was of 'the girl next door'—gentle, pure, sincere, nothing artificial. It had tremendous appeal. Always appearing to be vulnerable, with a hesitancy that made her audience worry whether she would make it to the end of the song. I was no exception.

RUBY—My Precious Gem!

Whilst still only 14 years of age, but with a wealth of performing experience behind her, an opportunity came along for her to join a professional summer season show on the other side of the Irish Sea. A famous Scottish comedian, Tommy Morgan, who staged annual summer shows in Glasgow at the Pavilion Theatre, was paying one of his regular visits to Belfast's premier theatre, The Opera House. He heard so many glowing reports about this talented young colleen, he asked to meet her with a view to her auditioning for his summer show. Ruby sailed through the audition, but there was the age problem to tackle. The idea was put forward that Ruby should use her sister Patsy's name. She was older than Ruby, and therefore Ruby could qualify for The Tommy Morgan Show the following summer using the name – Pat Murray. The show opened on the 7th May 1949. Remember that Ruby was just 14 years old at the time.

Before Ruby left Belfast for Glasgow 'Big Dan' and K.G.M. Promotions latched onto the idea of staging a tearful but celebratory farewell concert at the Ulster Hall in Belfast on 3rd May, just four days before the Glasgow opening. The souvenir programme stated: A 'Grand Farewell' Concert for Ruby Murray, the Stage and BBC Television Singing Star leaving Ireland to further her career.' The Ulster Hall was bursting at the seams that night.

Ruby needed a chaperone with her in Glasgow so her mother Winnie accompanied her for the entire run of the show. The weekly salary was naturally only a child performer's wage, so stretching it out to cover accommodation for two meant that there was only a pittance left over. Fortunately for them, there was a song and dance artiste in the show, Jimmy Hill, who befriended Ruby and he offered to accommodate them both, very reasonably, so they struggled through, but only just!

Dan, in the meantime, remained in Belfast, but he did cross the water to visit the show. However, signs were becoming apparent that all was not well in their marriage. In later years Dan and Winnie gradually drifted apart.

The popularity of The Tommy Morgan Show was always assured in Glasgow and the audiences took the child performer to their hearts. With numerous changes of programmes, sketches and scenes within the show, Ruby was managing to accumulate an abundance of valuable experience. Tommy Morgan, himself a seasoned artiste, was eager to assist Ruby with her career.

"It was through Tommy I learned how to use my hands." Ruby confirmed. "He stressed the importance of using them and demonstrated exactly what he meant. I never forgot that sound advice."

Ruby certainly benefited from Tommy's experience and her hands were one of the first things that struck me when I first saw her on stage. She had wonderful hands that were so expressive during her performance and even in photographic shoots they were a joy to behold. Most artistes, who go on to become stars have, at one time or another, worked with the likes of Tommy Morgan in their developing years and were fortunate enough to witness the tricks of the trade from some of the master craftsmen in show business.

Tommy's show regularly transferred each year from Glasgow to Belfast for another long run, with the same cast, the same scenery and sketches. Ruby had come back home flushed with success. On the completion of the run Ruby was to gain even more valuable experience, this time in an Irish touring and summer show called 'Holiday Express'.

RUBY—My Precious Gem!

Ruby's life long friend, Marie Cunningham, was also booked in the show, both as an accordion playing act and accompanist to the rest of the artistes. Another fine performer was booked to do a singing act in the show, an Irish tenor called Frank Murphy. He went on to marry Marie in later years. When the show toured the country as a 'fit-up' show, the cast was expected to perform, but also act as stagehands, ushers and usherettes, programme sellers and even sell raffle tickets during the interval. As was the custom, the cast had to travel on the lorry that transported the scenery and costumes, a very uncomfortable experience.

Winnie still toured with Ruby on occasions, but Ruby was now growing up rapidly and was mixing with a tightly knit bunch of show business troupers who were more than capable of watching over her, in particular Marie and Frank. These shows became part of Ruby's life and she thoroughly enjoyed working and performing in this environment. She had formed true friendship and comradeship with a group of people who respected her and treated her as an equal. They were honest and reliable. She was very comfortable with that.

During a time out period, Marie took a job in the city centre of Belfast, in The Gramophone Shop, run by a family called Solomons. Philip Solomons staged shows, from time to time. He was producing a show called 'Yankee Doodle Blarney' and was on the lookout for a good female vocalist. Marie had no hesitation in recommending Ruby to him. Again she passed the audition with flying colours and joined the show which was to tour the North and South of Ireland and was then destined to sail across the sea to England.

A weekend break during the tour in Ireland brought Ruby back home to Belfast. It came to her notice that an American singing star, Frankie Laine, was booked to appear at the Opera House Theatre. Ruby was thrilled at the chance of seeing an American super star in her local home town and promptly booked a ticket to see his performance. After the show, Ruby joined the queue of enthusiastic fans waiting at the stage door for his autograph. He chatted to the fans as he obliged each one with his signature or signed photograph. Ruby enthusiastically grabbed the opportunity to speak to him and even became bold enough to tell him that she too was a singer. He smiled at her, and engaged her in conversation, which resulted in him inviting her backstage to meet his accompanist, the famous pianist/song writer Carl Fisher.

One of our favourite songs, Ruby's and mine, was 'We'll Be Together Again' which was written by Carl. Conversation flowed in the star's dressing room and, to Ruby's utter delight, Frankie invited her to join his entourage for an after show meal at a local restaurant. Despite the fact that she knew that her father would be furious at being out late at night, she unhesitatingly accepted the kind invitation. It was an opportunity not to be missed. The American star unwound after his performance and showed great interest as Ruby excitingly related the details of her appearances in the touring show. At the end of the meal, Frankie requested that a taxi should be called to take Ruby home and even paid the driver in advance. I am lucky enough to still have the signed photograph that Frankie gave to Ruby on that unforgettable night.

When she arrived home, her mother quickly hustled her to her bedroom before 'Big Dan' came home. The next morning Dan learned of Ruby's invitation from Frankie Laine but instead of the anticipated outburst of anger, his false pride took him to his local drinking bars to boast to his pals about Ruby dining with the super star Frankie Laine. The drinks flowed even more freely that day.

Chapter 4
♪ 'There's No Business Like Show Business' ♪

In 1954 'Yankee Doodle Blarney' came to England and, once again, Ruby's mother Winnie came with her on the tour. The show played some provincial dates and then came to London where it was booked to appear at one of London's famous Variety venues, The Metropolitan Theatre, Edgware Road. It was a theatre that often featured shows with an Irish flavour, so 'Blarney' was a suitable attraction. Ruby's fairy godmother waved her magic wand, and as a result the same television producer, Richard Afton, who had seen such great potential in a young Irish colleen and booked her for television in London several years previously, came to the theatre to see the show. At the time, he was producing a highly successful series for the BBC called 'Quite Contrary', a television spectacular. It so happened that he was on the look out for a replacement female singer due to the fact that Joan Regan, the star female vocalist in the show, was leaving for pastures new. Joan had enjoyed great success in the first series and as a result she had been booked to do a nation wide variety tour throughout the British Isles.

At the theatre 'Dickie' Afton instantly recognised Ruby and could see that she had blossomed into a very beautiful young lady with a natural 'girl next door' image and a very pleasing style. Her husky voice had an endearing quality which, when coupled with her charm, added up to star potential for his television show. Her appeal was enormous. She came across to the audience as being vulnerable but with the aura of a star. The producer had found his replacement singer and immediately booked her for 'Quite Contrary'.

This turned out to be the turning point in Ruby's remarkable career. It also highlighted the need for Ruby to have that experienced person to represent her and to negotiate on her behalf. Someone needed to establish her fee for the television appearance, the number of appearances she was being asked to make, what billing arrangements would there be, would it be for one appearance or for the series, would there be another series, and would the BBC have an option on her services, etc. etc. In later years when I questioned Ruby about who negotiated for her at the time I discovered that she had no one. The only person with her was her mother, who had no experience at all in the business.

After her very first performance in the studio, it was plain that 'Dickie' had chosen well. The reaction from the television audience was overwhelming. A STAR had been born. From that moment Ruby's entire life

RUBY—My Precious Gem!

changed dramatically. She became instantly famous as millions of television viewers throughout the British Isles had taken her to their hearts.

The musical director for the series was Ray Martin, who also happened to be an A & R man (Artiste and Repertoire) at Columbia Records, a label within the EMI group. He too had been bowled over with the impact that Ruby had made in the studios. After establishing that she was not signed to any recording deal, he invited her to come to the famous Abbey Road Studios for a recording test. He was convinced that she had a great recording career ahead of her and signed her to Columbia Records. Once again, Ruby needed representation, someone to establish how long the contract would be for, how many records would Ruby cut in a year, what would the royalty be on each record sold, who chose recording material, would the artiste's choice of material be taken into the reckoning, and many more details that should have been negotiated. Once again the only person with her was her mother!

Ruby signed the contract that was placed in front of her without a question being asked. Then she entered Abbey Road Studios to make her first record and Ruby was about to create history in the recording world. Her first recording was of a song called 'Get Well Soon' which enjoyed moderate sales in the shops. However, her next record was a song called 'Heartbeat.' It shot straight into the Top Twenty and reached the number three slot in December 1954. It stayed in the charts for 16 weeks. From that moment on, Ruby became known as 'The Heartbeat Girl.'

Following close behind her first hit came a plethora of successes, which included her biggest selling record of all—'Softly, Softly', written by Paddy Roberts. It was given a typical Ray Martin touch with shimmering strings, harps and gentle voices, all blending together to make a beautiful backing to Ruby's very attractive husky voice. The result was outstanding. It had joined 'Heartbeat' by entering the charts in January 1955 and reached the coveted No. 1 position and stayed in the charts for an incredible 22 weeks. A complete change of mood and tempo came with the next hit, an upbeat arrangement was given to 'Happy Days and Lonely Nights.' It became the third hit record and reached the No. 6 position and remained charted for eight weeks. There were no less than 11 different recordings of the heart wrenching 'Let Me Go Lover' and Ruby joined the long list of star names who recorded it. The list included 'Little 'Ole Wine Drinking' Dean

Martin, Teresa Brewer and songstress supreme Lita Rosa. Ruby out sold them all with her version and took the No. 5 spot in the Top Twenty where it enjoyed a stay of seven weeks. It became her fourth record in the charts. The fifth hit record was 'If Anyone Finds This I Love You', a charming and appealing song which tells a sad story with a happy ending. It climbed to the No. 4 position, was a chart entry for 11 weeks and became part of an historic achievement.

Ruby had created a unique world record. Nobody before, or since, has broken that record and, with the changes made in single sales, nobody ever will. It will forever remain Ruby's own personal record. During the week

RUBY—My Precious Gem!

18th March 1955 there they were nestling all together in the Top Twenty and every music paper heralded this magnificent achievement. Looking back at it 50 years later, it must have seemed an unbelievable happening for the still shy, unassuming Irish girl, who was only 19 years old.

During the same year Ruby went on to gain even more Top Twenty success with 'Evermore' and the hauntingly beautiful 'I'll Come When You Call'. She was so spectacularly successful that for one whole year from December 1954 right through to November 1955 she was never absent from the Top Twenty. The following year, 1956, brought her another chart entry, 'You Are My First Love' the track of which was featured in the opening sequence of the John Mills film 'It's Great To Be Young'. In 1958 (momentarily leaping ahead in the story) Ruby and The Jones Boys were appearing in Great Yarmouth at the Wellington Pier with Ruby's co-star Tommy Cooper. Ruby  was concerned by the lull in her recordings and after a long confidence building chat that I had with her, I persuaded her to press Norrie Paramor, who had replaced Ray Martin as her A&R man at Columbia, to come up with some good material. As a result Ruby recorded a Bobby Darin song 'Real Love' in which she double tracked with her own voice. It put her back in the charts at No.18. In 1959 Ruby was back again, this time in the Top Ten with a smash hit song called 'Goodbye Jimmy, Goodbye'. It became so popular with her fans she featured it regularly in her cabaret act right up to her last performances.

I now return once again to the story.

Bernie Burgess & Frank Bowles

During the height of her record success, an agent who represented the beautiful Joan Regan approached her. One must assume that he got to know that Ruby had no agent or representation and an approach was made for her to go along to his office to discuss agency and management. Yet again, there was no one to negotiate on her behalf, no one to establish how long the agency contract would be for, what commission would the agency take, what guarantees could they offer her by way of further television engagements, etc.

Picture the scene. A young 19-year-old girl from Ireland had taken television by storm. As a result of the impact she had made, she was signed up by a major record company and instantly created music history. Here was a hugely successful star with a succession of major television appearances and multi hit records in the hit parade which combined to create massive box office power. She had no agent, no manager, no one to represent her, no-one to negotiate for her and she had walked into the London office of an agency/management company to discuss a contract. There was of course the little problem of the contract that Ruby had signed in connection with 'Yankee Doodle Blarney'. However, that was to be no obstacle and would be quickly nullified. Ruby's recording contract was already in existence. They were not involved in negotiating that and obviously they would not have wished to change it. Besides, as I was to discover, the office had no one knowledgeable enough in the music and recording world to change anything. In my opinion, they didn't know an 'A' side from a 'B' side, or even a waltz from a tango, so their advice musically would have been meaningless. She desperately needed a mentor who was musically aware. This was the job for an expert who understood recording and the music business. As for building her into a star, they had nothing to do. She was already there, massively so. A contract was drawn up for her to sign and, completely unchecked, she innocently put her signature to it. Nothing more needs to be said. Of course, Ruby did have her mother with her, but hardly a match for a huge London agency organisation. Again, the fact is she was ripe for exploitation. She certainly didn't appreciate her own worth regarding box office value. Rocketing from a hard working £15.00 a week 'rookie' to be offered a contract of larger proportions simply took her breath away. How could she have possibly understood the deal that she was being offered. In her eyes it was more than enough for a

RUBY—My Precious Gem!

young girl from Belfast. All her performing experience didn't equip her for doing business with a powerful London agency. Winnie, understandably, was completely out of her depth.

Amid all her success, both on television and in the recording world, her other achievements included co-starring with Norman Wisdom at the London Palladium in a show called 'Painting The Town.'

This spectacular show enjoyed huge acclaim and stayed in the west-end's premier venue for seven months. At the orchestral rehearsal Ruby became filled with fear. She looked around her and the reality of what was happening began to dawn upon her. Here she was, singing at the most prestigious theatre in show business, one which was internationally famous, co-starring with the legendary Norman Wisdom, and with the famous impresario Val Parnell and other dignitaries looking on. Her throat dried and she had great difficulty singing with the orchestra at rehearsal. She turned to her mother, who again was with her, and said: "I really don't want to be here Mummy, I'd rather be back home in Ireland!"

In readiness for the opening night Ruby's family and friends arrived from Belfast in vast numbers. Ruby was overwhelmed. At the time she was renting a small apartment overlooking Regents Park, by no means big enough to accommodate the large numbers of relatives and others that had arrived. "They were happy to sleep where they could," Ruby told me.

Partying commenced and the drink started to flow, and in Ruby's own words: "They slept where they fell."

The show opened but Ruby was still having problems with her voice. A doctor was consulted and he advised her to give her voice a rest. His advice had to be delayed whilst Ruby completed the heavy week-end schedule of shows, then she was admitted to hospital .She was taken by ambulance and of course the entire family travelled in the ambulance with her. Once Ruby was admitted, they all returned to the apartment to continue their merriment. As her mother turned to leave the hospital ward, she said to Ruby: "You'll be alright now love, I'm going back to the apartment with the others."

After her recovery she returned to the show, overcame her fear and by using her years of vast experience, she fulfilled a momentous season at the Palladium. Then the ultimate accolade was bestowed upon Ruby, that of being invited to join an international cast on the 'Royal Variety Command Performance', appearing before Her Majesty Queen Elizabeth. All of her show business experience was slow to come into play when having to carry out the Royal protocol of curtseying to Her Majesty as she was being introduced. A very tentative, nervous Ruby managed the recognised procedure and was then put at ease by kind and considerate comments from Her Majesty the Queen.

RUBY—My Precious Gem!

Around this period there was an international poll for female singers, and Ruby came second in the entire world to the delightful Doris Day.

In 1956, Ruby had the enviable task of presenting an award to another worldwide poll winner, none other than the most successful singer of all time 'Ole Blue Eyes' Frank Sinatra. Ruby, who was accompanied on her promotional tour of the USA by Norrie Paramor, her new A&R man at Columbia, was introduced to Frank at one of his recording sessions. In conversation with the great man, he commented: "It's a good thing you're not recording today with a cold like that." She spared him any embarrassment by not telling him that it was her natural voice!

Nationwide variety tours were being arranged for her and, with Ruby being at the height of her fame, they were destined to be sell-out performances. Her Agency/Management team was the promoter of these bills and of course they told her what salary they would pay her, as opposed to someone telling them what salary she required and deserved to receive. The schedule was, twice nightly performances, Monday to Saturday with matinees on Saturdays and sometimes Wednesdays. They were about to make a killing. Occasionally 'the office' arranged a road manager to tour with the show and to look after their 'star' attraction. Ray Lamar, an ex-member of a dancing act who had been working in the office, carried out this duty. He was to play a major part in Ruby's life later on. It was his duty to collect the box office figures after each night's performance and convey them to London. They insisted that he 'keep a close eye on Ruby.' So too were other artistes appearing on the bill who were represented by 'the office', artistes such as Morecambe & Wise. At the same time these artistes were dissuaded from talking any kind of business with Ruby. This became very ominous to Eric and Ernie. They quickly realised that Ruby was being exploited and not receiving her true worth. Word spread around that Ruby was being manipulated and opinions were being expressed within the business by such artistes as Frankie Vaughan that they understood what was happening. He was quoted as saying: "There were artistes that were not receiving their true value" and he felt that Ruby was one of them. Another star name Dorothy Squires made it generally known that she had severe doubts about what could be happening to Ruby. The Variety bills that she 'topped' produced very high revenue, but relatively little of that came Ruby's way.

There was a very amusing incident at one of the venues, It was normally a cinema but the occasional Variety bill appeared there. A couple of ladies passed the front of the cinema and the posters showed Alan Ladd in western film. One lady enquired of her friend "What is on there this week?" Her friend looked up and saw a poster and read it out to her friend "Ummm, it's Ruby Murray" to which the other lady replied "It must be one of those cowboy pictures."

The agency arranged for someone, within the office accounts department, to look after Ruby's finances and also appointed someone to take care of any legal matters. Both of these appointments proved to be highly costly to Ruby later on. In 1958, a year after our marriage, a huge tax demand dropped onto the mat. Whoever was supposedly looking after Ruby's tax matters had failed in his task and Ruby was left to pay a massive tax bill. It then became a high priority for me to find an independent accountant to look after both our tax returns.

From the very beginning of her success, Ruby wanted to buy her parents a new home and it became her main aim as soon as she could afford it. With record royalties, television fees and her variety engagements, Ruby had the means to carry out her wish. She signed a cheque for £5000, enough to purchase a beautiful house in Belfast in the fifties. Innocently,

RUBY—My Precious Gem!

she made the cheque out 'payable to Dan Murray' instead of the vendor's solicitors. Her trust in her father continued to spell grief. He found a house, placed £1200 deposit and took out a mortgage for the remainder. It doesn't take too much imagination as to what could have happened to the balance. A familiar cry was heard in the bars around Belfast: "I'm Dan Murray, Ruby Murray's Dad. Everybody can have a drink on me!" Winnie, her Mum, joined in with the lavish spending. She set about furnishing their new home with Venetian blinds, carpets and curtains and dispatched the bill to Ruby for payment. Dan told Ruby he was going to buy her a new piano for her 21st birthday, a thoughtful gesture. He had one delivered and, once again, the bill was sent to … guess who?

Chapter 5
♪ 'You're A Star, You're A Star' ♪

During 1956, Ruby was back on the variety trail and the same year she undertook a tour to entertain British Forces in the Middle East for Combined Services Entertainments (C.S.E.). Her best friend Marie was free to go along on the tour to play piano for the entire show so, to Ruby, it was like going back in time to the fit-up shows on the road in Ireland. The main difference was that, instead of travelling in the back of a lorry, the show and its cast were transported from one service posting to another by aeroplane. Artistes who chose to take part in entertaining the forces in those days were not paid their usual fees but only a nominal fee. However, the satisfaction that they gained by entertaining men and women serving in the armed forces away from their homeland, more than compensated for the loss in revenue. It also gave the artistes an opportunity of seeing parts of the world that they possibly hadn't seen before.

The venues were usually makeshift, with no proper stage facilities and at times they literally performed in the open air on temporarily constructed platforms, on the back of military vehicles or sometimes in a NAAFI canteen. Upon reaching Cyprus, Ruby was fortunate enough to be able to look up her brother Jack who was stationed there. Whilst the show was entertaining in Malta, Ruby met up with a dental doctor, a Scotsman named Jack Creighton, who was serving in the RAF. They became very friendly and Ruby grew quite fond of him. In a short period of time they formed a warm relationship and arranged to write to one another. The media got to hear about their relationship and soon had them romantically linked, a familiar press manoeuvre. They had previously tried to link Ruby with other likely suitors such as Ronnie Carroll, Danny Purches the

RUBY—My Precious Gem!

Romany star and a member of an American vocal trio, The Three Deuces namely, Shane Rimmer. Whilst home on leave, doctor Jack arranged to meet up with Ruby and asked her to marry him and bought her an engagement ring. Ruby hesitated and thought very carefully about becoming the wife of a serving military doctor. After deliberation she realised that she was not sure and therefore left things in abeyance. It was not until I met Ruby in the summer of 1957 that she made the decision she was not sufficiently committed to their relationship. She decided to write to him, explaining everything and returned his ring.

Ruby with Marie Cunningham and Joan Winters

In the summer of 1956 Ruby was to star in a summer season show with Reg 'Confidentially' Dixon at the Hippodrome Theatre, Brighton. Again Ruby's agency office was the promoter of the show and again it played to packed houses.

Up until this time, Ruby travelled everywhere by train and taxis but Marie, her close friend, who was asked by Ruby to join her as secretary and travelling companion, suggested that Ruby changed her mode of transport. Winnie, in the meantime decided to return to Belfast. Marie pointed out to Ruby that she should have her own car, despite the fact that neither she nor Marie could drive. At the end of the season Ruby was booked for more variety dates. Taunton was one of the venues. The two girls went shopping and Ruby spotted a glistening, brand new, powder blue, Vauxhall Victor sparkling invitingly in the window of a car showroom. Marie seized upon the opportunity to persuade her friend to go inside to make enquiries.

"You're a star Ruby. You should be driving a car like that, not using trains and taxis." They asked the salesman if they could sit inside the car.

"Of course ladies, please do," sensing the possibility of a sale. Ruby ran her hands along the beautifully finished seat. The smell of newness was appealing to her.

"You're right Marie, I should have a car like this!"

Calling the salesman over Ruby said: "I'll take it."

The salesman was slightly taken aback by the speed of their decision but politely explained: "Sorry madam, there is a waiting list for these new Vauxhalls. Shall I put your name down on the waiting list?"

Marie pointed out to him: "We're only in Taunton for the week, at the theatre."

The salesman suddenly realised who Ruby was and hastened off to find the garage owner. As a consequence, the shining new Vauxhall Victor was delivered to the stage door on the Saturday morning.

Of course, there was a problem. Who was going to drive it. On the bill with Ruby was a comedian called Tommy Locky. He could drive so he offered to chauffeur both Ruby and Marie around until alternative arrangements could be made. At that time it was possible to actually purchase a driving licence over the post office counter in Belfast. Apparently

RUBY—My Precious Gem!

no driving test was required, so arrangements were made for the two girls to have licences issued. They soon learned the art of driving and both became competent drivers. Arthur Helliwell, a well-known journalist for a national newspaper, arranged to interview Ruby in London early on in her driving days. His piece in the newspaper was entitled 'Bumper car riding around Regents Park with Ruby Murray!' Happily, it was done with tongue in cheek although he didn't easily forget the experience.

Whilst Ruby was in Brighton for the summer season in 1956, she entered the film making world and became involved in acting in three films. One was a film that starred John Mills 'It's Great To Be Young'. Ruby's recording of 'You Are My First Love' was featured in the opening scenes of the film. The second was a documentary film by Pathe, about the making of a record. It was shot partly in a music publisher's offices in Denmark Street and the recording studios at Abbey Road. Co-starring with Ruby in the Pathe documentary was a very fine singer who had enjoyed great success with a song called 'The Story Of Tina'—Ronnie Harris. The third film was 'A Touch Of The Sun' which featured the star comedian Frankie Howerd.

In the film Ruby played the part of an Irish chambermaid and she sang two songs 'O'Malley Tango' and 'In Love'. Her schedule during that period was hectic, to say the least. She was up at 4-30am every morning and journeyed to Nettleford near Walton-on-Thames in Surrey. There followed a session in the make-up department and then on to the set for an 8.30am start. Sometimes, after completing a morning at the film studio, Ruby would be whisked off to Abbey Road for an afternoon recording session before the return journey to Brighton for the first of the two evening performances of the summer show. Some schedule! That's show business!

Bernie Burgess & Frank Bowles

Returning to variety tours, Ray Lamar, the road manager, became very friendly with Ruby. When she was about to set off for Blackpool in the summer of 1957 he offered to garage her car until she felt confident to drive herself. It would have given him the opportunity to pursue her romantically, but Ruby felt that she would be in need of the car during the season. Before departing, he asked her to marry him. Ruby's reaction was to suggest to him that they both think about it during the summer and see how they felt after a period of several months' separation. In truth, Ruby was not sure how she felt and was stalling. This was fortunate for me as it proved later.

Rehearsals started for the Blackpool summer season show in a rehearsal studio in the Marylebone Road. The cast assembled and the usual 'getting to know one another' took place. This show was to be the first one in Blackpool for the Bernard Delfont office and he made quite sure that it was impressive. The show was to be lavish, with spectacular scenes, beautiful costumes, and a huge cast. He engaged TVs Ernest Maxim to produce the show, and what a show it turned out to be.

The cast included three star names: Ruby Murray, Tommy Cooper, and Ken Platt plus a very strong supporting cast including The Four Jones Boys ('The whole town's talking about them' – this is where I make my appearance), The Morton Fraser Harmonica Gang, Neil and Pat Delrina (a fantastic dancing act) and the Vernon Girls. The musical director for the show was our (The Jones Boys)

RUBY—My Precious Gem!

personal M.D. Paul Burnett, a brilliant pianist/arranger and musical director. He had a 12 piece orchestra under his command and he made full use of them with some brilliant arrangements. He had a very amusing tale to tell concerning the show. After he had conducted the first half, which was packed with spectacular and beautiful costumes, sketches and production routines, all worthy of a west-end production, he came out of the orchestra pit for the interval. There was a tap on his shoulder. A member of the audience wanted to ask him: "Do you think we could have a 'sing song' in the second half?"

Paul had an abundance of amusing tales like that one to tell. He was a riot.

Ernest Maxim, the producer, was a very good dancer himself and always included many fine dance sequences in his productions. He planned to get Ruby involved in a dancing role. Although Ruby had managed some dance routines in the London Palladium production, it was only in a minor way. She was always terrified of dancing on stage. It became a major concern for her when Ernest revealed that she was to be involved with The Jones Boys in a hectic Rock n' Roll routine to 'See You Later Alligator.' He demonstrated the routine and Ruby started to learn it. She spent a lot of her spare time practicing the dance sequence. Other problems manifested themselves whilst the rehearsals took place. Her family and some other relations from Canada descended upon her and occupied the house that Ruby had rented for the season. Such were the numbers there was not enough beds to go around and Ruby found herself, once again, stepping over sleeping bodies. Despite having also engaged a domestic help for household duties during the season, the heavy workload that entertaining this 'crowd' of people entailed, became a great burden that bore down on her. To add to her problems, she had a visit from a man who worked for Boosey & Hawkes, the publishers of 'Softly, Softly.' Maurice Taylor was a very handsome man with a smile that was capable of melting any girl's heart.

He had become friendly with Ruby during the heady days when the song was in the No. 1 slot. He invited Ruby out for a quick lunch in a break in rehearsals, and during the conversation he spun her a hard luck story in which he explained to her that he had foolishly left his wallet and cheque book behind in London and he was in a difficult position. He had

Shirley Eaton, Maurice Taylor and Ruby

arranged to meet and entertain a business colleague and needed to rent a car to keep the appointment but, of course, had not got the means. Always ready to help Ruby took out her cheque book and offered to loan him some money until his own arrived from London.

Somewhat taken aback by the size of the sum he required (£500) Ruby, a trusting soul, handed him her cheque for that figure. He took it and vanished. It came to light later that the 'smoothie' had taken another female star 'for a ride.' He had also 'borrowed' money from Shirley Eaton, the film star. Ruby would have to work very hard to be able to earn that money and she was deeply upset by the cunning shown in this miserable incident.

In later years I was destined to catch up with Maurice Taylor myself.

The tally of problems mounting up for Ruby looked like this. She had to learn new songs and dance routines for the show, entertain her family and guests from Canada, do the shopping and cooking and then to have a confidence trick played upon her. It was all too much. As if that wasn't enough, the family members started their usual 'celebrating' in a very noisy and rowdy manner, which deprived her of sleep. Ruby felt over tired and extremely frayed, and it showed. Ernest Maxim noticed that Ruby was distressed and tried to help ease her concerns. Seeing that Ruby was looking drawn and very tired, the domestic lady, Renee, tried to help Ruby by suggesting that she had a spare bedroom in her house and would be more than pleased to let Ruby use it. It was an offer she couldn't refuse, Oh! to get some sleep! The offer was gratefully accepted.

RUBY—My Precious Gem!

Let's leap forward in time to complete the Maurice Taylor saga. Ruby was booked to appear on television in Toronto, Canada in a television series called 'The Pig & Whistle.' It was the equivalent to the series in England called 'Stars & Garters'. The anchorman in the Canadian series was the British actor from the television commercial made for Birds Eye Fish Fingers – Captain Bird's Eye. Before we left England for Toronto, I had picked up a story that Maurice Taylor was believed to be in Canada and was connected to a property company, possibly in Toronto. I kept the story to myself in the hope that I could seek him out whilst we were in Canada and pay him a surprise visit, without telling Ruby. I remember the incident well. Ruby had completed her television engagement and with our two children, who were on the trip with us, we were spending a few days with Lilian and her husband, Bill Zwicker, at their farmhouse home. I had brought my camera on the trip and made the excuse to Ruby that I wanted to go into Toronto, a few miles way, to take a series of photographs. Leaving Ruby and the children with Lilian, I made my way into the centre of Toronto and started to make enquiries. The Property Company that he was associated with was a name similar to Evergreen. In no time I picked up a trail and followed it and to my amazement I found myself standing outside a very tall building with the name I was looking for emblazoned across the front. I was then confronted with the problem of how to get inside the building. It had electronic security doors. I stood and watched as people came and went to see how I could gain access. I decided to chance it and I followed a man with a briefcase through the front door. I fumbled in my pockets, giving the impression that I was searching for my security card and a few other people arrived. I simply joined them and walked through without being challenged. I was in. Scanning the list of names in the foyer I found Mr. Taylor's name with the floor and number of his office. I ascended in the lift, entered the office, walked up to the reception secretary and asked to see Mr. Taylor.

"Your name sir?" She asked. I explained that I was an old friend of his from England and that I was in Toronto on holiday and I hoped to surprise him.

"I must have a name, sir," she said. I stuck to my guns "I really would like to surprise him." Fortunately she didn't press me further, left her desk and went into his office. When she came back out of his office she ushered me in.

Bernie Burgess & Frank Bowles

Taylor rose from his desk and walked towards me. He said that he couldn't remember meeting me and asked where I came from and what my name was. I told him that I was from Surrey and that he probably would not remember my name but he would be sure to remember my wife's name. He invited me to sit down and then enquired what my wife's name was and I replied: "It's Ruby Murray."

I held my hand out across his desk. His face turned white. He was speechless. He knew instantly that he had been duped. I went on to tell him that I had called for the £500 that he had 'borrowed' from my wife some considerable time ago. He spluttered quite a bit when telling me that he hadn't got that amount of money in his office to which I replied that I was quite prepared to wait in his office until he fetched it! I also made it abundantly clear that I wouldn't be leaving his office until I had the money in my hand. He used the telephone on his desk, turning his back as he did so, preventing me from hearing what he was saying. A few seconds later he told me that he would have to go to get the money for me. I assured him that I was in no hurry to go anywhere and that I would remain in his office waiting for him. Ten minutes or so went by and he then came back into his office with an envelope in his hand. Handing the envelope to me he suggested that I checked the money. I agreed that it was a good idea by counting the money carefully in front of him then slid the envelope into my inside pocket and bade him 'farewell'.

Returning to Lilian's home, Ruby greeted me and asked how my photographic trip had gone. I told her that it had been interrupted when I met up with an old friend of hers, a certain Mr. Maurice Taylor. Ruby stared in disbelief. I told her that I had brought up the subject of the long outstanding 'debt' and that he had given me some money. I had prepared my little surprise for Ruby by discarding the envelope. I reached into my pocket, produced two £50 notes and placed them on the table. Her mouth opened and I then proceeded to produce one note after another until the whole £500 was displayed in front of her. I was given an extra special hug that day!

Chapter 6
♪ 'Love Is Just Around The Corner' ♪

Amid all the pandemonium that surrounded her, Ruby had arrived at the opening night.

The show opened at the North Pier Pavilion Theatre, Blackpool, in May 1957. It was a tremendous success and the press gave it 'rave' notices. Ruby herself was in great demand by everyone on a daily basis, doing personal appearances, photographic shoots, opening fetes, shops and supermarkets, whilst all the time trying to cope with personal problems. At that time I was unaware of the huge difficulties that she was experiencing.

Perhaps I had better explain about how we, The Four Jones Boys, happened to be in the same show as Ruby that year, 1957.

Bernie Burgess & Frank Bowles

We had recently been subcontracted to the Bernard Delfont Organisation after Bernard Delfont himself had seen us in one of his summer season shows at the Theatre Royal, in Southsea, the previous year. We had been a hard working vocal group who had scaled our way up the ladder of success via television, concerts and variety performances, to a position of being able to top the bill in our own right. As a direct result of Delfont seeing our act, he booked us to appear on a fortnightly variety bill at the Prince of Wales Theatre in the West End of London. It was originally supposed to be headed by Mel Torme but he was taken ill and could not appear. The replacement top of the bill could not have been more contrasting—Hylda Baker. Amongst the supporting acts, apart from ourselves, were Charlie Carioli & Paul, Peggy Ryan (who partnered Donald O'Connor in films) with Ray McDonald, Morecambe & Wise, Joe Church and a host of other artistes. We had appeared on numerous television shows such as The Dave King Show, The Jimmy Wheeler Show, the Charlie Drake Show and The Michael Holiday Show etc. We had a recording contract with Decca records.

Directly after the West End performance in November 1956 we were informed that we would be booked for another Bernard Delfont summer season show the next year, but not told where it would be. We were about to experience a little slight of hand by 'the office'. Christmas came and went, and still no word as to where we were going for the summer. By this time, most of the summer shows throughout the country were fully booked—artiste wise. We pressed our agent very hard to get information, due to the fact that if their promise fell through we would need to get booked into another show. It was well into the spring before we were told that it would be Blackpool. We were relieved to hear the news because we had visions of being left stranded without a summer show. The contract finally arrived for signing but, much to our dismay, the fee was not what we expected and well below our usual money. To top that, we discovered that we were expected to appear in all the scenes and do two Sunday Concerts each week throughout the summer, at the same venue, but with no additional fee. It meant that two more performances were merely tacked on to the 14 performances we were already committed to at the Pavilion Theatre. (Twice nightly—Monday to Saturday with matinees on Wednesday and Saturday.) A pistol was being held to our heads. Take this offer or miss out on the summer season. We had been 'conned' and could do nothing about it. We gritted our teeth, signed the contract and pressed

RUBY—My Precious Gem!

on with the show. Manipulation is rife in many businesses. We had suffered it, and so too had Ruby, as I was to discover later. We were involved throughout the show in scenes and production numbers, including the dance routine with Ruby. We received very good press notices for our efforts and looked forward to a happy season. Little did I know that it was to be the most important time in my life.

I had spoken very little to Ruby throughout the rehearsals and didn't realise what she was going through. I had every respect for her and enjoyed what little conversation we had albeit on matters concerning the show. Getting Ruby's new car to Blackpool was a problem that was solved when Ron, one of our group, offered to drive it up from London. As in most summer seasons the artistes would usually find a suitable restaurant in the town to have a meal after the shows. It was a way to unwind and get to know each other better.

I began to have regular conversations with Ruby and discovered what a wonderful person she really was. I enjoyed her company and her sense of humour very much and began to feel that I would like to get to know her better. I knew that I was attracted to her but could never make any kind of approach, after all she was the star of the show. I must also admit that the fear of being rejected, if I had made an approach, was foremost in my mind. I could not have faced a situation of being rejected and then having to spend the rest of the season feeling totally embarrassed.

Ruby had a remarkable ability of making you feel at ease. One memorable occasion was on a wet and windswept night as a group of us left the Pier and looked for taxis to go to our chosen restaurant. Being the star of the show, Ruby was allocated a parking space for the season close to the top of the Pier. She chose to leave the car where it was and look for a taxi with the rest of us. Purely by chance, I finished up sitting next to Ruby in the back of one of the taxis. The taxi drove off, through the miserable rain, and we started to chat.

"I'm hungry!" she said. "Are you?"

I replied: "I could eat the hind leg off a donkey."

She threw her head back, laughed and placed her hand on my knee. A friendly gesture, one which was perhaps meant to put me at ease, as was her way. It encouraged me, and some of my inhibitions were dispelled. We arrived at the restaurant and alighted from the back of the taxi into the rainy night. We needed to cross what was still a busy road, so I offered her my hand and she took it. I felt that she didn't want to let go when we reached the restaurant door. We ordered our meal and Ruby started to confide in me about how several of her family had arrived and why she had to leave her overcrowded house.

"The partying became all too much for me in the house. We're all Irish you see!" she said. "Renee, my domestic help, is a wonderful lady. She is so considerate and offered me accommodation in her house. I gratefully accepted. I simply had to get some peace and quiet and desperately needed sleep."

The meal was thoroughly enjoyable so was the company. By the end of the evening I was again holding her hand and felt that there was a great deal of warmth coming from her filling me with hope that we could enjoy many more evenings such as this one. At the end of the meal we left the restaurant and searched for a taxi to take us back to where her car was parked. We arrived, and I was just about to ask the driver to take me on to the hotel where I was staying when Ruby enquired "Where is it you're staying?"

I replied: "The North Bank Hotel, just along the seafront" to which Ruby suggested: "Why not let me drop you off there? I can go that way."

This really was an offer that I couldn't refuse and it was coming from a very pretty girl, who just happened to be the star of the show, and she was offering to chauffer me back to my hotel.

"That is very kind of you. Thank you," I said.

It was still raining so we walked quickly to where her car was parked, and within a couple of minutes we arrived at my hotel. We said goodnight and I gave her a peck on the cheek, as most artistes do when departing.

"Goodnight Ruby," I said. "And thanks again for the lift".

RUBY—My Precious Gem!

She smiled and said: "Oh hell, that's alright," which was an 'in' joke that she had related to me earlier. Turning her car around, she drove off in the direction of Renee's house, where she was staying.

The next morning we ran into one another as we were both looking for mail in the post box at the stage door.

"Care for a coffee?" I asked. Ruby seemed pleased to accept. Soon we were discussing each other's problems and aspirations. Gradually she began to open up and I was to learn about some of the difficulties that she had experienced, for example with the dance routine, the 'conman' and her rowdy family. She told me that she visited her family each day at the rented house and she was to learn that major differences had arisen and heated arguments had broken out.

"Shades of The Fighting Connollys," she said.

The Canadian members of the family had decided to leave and go back to London where, presumably, they would catch their flight to Toronto. Other family members were due to arrive so the accommodation situation did not ease. Finishing her coffee, Ruby explained that she had an appointment that she needed to keep. I really didn't want her to go. As she was leaving she turned to me and said: "Thanks for the chat … it's good to talk" to which I replied "Oh hell, that's alright". She laughed, turned on her heel then hurried along the pier toward the main street.

We dined regularly together after that, and then one day Ruby suggested that instead of going to the restaurant one night, she would cook us a meal, with Renee's permission, back at her place.

"That would be wonderful but when? I asked.

"What about Saturday? she asked.

"Great, I shall look forward to that," I said.

Back again came the 'in' joke, "Oh hell, that's alright." She had prepared a meal before leaving to come to the theatre to do the three Saturday performances and left Renee to light the oven at an appropriate time. When we got 'home' Renee had laid everything out beautifully for us and then retired to another room allowing us to dine quietly together. What bliss, a delicious meal, peace, and delightful company. On this occasion it wasn't just a peck on the cheek when I departed, we embraced and I experienced her kisses for the very first time, thrilling moments indeed. Despite the fact that we had only known each other for a brief period of time, I had fallen for her completely and felt that she had deep feelings for me. I simply couldn't believe what was happening, I was experiencing love, real love, for the very first time.

Music was always a favourite topic of discussion and who were our favourite singers and what type of music we liked. Ruby had a wide preference in both music and singers, but I was thrilled to learn that her first choice of singer was, the 'guvnor' – Frank Sinatra. Being a member of a vocal group I loved harmony, so harmony groups were my first choice. The Four Freshmen were far and away the finest group that I had heard up until then, and I had a large collection of their records. The 'Frosh,' as they were nicknamed, had a great influence on our quartet and we strove hard to achieve a mere part of their musical ability, but sadly we had not got a lead singer with the voice like Bob Flanagan. Neither had we their supreme musical and instrumental talent. There was one song amongst the hundreds that they recorded that seemed so applicable to our relationship, Ruby's and mine— 'How Can I Tell Her'. I took the recording with me one night and played it to Ruby. She loved it, and from then on it was 'our song' and it had a very special meaning to us both.

This is the lyric –

Should I try to hold her near me, or how should I try to tell her?
Should I sigh and hope she'll hear me, or should I wait, would it break?
Or should I simply say that she's the love I've dreamed of always,
The only love I long to hold,
It's hard to hide, deep inside, the things that should be told
But how to tell her, how should I tell her
How can I tell her of my love.

RUBY—My Precious Gem!

It was becoming a deeply emotional period in my life and I was trying to pluck up enough courage to actually tell Ruby of my love, and my feelings towards her. Then, the decision was about to be made for me. By this time the Connollys had gone, Ruby's father had returned to Belfast, leaving Winnie and various other members of the Murray family to come and go as they wished to the rented house. It had become like an hotel for them all. I was unaware of it, but relentless telephone calls were being exchanged between Ruby and her mother. It became apparent that Winnie had found out about her daughter's involvement with me. I didn't know either that Ruby had told her mother that she had met the man she wanted to marry. To Winnie that was explosive. She telephoned Dan in Belfast and all hell broke loose. Dan declared that he would return to Blackpool immediately, to find out all about me. He called Ruby and demanded: "I want to meet this man. In the meantime you must return to the rented house and don't make any move until I get there".

When he arrived he was ready to vent his anger. He had discovered that we were seeing each other after the show and going back to Renee's house. He called Ruby from the rented house and told her that he was coming over to Renee's, I was there when he arrived. He was furious and directed his anger at Ruby. His finger wagging and his verbal tirade of abuse became offensive. I was stunned. I couldn't believe this man's behaviour towards his own daughter, who happened to be the star of the show, and in front of company. Most of his demands were centred on Ruby returning to the other house.

"I don't want any arguments. You're going and that is it!"

Ruby pointed out: "Daddy, I have a heavy schedule, which includes carrying out loads of personal appearances here there and everywhere and two, sometimes three, performances each day. I need to rest and to be able to get sleep and I was not getting that back at the other house with all the noisy parties that were going on. Whereas I am able to get peace and quiet here with Renee."

He wasn't going to listen. "You're going, I don't want to hear anymore," he said.

Inside I was fuming with anger myself but could not interfere, at least I couldn't then. He carried on with his dictating until it reduced Ruby to tears. I could see that she was embarrassed for Renee, her husband Wally and also concerned about me seeing this unbelievable behaviour from her bullying father. Ruby at this time was 22 years old, an adult capable of deciding what she wanted to do, when, how and with whom she wished. Her father had no right to dictate that she should do his bidding. I felt compassion for this lovely lady and certainly couldn't understand how any father could treat his daughter in this objectionable way.

His hateful behaviour continued a couple of nights later when he returned to Renee's to take up the fray. Obviously totally embarrassed by the scene, Renee and Wally diplomatically retired to the kitchen. I was present and becoming increasing uncomfortable myself, especially when Ruby started to cry. In an attempt to get a moment or two alone with Ruby's father, I carefully suggested that 'I think that a cup of tea wouldn't go amiss' and planted the idea to Ruby.

"Do you think that Renee would be kind enough to make us some tea, Ruby?"

Ruby left the room, as I had hoped, leaving me the opportunity to try to put a stop to this ceaseless bullying. I turned to him: "Mr. Murray, you can surely see that Ruby is obviously very upset. This is the second time you have reduced her to tears in front of Renee, her husband and me".

His immediate reply was: "What's it got to do with you?"

We exchanged more words and he refused to stop his abuse which ended with "I think you and I ought to step outside."

I responded to his challenge by telling him: "Up to now Mr. Murray, I am willing to take into consideration the age difference that exists between us."

I estimated that he was perhaps 60ish whereas I was just 28 years old. I went on "... but if you continue to upset Ruby in this manner, I will

RUBY—My Precious Gem!

ask Ruby to marry me and if she accepts my proposal you would be upsetting someone who has agreed to become my wife. It would then be an entirely different matter. I would then be severely tempted to accept your offer."

He backed down, and with my proposition ringing in his ears he departed. I knew instantly that I had made an enemy, in no uncertain terms. Nobody had stood up to 'Big Dan' in this way before and got away with it.

I was to receive praise from Renee and Wally for the way I stood up for Ruby against her tyrannical father. I fervently hoped that, after the initial upset of seeing her father leave, Ruby would grow closer to me.

Our meetings continued and feelings between us deepened. Unfortunately, the torrent of abuse didn't stop. Now Winnie joined the fray. She made it clear that she wasn't going to accept the situation. Vitriolic telephone calls were a regular occurrence, and we both realised that war had been declared. This war was to last for years, throughout our married life, without respite. It became clear that Ruby's parents were scared that I would take over from them, as Winnie was quoted in the press as saying, and later I realised that Ruby to them was a pot of gold, which they might be in danger of losing.

The arguments that they thrust at Ruby included: "You should have married Dr. Creighton not him!" and " Who is he anyway? A nobody" followed by "You don't even know him."

It was true that we had only been 'courting' for a few weeks but in essence their behaviour helped to cement our relationship. The "You don't even know him" statement was to come back again and again in the future. It was obvious to anyone that whoever married Ruby would be a 'threat' and in the way, future events proved that quite conclusively. I was to become aware of the strength of influence that Winnie had over her family and in particular over Ruby. They were not called 'The Fighting Connollys' for nothing. Their reputation went before them.

Happily, our relationship went from strength to strength in a very short time. It blossomed into a very loving relationship, despite family interference. We were both blissfully happy together. Soon we were engaged to be married. I went out and bought Ruby an engagement ring, one which to this day is a treasured possession of mine. It became painfully obvious that we were not going to win with Dan and Winnie, but it was our hope that when they came to terms with the fact that we loved one another, and that we were adults capable of knowing our own minds and that it was not some teenage flirtation, they might relent and give us their blessing.

On the contrary, the pressure that they exerted was unrelenting. As a direct result it pushed us closer to one another and we decided to get married and tell them the news afterwards. Renee and Wally were diamonds to us both and Wally suggested that, with the aid of a special licence we could obtain a very speedy wedding—a matter of days he thought. They also knew of a church minister by the name of The Reverend Alcock, a very charming man, whose Baptist church was quite close to where they lived. We agreed to meet up with the minister to discuss arrangements and discovered that he was quite willing to be discreet when it came to our need for secrecy. We were both deeply in love and deliriously excited with all the arrangements and with the way in which

we received so much assistance from those involved. Our engagement lasted just nine days. "Everything is pink and feathers!" were the words that Ruby used.

The wedding took place on 23rd August 1957 at Whitegate Drive Baptist Church in Blackpool. The entire congregation, other than Ruby and myself, numbered just 12 adults plus two children.

RUBY—My Precious Gem!

My best man was one of my partners in the act, John Padley. The other two partners were present together with their wives, plus of course dear Renee and Wally. Because it was a secret, as far as Ruby's family were concerned, I contacted my family and explained exactly what was taking place and why I could not invite them to the wedding. They understood completely and were very happy for us both and sent their blessings and good wishes. With the help once again of Renee and Wally, the management and staff of the Carlton Hotel along the promenade, arranged a fine wedding reception.

The memorable day arrived and everything ran smoothly. We both remembered our lines. Then the usual signing of the register and the wedding photographs took place. We thanked the Reverend Alcock for all his help and understanding and then everyone made their way to the Carlton Hotel for the reception. Unbeknown to most of us, Ruby and the girls—the other Jones Boys partners—dreamed up something amusing for after the speeches. Her wonderful sense of humour rose to the occasion. Using the age old expression, something old, something new, something borrowed, something blue, Ruby, to everyone's great amusement, informed those present of the details of how she had accomplished that. She was wearing a two piece suit that was old, a hat that she bought for the occasion that was new, an ornate garter that she borrowed and was wearing it discreetly beneath her skirt and finally she had bought, especially for the fun of it, a pair of old fashioned blue satin, knee length knickers equally discreetly concealed. Every one was in stitches with laughter as Ruby revealed the garter on her leg and then slowly pulled the leg of the blue satin knickers down to cover the garter. This was Ruby sense of humour and it was done with a theatrical flourish and panache.

With the reception over, it was time to dash back to Renee's so that we could both change in readiness for the evening performances. Before leaving for the theatre, it was time for Ruby to call her parents to tell them the news, before the media got hold of the story and splashed it across their headlines and the air waves. She stood hesitating with her hand hovering over the telephone receiver, knowing that she must pluck up the courage to dial their number. Several attempts were made to pick up the 'phone before Wally came to her rescue.

"Here," he said, "drink this" and offered her a glass of brandy. "It will give you 'Dutch' courage". She sipped the brandy, shuddered, then picked up the 'phone to call Winnie and Dan. I often wondered, in later years, whether that offer of 'support' under pressure played a part in her problems in the years to come. I never did know exactly what the response was to the news but I do know that it was not in the least bit favourable. As we arrived at the Pier for the shows, a host of reporters had gathered and were waiting for us. Fortunately we had a legitimate reason for not hanging around too long. We had shows to do.

That night, after the final curtain had descended, the whole cast gathered backstage for champagne and wedding cake.

Then it was off to a secret hideaway that Renee and Wally had cleverly arranged for us in a beautiful house belonging to a friend of theirs in St. Annes. A certain Daily Express reporter, who had always been kind to Ruby with his articles, was invited by Ruby to accompany us to the house so that he could have a scoop for the following morning.

He was delighted and said: "I think that Mr. and Mrs. Burgess must be the only show business couple to have a member of the press present on their wedding night."

Now, we were married, it seemed like a dream to me. I had found love, wonderful love and the whole world was at our feet and our future seemed assured. There was of course the ongoing unpleasant situation with Ruby's parents and their deep resentment and opposition towards me, but I was hoping that, in time, their objections would eventually diminish and that

RUBY—My Precious Gem!

they would wish their daughter 'Good Luck and a Happy Marriage'. It was destined to be a forlorn hope. I was a definite threat in their eyes, one that they were determined to eradicate. However, Ruby was a happy bride and she blended in easily with the other Jones Boys and their respective partners. A new era was dawning for both of us, a lifetime of love and devotion lie ahead, but we were not destined to walk off into the sunset for a happy ending.

Chapter 7
♪ 'You Always Hurt The One You Love' ♪

Dan, who was still in Belfast, obviously decided to open up a new front. Now he made totally different demands. This time he told Ruby that she should come to Ireland 'to be married properly in a church in Belfast'. Again, he wasn't going to take no for an answer. Where, I wondered, was the man's thinking. It simply isn't possible for a couple to marry a second time, once they had married in a church, unless they had divorced in the meantime. He didn't agree, and continued with his insistence. It was more than likely he wanted his pals to be able to come to the church to see his daughter get married and for her father to give her away. He didn't take too easily to the fact that, in his pals' eyes, because his daughter had married without him being present it would give them the impression that he was not in charge of everything.

Winnie was also making her voice heard in Blackpool. One quote that was printed in the press was 'I hope we are not going to be pushed into the background and forgotten'. That quote was eagerly picked up by the press and expanded quite considerably in later stories. The actual quote was not exactly portraying a picture of a loving mother's response to her daughter's wedding. The press had now got their teeth into what was for them a newsworthy story. A whole string of unkind remarks were picked up and used. A quote from Dan to his daughter was: "Well, you've made your bed...". Winnie revived a previous one, again to her daughter: "You don't even know him. Who is he anyway? Just a nothing!" a remark which she was to use all too frequently later on.

RUBY—My Precious Gem!

In the meantime, both Ruby and I were deliriously happy to be man and wife. We managed to snatch precious moments alone together, despite all the pressures of engagements, performances at the theatre and the family feuding. Ruby was a warm and tender person and I felt privileged to have such a delightful, loving person as my wife. After the stay at the 'hideaway' house in St Annes, we returned to stay in Renee and Wally's home and they were wonderful to us. They went to great lengths to make sure that we had privacy, peace and quiet. We were very grateful to them for that. They made sure that we had romantic candlelight meals alone after the shows, which we took full advantage of with soft lights, sweet music and love.

Our story, in the press just ran and ran. At one photo shoot they arranged for Ruby to be photographed with her mother and they came up with a 'hum dinger—'Ruby Meets her Mum, Bernie Stays Away!' That certainly fanned the flames. The truth was that we, Ruby and I, had decided that I should not be present for fear that a public disagreement might emerge which could possibly prove to be an ugly situation. As it turned out, the press created even more friction. Meanwhile, one of my singing partners in The Jones Boys—John, my best man—had got married to another show business personality Anne Hart. Between us we decided that when the season came to an end in October we would all go to Paris on a belated honeymoon. Hotels and flights were booked. It was to be a very romantic, thrilling and memorable occasion.

Both Dan and Winnie kept up the incessant telephone calls, Dan from Belfast and Winnie from Blackpool. Their conversations were deeply upsetting for Ruby and I was trying to restrain the urge to step in and take control of the ugliness, whilst all the time taking into account that, despite it all, Ruby still loved her parents very much. The difficulty for me was the fact that Ruby was taking all the flack, whilst I was reduced to being a bystander. She took the full force of their anger because of course they would never ask to speak to me. It was clear that Ruby and I had to discuss what could be done to bring about an end to this desperate situation. Eventually we did discuss the matter in depth, on many occasions, and we mutually agreed that some decisive action would have to be taken to put a stop to their hostile attitude. We were a young married couple devoted to one another, very much in love and hoping to live a happy, carefree life together.

The outcome of our discussions was that we should both agree that a stand must be made to bring to an end the whole deeply upsetting affair. It meant that if I stood up to both Dan and Winnie, Ruby would need to back me up wholeheartedly. Crunch time finally came one evening when Dan telephoned from Belfast. The telephone at the Pavilion theatre was not inside the theatre, as is a normal situation, but it was in fact a public telephone box outside the stage door, which was in full view of members of the public passing by on the Pier. The call came in at a difficult time in the show for Ruby to take it and considering that previous calls were so distressing Ruby was again being reduced to tears, which in itself was awkward because of the mascara that Ruby was wearing. I decided to take the call and notified Ruby that I was going to do so. I could no longer see Ruby being subjected to such a bombardment of abuse and being reduced to tears in full view of the public.

I explained to Dan that Ruby was unable to take the call but he didn't believe me. Within a few moments heated words were being exchanged which then developed into an argument. During the exchange Dan made a threat— 'I made Ruby Murray and I will finish her'. I didn't take too kindly to that remark. In fact I saw red. As Ruby's husband it was my duty to protect her and care for her well being so I parried his vicious threat by saying: "Dan, don't even think about trying, because I will be here to stop you".

He was furious at being challenged and then made the ultimate threat: "I'll send the 'boys' over from Belfast to take care of both of you." I considered that to be a very serious threat indeed and the last threat he was going to make. Now I must act positively. Threats themselves were bad enough, but threats of physical violence simply could not be tolerated. For a father to physically threaten his own daughter was beyond belief. I called an immediate halt by saying to him: "That is it Dan. You have said and done enough. Just get out of our lives, and stay out".

I had made my stand, now I just hoped and prayed that Ruby would be strong enough to give me the support that we had agreed to in our discussions. Desperate situations had called for desperate measures to be taken, but I feared inside that Ruby would give way under pressure. She feared her father's wrath, and that she would not go through with the total ban that I had called for. Unfortunately, I was right. The crumbling start-

RUBY—My Precious Gem!

ed almost straight away. Perhaps I was expecting too much from a very gentle Ruby. The alternative was for us to continue with the war, their hatred towards me and Ruby's tears, all of which could eventually ruin our marriage completely and possibly even separate us, which was quite evidently their aim.

The Jones Boys' commitment to the weekly Sunday concerts on the North Pier came to an end and we were free to accept other offers. An engagement came along for a Sunday concert in Rhyl, North Wales on a bill with Marty Wilde. The three other Jones Boys female partners would be travelling there with us so Ruby wanted to be included in the party, which delighted me. We were becoming like one big happy family and life was a big adventure. Four young couples for whom life was eventful, successful and very colourful. We were all bubbling with fun and excitement.

We arrived at Rhyl to do two evening performances. The press had done their homework and guessed that there might be a possibility of Ruby being present. Quite a gathering of reporters and photographers were assembled at the stage door waiting for our arrival. We were travelling in two cars. Ruby and I got out of the car that we had ridden in and I started to unload. I suggested to Ruby that she might care to go inside with the other girls whilst I attended to the baggage.

"I'll get the suitcases Ruby. Why don't you join the girls inside?"

One reporter enquired: "I suppose you'll be making all the decisions now then Bernie?" to which I replied "Of course. I will do my best to take care of Ruby".

A huge headline in one national newspaper the next morning read "I am boss," says Bernie." I'll be making all the decisions from now on".

A typical press manipulation of facts. This was just the ammunition that Ruby's family needed. No such words ever came out of my mouth. Nevertheless, it had the effect of stoking the flames. The headline was taken up by other newspapers and further distortions were added along the way. Another headline—'Mr. Ruby' says: I'm the boss!" The line below went on: "From now on I take charge of her life and career".

A female reporter had a piece where she (quote): 'Hits out with 'a warning to husbands' —after reading about Ruby Murray'.

She goes on to say that Ruby had been doing very nicely on her own efforts, but what happens now when she gets herself a husband? After only three days of marriage he is beating his masculine chest and lording it. Not so Softly, Softly with "In future I will take all the decisions regarding Ruby's life and career." She even called it 'Stone Age' technique. The piece got even worse after that. Yet another newspaper claimed that I had dealt a second blow to Ruby's parents, the first was not telling them about the wedding—" ... they were not there" it said. The blatantly untrue news headlines that appeared after the Sunday concert at Rhyl, massively contributed to creating division between me and Ruby's family. Here was an example of how the press can destroy a person's life without a modicum of care. They most certainly had a major effect on our married life and to our individual lives.

A photographic appointment was made for Ruby to be photographed with her mother about the same time. They published a photo of Winnie kissing her daughter and the headline read —"Ruby kisses Mum, but Bernie stays in his room." The truth of the matter was, Ruby and I agreed that after all that had taken place it would be better for me not to get involved in the photo shoot in case something explosive took place. It was advisable for me to keep a low profile. Ruby was to meet her mother alone and on neutral ground. The press made up their own stories, as they are well capable of doing. The business of selling newspapers can be a ruthless one. It is possible to completely destroy someone merely with the use of words and at times they never hesitate to use them, irrespective of what effect it may have on their victim. In a very short space of time they wreaked havoc upon our relationship by dreaming up stories about things that were completely untrue. When the media onslaught had subsided, Ruby and I returned once more to married bliss.

The demand for Ruby to be here, there and everywhere, plus 14 performances and concerts on Sundays, left us with very little time on our own but we were determined to have precious time alone and we succeeded. Despite the pandemonium that reigned around us we had fun together. We exchanged stories, explored our individual likes and dislikes, played

RUBY—My Precious Gem!

our favourite music and thoroughly enjoyed each others company. Ruby was a beautiful person with a wonderful sense of humour and laughter was plentiful.

The Blackpool season ended in mid October, but in the meantime, we were looking forward to our belated honeymoon, which we would spend in Paris together with our friends John and Anne.

We really had a ball. As most tourists do, we went sightseeing around the French capital, thoroughly enjoying our nights out at the Bal Tabarin, The Lido Night Club and The Follies Bergère. A memorable moment happened at the Follies Show. During one spectacular scene, which involved dozens of show-girls, all in various degrees of nudity, posing on pedestals. One topless blonde, who had obviously fallen out with one of her friends, was also in a state of nudity facing her on the other side of the stage. She turned to her and, in full view of the audience, poked out her enormous tongue. Ruby turned to me and said "That's show business!"

Being the out and out romantics that we were, we had to go to see the film of that magnificent love story 'Porgy and Bess' which was showing at a cinema on the Champs Elysée. John and his wife Anne joined us. At the very sad ending of the film, when Porgy rode off in his hand made cart to find his great love Bess, Ruby, in floods of tears, made a classic remark. She said out loud: "No... it can't end there!"

Bernie Burgess & Frank Bowles

We returned to England, having spent an unforgettable stay in the world's honeymoon capital, bringing back a wealth of memories and precious photographs. There was to be one blemish on the horizon, which took place on the plane flying back to London. Ruby showed signs that she wanted to reverse the stand against her parents. I carefully and diplomatically reminded her that we had made an agreement that she would back me up 100%. I had hoped that she would see that if our marriage was to succeed, they would have to stay out of our lives as they had no intention of letting up. However, now it was becoming apparent that it wasn't going to happen. I felt disappointed and to be honest, rather let down, but they were her parents when all is said and done, despite their campaign of abuse and hatred towards me. I thought that there must be a way of finding a compromise, which I suggested to Ruby when we bought our first home in 1958 in Oxshott, Surrey.

Immediately following on from the belated double honeymoon in Paris, The Jones Boys had a contract to appear in cabaret at Wiesbaden in Germany at the General Von Stuben Hotel. It was a quality hotel, built by the Germans for the use of American Officers serving in Germany. Two of The Jones Boys wives were joining their husbands for this gig and, of course, there was now another new wife on the scene, Ruby. I was delighted to have her with me.

Our musical director, Paul Burnett, joined us for the engagement and we became a very happy band of show people. We had played to American audiences before and therefore catered to their tastes. "Hey! You guys are great. Have you ever been to the States?" We did the usual sightseeing, including a fascinating outdoor zoo. There was an Italian trio playing at a venue in Wiesbaden who sounded fantastic. It was the first time we had heard a sound system with a built

RUBY—My Precious Gem!

in echo unit. The speakers were concealed in the ceiling and the overall effect was quite stunning. We were quite envious of this wonderful new sound.

At the end of 1957 Ruby and I were booked for pantomimes in two different parts of the country. Ruby was to star in 'Robin Hood' at the Empire Theatre in Liverpool with Jimmy Jewell and Ben Warriss and Lynette Rae (who later became Mrs. Val Doonican). We, The Jones Boys, were booked to appear at the Alexandra Theatre in Birmingham with Arthur Haynes and Freddie Frinton (the famous drunk with a droopy cigarette in his mouth singing 'Sugar in the morning, Sugar in the evening'). Being the newly weds that we were, we didn't cherish the idea of being parted, not only for Christmas but for several weeks after, so we came up with a solution. We booked a flat in Crewe, a halfway point, and both commuted each night after the show which sometimes involved leaving our make-up on to avoid missing the last train. I got some very strange looks on the train, being as conspicuous as I must have been. It proved to be no easy task with British Rail's reputation for punctuality. Fog, ice and snow didn't prevent us from meeting up each night. We overcame it all and it became all worthwhile when we embraced in the rented apartment after suffering many hazardous journeys.

Soon we were to be confronted with more innuendo and rumours, from both the press and Ruby's parents. This time they picked on an obvious target, our financial status. Of course it was a case of— "He married her for her money". I had anticipated that and wondered how long it would be before it was used. Ruby, from day one, had been absolutely wonderful to me regarding finance. Obviously there was a huge difference in our respective earning power, but Ruby made it easy for me to accept and live with the reality. She made quite sure that I could feel on an equal footing by allowing me, whenever possible, to pay my share and to dispel any bad publicity that I had married her for her fame and fortune. We never once had a difference of opinion whenever it came to financial arrangements. The imbalance simply made no difference to either of us. I was still earning well with The Jones Boys as we continued to be fully booked in variety, Sunday concerts, and television appearances, enabling me to pay my share.

Bernie Burgess & Frank Bowles

Shortly after the Liverpool pantomime a contract came in for Ruby to go to America to appear in 'The Patti Page Show'. This was to prove to be yet another fiasco that she suffered as a result of bad management on behalf of her agency office. The contract stipulated that Ruby would be guesting on the show and was to perform three of her recording successes. Once in the television studios, alterations started to take place. The producer arranged for Ruby to play a part in a scene with Patti Page, dressed up as her wicked step mother, wearing a grey wig with a bun at the back, ageing make-up and a horrible, full length grey costume. Then she was to learn that her three songs had been cut down to three choruses of just one song. Here was a classic case of what a management office should be doing to protect their artiste. The situation should never have been allowed to happen. There should have been someone to negotiate for Ruby. If the discussions ended in the production team, or Patti Page's representatives, insisting that Ruby carry out the tasks that they put to her, then Ruby's office should have withdrawn Ruby from the show. On the face of things, the Americans must surely have broken contract by reducing Ruby's songs in the way they did. That is of course providing the contract had been drawn up correctly in the first place. The accompanying agency representative's response to all this was to say to Ruby: "It's only one show Ruby. The money is good. Just make the most of it!" That's management?

Early in 1958, just before we bought our new home, we had been living in hotels and on occasions in my father's home in Northampton. My father and Ruby were great pals. She fitted in straight away with all my family and became a loving daughter-in-law. My mother had passed away in April 1953 leaving my father to live alone in a small three-bedroomed terraced house close to the town centre. He had suffered partial loss of vision whilst undergoing a surgical operation for a duodenal ulcer. His vision, being so badly restricted as it was, caused him to have difficulty with everyday life so my sister Jean sold her house and bought the house next door so that she could watch over him. Before our first stay in my father's house, I tried to explain to Ruby that his home was humble and working class. Typical of Ruby, she immediately attempted to ease my concern by reminding me that she too was raised in such a house in Belfast and I was not to worry. Star status had certainly not changed Ruby's values or her attitude to ordinary working people such as my father. Her

RUBY—My Precious Gem!

roots were always near the forefront of her mind. This was one of the many qualities that I loved about her. I know that she thought the world of my father and he thought the same way about her.

The summer of 1958 saw both Ruby and I, with The Jones Boys, back in summer season together. This time it was Great Yarmouth at the Wellington Pier in another summer season spectacular production and again with co-star Tommy Cooper.

The season was very successful and the box office receipts were tremendous. We rented a beautiful cottage outside the town that had a lawn laid out for croquet.

It had a summerhouse with a broken window and Ruby and I became fascinated by watching a nesting blackbird flying in and out of the window, building its nest and later feeding its young.

Once more the artistes that were appearing at the various venues in the town gathered at a local eating place for socialising. Amongst those who attended for after show meals and fun were Lonnie Donegan, Stan Stennett, Teddy Johnson and Pearl Carr, and The Hedley Ward Trio. The artistes gave their spare time freely to raise money for charity causes by appearing at fetes and publicity events. The more athletic amongst us played in charity football and cricket matches against holidaymakers' teams raising money for cancer research and handicapped children. I still have some 8mm film of some of those events. I was never very good at football, but I was better at cricket. Stan Stennett brought his aeroplane to Yarmouth and provided great excitement for his fellow artistes by taking them in turn for short flights around the surrounding areas. There is an island just off the seafront at Yarmouth called Scrooby Island which is frequented by seals, so Stan made return trips for anyone wishing to see the seals basking in the sun. To my utter amazement Ruby wanted to go on such a trip. I knew that Stan was a very good pilot and that he would take great care of her, so off she went. On her return I asked her: "Did Stan swoop low for you to get a closer look at the seals?"

Ruby's reply was, "Swoop low? … He left his tyre marks on one of them."

All went swimmingly until the arrival of Lilian, Ruby's Canadian sister. She had flown to England in the hope of starting a new life for herself and Janice, her young daughter. Her marriage had ended and she had become a one parent family. She moved into rented accommodation which Jack, her brother, had found for her in Gloucester, close to where he was stationed with the RAF. For the trip to see her sister in Yarmouth, Lilian had left her daughter with Jack's family so that she could make the trip. We had plenty of room in the cottage so we provided her with hospitality and comfortable accommodation. On the first night she came with us to the theatre to see the show. The next day Ruby had arranged to have a small party back at the cottage and had invited friends from the cast. We shopped for the provisions during the morning but there were three shows to do that day, a Saturday, two at night and a matinee in the afternoon.

Lilian kindly offered to stay in the cottage and do all the preparations for the party, a very kind offer which Ruby gladly accepted. We left her in the cottage and went to the theatre to do the shows. Between the matinee and the evening performances I decided to dash back to the cottage to see how Lilian was coping with the sandwich making etc. To my horror I discovered her slumped in a chair soaked in drink and thoroughly inebriated. In the short time I had I got her to her bedroom. I laid her on her side and placed two pillows so that she couldn't roll onto her back and be in danger if she vomited. I hastened back to the theatre dreading the thought of telling Ruby of my discovery. After the two evening shows we hurried back to the cottage fearing what we might find. To our relief Lilian had partially sobered up and we got through the party without too much embarrassment.

RUBY—My Precious Gem!

During the very busy season we enjoyed relaxing at the rented cottage, playing croquet on the lawn. What a vicious game that can be, hammering those hard wooden balls around the lawn with, above all things, a mallet. We had a photographic call from the press and some very humorous shots were taken. One was of me lying flat on the lawn playing snooker using the mallet acting as a cue and striking the wooden croquet balls through the large hoops. Another was yours truly wheeling Ruby around the garden in a wheelbarrow. We were happy, deliriously happy. Her parents were not present during the season and life was peaceful, apart from the Lilian episode. It was a hectic season, due to the fact that we, The Jones Boys, had Sunday concerts to do in Blackpool and with no motorways to use, the extremely long return journey became very hazardous. We were young enough and life was an adventure in those days, besides I had a very loving wife waiting for my return.

Shortly after Lilian had returned to Gloucester, she telephoned to Ruby asking for financial help. Bills had accumulated which she was unable to pay, including rent and the usual domestic bills for gas, electricity, water, rates and food. Out came the cheque book and sufficient funds were sent to cover all her debts and some extra to help her until she could pay her way. That was by no means the end of the matter. There was more to come. We discovered that Lilian chose to use Ruby's donation to her to buy plane tickets for her and daughter Janice to return to Canada leaving the unpaid bills! Wait for it….. for Ruby to pay!

Chapter 8
♪ 'Home Sweet Home' ♪

Apart from the bitter disappointment that we had with Lilian, the season at Great Yarmouth went smoothly and was highly successfully. Up until this time, we still had no home of our own, so when the season came to an end we devoted time to finding one in the hope of eliminating the need to live in suitcases and hotels. Being close to London seemed like a good idea, so we concentrated our efforts in areas around the capital. Ruby took delivery of a very nice looking new Vauxhall Cresta during the summer. We were very proud of its new design and striking pink and grey finish. It looked a picture as we drove around looking at houses when we got back to London. We both liked houses with big picture windows that gave plenty of light and after viewing numerous properties we came across one that really appealed to both of us. It was situated in Oxshott, Surrey. So many artiste friends that we knew in the profession had chosen Surrey as their base so we looked forward to joining them as neighbours. The bungalow that we decided to buy had the type of windows that we liked and just the right amount of garden that could be arranged in a labour saving way. Gardening did not go hand in glove with touring the country in show business. The time element also had to be considered, as well as the backache.

We purchased the new bungalow, with the services of a solicitor, Anthony Grant, who lived in a house on the opposite side of the road – known to us as Tony. He was a local politician serving in government and later he became Sir Anthony Grant. Buying the furniture was a very pleasing first time experience for us. 'G' plan furniture was all the rage and Ruby bubbled with excitement as we went from one shop to another, sitting in

RUBY—My Precious Gem!

chairs, lying on beds, as all young married couples do when setting up home. My experience working backstage, constructing sets and building scenery, came in extremely useful when it came to doing all the DIY tasks in our new home. I worked with enthusiasm as we combined ideas about interior décor and soft furnishings. My imagination ran wild as I visualised how it would all take shape and Ruby encouraged me and added the feminine touch as we progressed. When I look back, I cringe at the thought of some of the vivid colour combinations that we used. For example we had purple carpet fitted in the lounge and lemon velvet curtains

which I lit up by using concealed strip lights inside the pelmet boxes. Well, we thought it was great at the time! The garden was a little too open and didn't provide much privacy so we bought some of Ruby's favourite roses and I erected trellis fences to train them upwards. It was a quick and effective screen and we were soon able to sit and enjoy the privacy of our garden. Ruby loved flowers so we bought plenty of boxes of annuals that would supply a blaze of colour in late spring and throughout the summer. The fact that they attracted bees was quite a daunting prospect as far as Ruby was concerned. It reminded her of the bite on the leg that she suffered as an evacuee. Soon house, furnishing and garden were complete and we stood back to admire our work.

The compromise concerning the family was due to come into play now that we had a home of our own. The new bungalow in Charlwood Drive, Oxshott was to be our 'castle', our safe haven, our retreat. We had agreed that Ruby could visit her family whenever she wished and for as long as she wanted, but the new home was to be our own and no family fights, squabbles or wild parties should encroach its walls. It was envisaged that if and when Ruby chose to visit members of her family and unpleasantness broke out, she could take comfort in the knowledge that she had a safe sanctuary that she could retreat to and a protective husband ready with a pair of safe and loving arms. It seemed a sensible and ideal solution to us, but Winnie was having none of it. She had used her manipulative ways and soon arrived on the doorstep with a weekend bag, quickly followed in the coming weeks by Patsy and her new partner Henry followed by Jack, his wife wee Ruby and his family, then eventually 'Big' Dan.

The castle walls had come tumbling down and we were defenceless. Fortunately, at that time, neither Ruby or myself felt the need to have supplies of alcohol in the house so unless they brought their own drink there was a chance that feuding might not break out. Soon, every week-end, when we were at home and not working, members of the family would arrive and it wasn't long before friction appeared and Ruby was back under strain. During one such period of stress, to my horror I discovered that Ruby had taken a large dose of codeine tablets. Fortunately it was not enough to cause health problems but enough to cause me deep concern. Looking back to that incident I should have recognised that as a warning of trouble to come.

In an earlier book written about Ruby, it was stated that I would not allow Winnie to stay in various rented accommodation. As if I, or anyone, could tell Winnie what she could or couldn't do. The statement was completely untrue, as the situation at Oxshott so conclusively proved. Winnie would come and go as she felt fit, but invariably there was always some kind of trouble. It was also chronicled that Dan never visited Ruby when Bernie was around. He did! He came to Oxshott, and later, when he had started a relationship with a woman in Belfast, Ruby and I flew over to visit them. Yet again, when his health was declining and gradual liver failure became an ongoing problem, I went with Ruby to Belfast to see him in hospital. There was an enormous amount of incorrect stories in the same book but it was written at a time when Ruby was suffering with a problem herself. I will write more about that particular book at the correct point in the story.

Once we had consolidated our home, our discussions became centred around our future. It was painfully obvious that we could not continue to pursue two separate careers and hold our marriage together. Far too often we had to say goodbye to one another and then depart in different direc-

RUBY—My Precious Gem!

tions. All too frequently in the entertainment world, married couples suffered from the strain of only seeing each other occasionally. These marriages were often doomed to failure and we didn't want that to happen to ours. Nothing could be done straight away. There was so much commitment by way of existing contracts for both Ruby and The Jones Boys. The discussions concluded that one of us must give up their career. I couldn't expect Ruby to give up hers. It didn't make financial sense. I would have to give up mine. It would be extremely difficult due to the fact that I had three partners to consider. I couldn't just tell them I was leaving. I would have to give them time to find a suitable replacement. In the meantime there were contracts to fulfil so I needed to wait for the correct moment. Now it was time for me to think about pantomime, which was at the Grand Theatre in Wolverhampton, once again with Arthur Haynes and Freddy Frinton. Ruby was elsewhere so consequently we were parted. It hastened my decision to inform the boys that they needed to find a replacement. My marriage had to come first. I anticipated that the family and the press would both grasp the opportunity to say that I was living off Ruby's earnings, no matter what the real situation was, but I would have to live with that. In fact the family did better than that. They claimed that I had <u>decided to retire</u> (in 1959). What a terrible thing to say.

During our stay at Oxshott a discussion took place between Ruby, myself, Geoff Sanders, who played piano for Ruby, and Roy Castle, who Geoff was due to join as his Pianist/MD. The subject of going into the property business came up. At one time or another, we had all thought about creating future security by buying property. It was currently a 'buyers' market and we all agreed that the time was right to do something about it. Ruby had suffered with huge tax demands and her family had been bleeding her of her money. In my mind, if we could convert sums of money into bricks and mortar they would find it difficult to help themselves to piles of bricks. We formed a company and called it R.& B. Burgess Properties Limited. I made quite sure that the only person able to sign cheques was Ruby herself. I would not allow a situation to arise whereby I could be accused of anything to do with finance. We bought a house near Croydon that had been converted into three flats and they would provide some financial income. Later we used our newly created company to purchase more property and I worked hard renovating, decorating and finding tenants to rent them.

Chapter 9
♪ 'Chicago! Chicago!' ♪

Another overseas tour was offered to Ruby in 1959, this time for a tour of Irish American dates in the USA. I accompanied Ruby on the tour. Everything went fantastically well until we arrived at The Keyman's Hall in Chicago. It was a massive venue, but, as its name states, it was a hall and definitely not the best place for a stage performance as we were about to find out. When we arrived, to our dismay, we discovered the hall was completely devoid of atmosphere. It was dimly lit and gave the appearance of being run down and in desperate need of renovation. Oddly, there was a large bar slap bang in the middle of the hall where most of the audience(?) gathered. From there it was a very long way to the furthest end of the hall where the management intended Ruby to perform. As a general rule, artistes with only a modicum of experience, can instinctively know when there is going to be some difficulty regarding getting across to an audience. An exchange of glances between us said it all. That was all that it took, nothing needed to be said. I had grave reservations about Ruby's chances of overcoming the difficulties confronting her, but I knew that Ruby would refuse to be intimidated in any way.

The management of the venue had hired the services of a local radio D.J. specifically to introduce Ruby to the audience. He proved to be lacking in professional ability when it came to a 'live' performance and was unkempt, uncouth and undiplomatic. His opening remarks, preceding the actual announcement, were destructive to say the least. It began with an apology for the fact that "Ruby was from Northern Ireland, not the South", and then asked the audience not to hold it against her. He could not have said anything more antagonising to this particular audience. He went on

RUBY—My Precious Gem!

to tell them that the management of the establishment — "had to pay megabucks to bring her to the U.S.A" Yet more antagonism. This man was supposedly a professional radio presenter. There was a crowd of unruly heavy drinkers gathered at the large bar in the middle of the hall, and by the time he had finished his inflammatory introduction Ruby turned to me and remarked: "They're ready to lynch me now."

To add insult to injury, once announced, Ruby was committed to walking the whole length of the hall, from her makeshift dressing room at one end, to an even more makeshift stage passing what had become a very hostile crowd. The majority of the audience were full blooded Irish/Americans, and there is nobody more Irish than they are, who showed that they didn't want to listen to anything that wasn't rebel Irish. They were going to be an almost impossible crowd to win over but Ruby with her true professionalism stuck to her task and made it through to the end of her act.

When Ruby had completed her performance I was seething with anger and made straight for those in charge of the evening's entertainment. I exploded all over them and I let them know, in no uncertain manner, that "they had no idea at all how to present a show, that the Radio D.J's introduction was a disgrace and that the venue was not a fit place for 'live' entertainment."

I was proud of Ruby for the way she battled against impossible conditions and told her so in front of them. They could see how very distressed we both were and tried to apologise. I was disgusted and we departed feeling full of frustration and annoyance. Looking back later, I realised that by challenging such an unruly mob I was tempting providence in a big way. After all, we were in Chicago of all places. Perhaps we were lucky to escape.

In the Autumn of the same year Ruby was asked to do a three week engagement for C.S.E (Combined Services Entertainment), in the Middle East, taking in Malta, North Africa and Cyprus. I was asked to act as compere/link man for the show and to do a couple of solo numbers, which I looked forward to doing. It was a well balanced unit which included Hal Roach, an Irish comedian from Dublin. Also in the party was Ronnie Collis, a very talented artiste who was an all England tap dancing champion as well as being a fantastic ukulele player and a superb Charlie Chaplin impressionist. Ronnie was a life long friend of mine and Ruby's. The cast was rounded off by a superb instrument/comedy act Guy Holloway and Pat. The pianist for the show was also Ruby personal pianist Geoff Sanders. As a unit we were flown from one service station to another in an aircraft specially delegated for this purpose. We flew in a Valletta aircraft presumably from RAF Command, with the same crew for the entire tour. We got to know the members of the crew and had quite a lot of fun with them. Even the piano travelled with us yet I don't recall seeing how it was loaded and unloaded, or who did it!

Life was bliss on this very happy tour. We were away from family squabbles and amongst good 'pros'. Ruby was happy being back in the 'fit-up' show environment with good friends and it was wonderful to visit so many interesting places in the world. The rapport amongst all of us was thoroughly enjoyable and between us we generated plenty of fun and laughter. A real tonic. In our leisure time, Hal, the comic, and Ruby provided everyone with excerpts from an Irish star act of light years ago — Old Mother Riley (Arthur Lucan) and her daughter Kitty (Kitty McShane). Ruby played the part of Kitty very well, despite being only a child when this act was at the height of its fame. She had an uncanny way of memorising her favourite film and stage stars.

At one of the RAF stations, Hal had to compete with the roaring engines of jet fighters taking off and landing during his patter act. They had a great sense of timing. They would go screaming up the runway just as Hal was about to deliver the punch lines to one of his gags. It played havoc with his own timing. At one point on the tour our aircraft was commandeered for official military duty transporting service families. We became stranded at an RAF station on the North African coast, namely El Adam, which was merely a refuelling stop in the desert with only a small number of personnel stationed there.

There was nowhere for us to go and nothing to do. Fortunately we were given very comfortable accommodation which enabled Ruby to catch up on the female necessities such as hair washing etc. I left Ruby carrying out these chores and took the opportunity to take photos of a visiting aircraft. We had been informed that a Vulcan bomber was coming in to refuel. I had always been fascinated by this incredible delta winged aircraft so I was eager not to miss out on the chance to get some photos. It arrived

RUBY—My Precious Gem!

with a deafening roar as it thundered down the only runway. I took my snaps and returned to our accommodation to find that Ruby had prepared a little surprise for me. During the tour we had purchased an Andy Capp cartoon book which we both enjoyed reading. I entered the room to find Ruby reclining on the bed doing an impression of Andy Capp's wife dressed in a dressing gown, with her hair in a net, a hair dryer conveniently perched, a cigarette hanging from her lip and the Andy Capp book in her hand. Her greeting was "Where 'ave you bin?" to which I replied "Give us a drag of yer fag Flo!" With my camera already in my hand I couldn't miss out on the scene. The shots that I

took still remain very precious to me. They permanently remind me of the enormous amount of fun that Ruby created in our lives especially when we were on our own as a married couple.

Our itinerary included a stop over and a show in Benghazi, a name that was so much in the news during WW2 when General Montgomery was chasing after Rommel's Africa Corps. As our aircraft made its approach, our attention was drawn to a raging sand storm that was taking place below us. It became apparent that we could not descend into Benghazi due to the sea of red desert sand that obliterated the whole area, which included the landing site. We were forced to fly on to the next stop. A hasty rearrangement of our schedule was made and we flew back to Benghazi two days later so that the service personnel there didn't miss out on the entertainment. We landed safely only to discover that the building that we were due to perform in had been badly damaged by the storm. Whilst Ruby was being shown around by the commanding officer I went to survey the devastation. There was very little hope of being able to stage a show in the badly damaged building so I decided to set about the task of constructing a mock-up stage in the open air. My backstage knowledge came in useful once again and with the assistance of a few 'squaddies', who were on 'jankers' (only service personnel would understand that term!) we built a temporary stage from pallets and whatever we could lay our hands on. We even found some bunting to drape around the area when it was completed.

Ruby enquired: "You won't be expecting me to sell raffle tickets in the interval will you?" That's my girl! The alfresco show was finally greeted with great enthusiasm by the servicemen and women on that desert post.

We returned to England with a wealth of stories, anecdotes and photographs of that happy experience in the Middle East which we treasured for many years. After unpacking and settling back in our home, a situation arose which made it necessary for a financial appraisal. Our nest egg planning needed safeguarding. Since Ruby's rise to stardom she had funded her family to the tune of many thousands of pounds. In the fifties, when the average wage was less than £20 per week, Ruby had given away vast sums of her money to Dan and other members of her family. Cheques had regularly been sent to him as well as Winnie, Jack and Lilian, all of which had been carelessly squandered. Winnie and Patsy considered that they had a divine right to open house at the bungalow.

Ruby's wardrobe was necessarily extensive due to her many personal appearances and frequent television shows. I had always encouraged her to spend money on her own needs, especially for her personal wear. She had previously hesitated about asking her dressmaker to make her a two piece suit with mink trimming. I had persuaded her to enjoy owning, not just one but two. The first one he made was a silver grey material with matching mink trimming and the second was in a toffee brown, again with matching mink. They were exquisite and Ruby looked a million dollars in them. Patsy noticed them hanging in the wardrobe, on one of her visits to our home, and admired them. Sometime later I was to see Patsy wearing one or the other, which proved that Winnie was not alone with her powers of persuasion. It was obvious that Ruby was being bled dry financially and something had to be done to stop the drain on her resources. An opportunity came along that just might provide a sensible solution.

From the outset of Ruby's stardom her parents were receiving a weekly allowance which was paid direct from Ruby's bank. Winnie had left

RUBY—My Precious Gem!

home and had been living in London for quite some time so the allowance was going to Dan who was simply drinking and gambling it away. His health was suffering badly from his drinking but he ignored the warnings. I was trying to find a way to put a halt to Dan's unnecessary extravagancies. Out of the blue, Dan came up with quite a strange idea. He wanted to run a parcel office and he needed money to set up the business in an office or a shop. Deep down Ruby knew that if Dan continued the way he was going he would become a very sick man.

I put forward an idea to Ruby that might solve the problem. Rather than simply handing over yet another big cheque she could achieve two things at the same time by putting a proposition to Dan. He should accept a sum of money equal to the family allowance to the end of the year, which was some months away, and that would be the final payment. He could then open his business and earn his own money. This might then bring him to his senses about throwing it all away on foolish weaknesses. At the same time, we were putting a stop to the continual drain on Ruby's resources. Ruby agreed. She saw the sense in the proposal and was willing to go ahead. I knew that Dan would never listen to any suggestion put to him by me. He hated to think that I, as Ruby's husband, had any say about her finances and where she spent it. He still considered himself as head of the family and what he said was final. As far as he was concerned I was just an intruder that needed to be eliminated. The proposition must come from Ruby. He listened to it and agreed to accept it. Here we go again!

We later learned that the cheque was cashed but there was never any hint as to what happened about a certain parcels agency. Not long after this episode, his health dramatically declined and he was admitted to hospital.

Chapter 10
♪ 'Yes Sir! That's My Baby' ♪

The Christmas season of 1959 saw Ruby in pantomime at the Hulme Hippodrome in Manchester. She was starring alongside a comparative newcomer to pantomime, the ex-champion boxer Freddie Mills, a great character. The subject was 'Dick Whittington & His Cat' with Ruby playing Alderman Fitzwarren's daughter Alice, whilst Freddie was playing 'Idle' Jack.

Before the season started, we had been delighted with the news that Ruby was expecting our first baby. In fact, during the panto Ruby past the five-month stage and became affectionately known to the cast as 'Fat' Alice Fitzwarren!

As a surprise Christmas present, I decided to buy Ruby a Singer sewing machine which I christened myself. With the expert help of the show's Wardrobe Mistress, I managed to make Ruby three maternity outfits on the machine. I went out and purchased the patterns that I thought that Ruby would like and started to 'run them up'.

RUBY—My Precious Gem!

One was in black satin with a mandarin collar and three fairly large diamante buttons at the neck opening. To my surprise and great satisfaction all three garments turned out fine and Ruby was thrilled. She looked positively radiant in them.

Freddie and Ruby were staying at the same hotel, whilst I was travelling back and forth from another panto engagement. During the run of the show several amusing stories came about. One concerned an incident at the meal table in the hotel. An autograph hunter came over and reached across the front of Freddie placing an autograph book in front of Ruby for her to sign. Ruby was slightly concerned at the way the book was pushed across Freddie's face. As she was signing the book she began to wonder whether she should pass the book on to Freddie for him to sign but then decided to leave it to the owner of the book to ask Freddie personally. To her dismay, the person again reached across Freddie, snatched back the book and departed. Ruby hoped that Freddie had not taken any notice of the incident. A day or so later the exact opposite happened. It was Freddie who was recognised and was asked for his signature. Across came the book, right under Ruby's nose, and as Freddie was signing a smile appeared on his face as he waited for the book to go back the way it came. It passed across Ruby and the owner walked away. Freddie, with a sly smile on his face, turned to Ruby and just said "Now you know how it feels!"

He had a very funny story to tell about a drunken Irishman that he passed in the street. Hanging on to a lamppost for support, the drunk was looking up at a tall tenement building and yelling "Come down here and I'll fight the lot of yuz!" He repeated his challenge again, then noticed Freddie passing by and said to him "'ere, I know you, aren't you Freddie Mills the boxer?"

Freddie replied "Yes, that's right" And the drunk said "I thought it wuz you" then turning to the building again he yelled "Come down 'ere! Freddie Mills and me will fight the lot of yuz!"

The weather was positively dreadful on the homeward journey after the closing night. I chose to travel when the roads were quiet but I was soon to regret making that decision. As we left Manchester, it started to snow and the freezing conditions became gradually worse on the journey. I was very much aware of the fact that I had a very precious cargo on board, so my concentration had to be 100%.

I drove with meticulous care through the icy conditions and after hours of precarious driving, we arrived on the outskirts of Northampton where my father's home was waiting for us. As I approached a dual carriageway with a thirty mile an hour sign, I was confronted by a bend in the road. I momentarily relaxed my concentration for just a second and touched the brake pedal. The car slewed sideways. I corrected the slide but by too much! The car swung around in the opposite direction, mounted the central reservation and finished up on the other side of the road facing what could have been oncoming traffic. Thankfully the road was empty as it was in the early hours of the morning. No damage had been done. Mother and baby were unharmed, so too was the car.

Towards the end of the pregnancy we became very concerned when one of Ruby's legs began to swell. The gynaecologist at the Barratt Maternity Home in Northampton was a highly respected consultant, Mr. Watson an Ulsterman. I took Ruby to see him and he diagnosed a thrombosis in the vein. He admitted Ruby into the Home for observation immediately. I knew that Ruby was in the hands of a first class man and she was completely at ease and confident in his care. The problem was brought under control and from there on he took complete charge of Ruby's pregnancy and towards the end of the ninth month he advised a caesarean operation. After the birth the nurses handed Ruby a baby with flaming red hair after a successful operation carried out by Mr. Watson. Julie Amanda was born on May 5th 1960. A really bonnie baby she was too. Within a matter of just a few weeks, Ruby was due to appear in a summer season with Harry Secombe and Harry Worth at the Palace Theatre in Blackpool.

For quite some time Ruby had been going through a quiet spell with her recordings. At Yarmouth in 1958 we chatted together about the lack of suitable recording material and the need to perhaps give Norrie Paramor another prod!

I was not Ruby's agent or her manager at that time, so it was difficult for me to get involved but I felt I could advise her as her husband although I didn't want her agency to think I was interfering. The 'office' didn't ever get in touch with Columbia. They were out of their depth in the recording business but hoped things would happen as hit records could only

RUBY—My Precious Gem!

enhance 'their' client. Something needed to be done to invigorate the recording side of Ruby's career. We were both aware that Norrie Paramor was a very busy man. He had a sizeable stable of recording names, apart from his own personal orchestral recordings with The Big Ben Banjo Band.

After a long confidence-building conversation with Ruby I accompanied her to the telephone to call Norrie. We had in fact rehearsed what she was going to say, now it was a question of whether she would be bold enough to say it. Norrie knew Ruby as being the gentle, meek lady who would not dare to give someone a ticking off. However, she nervously spoke out, albeit in a gentle way, and it worked like a charm. Within no time Ruby was given a Bobby Darin song to record titled 'Real Love'. Double tracking her own voice on the session, it turned out to be very pleasant track indeed and ended up in the Top Twenty at number 18. It was followed not long after by a 'smash' hit with 'Goodbye Jimmy, Goodbye', which got into the top ten and proved to be so successful she kept the song in her act right through until her last performances.

All of this underlined that from a management and agency point of view Ruby's career was never given the proper attention and that sooner or later there needed to be some changes.

Bernie Burgess & Frank Bowles

In 1960, Ruby returned to Blackpool to appear at the Palace Theatre with the two Harrys. Blackpool was THE place to be in those halcyon days when millions of people headed for the seaside resorts and enjoyed live 'family' entertainment. Audiences were treated to good clean fun in spectacular and lavish productions which packed the theatres night after night. Ah! Happy days.

We rented a house and employed a nanny to help with baby Julie. Edith, who was a staunch member of Ruby's fan club, was asked to carry out the duties and to assist Ruby with the domestic chores. Naturally Ruby wanted to spend as much time as she could with the baby but needed someone to be there with Julie when she had to be at the theatre. The baby was bottle fed, for obvious reasons, and Ruby thoroughly enjoyed those precious moments cuddling her at feeding times. Disposable nappies were non-existent at that time so the clothesline was always full of Terry Towelling nappies wafting in the breeze. We had purchased a beautiful high 'pram' which gave me plenty of opportunities with my camera and mother and baby made excellent subjects. The christening party was a huge success with the garden filled with celebrities. Ken Morris and Joan Savage also had a new baby at the same time as us named Kelly and they joined us in the celebrations. Harry 'Goon' Secombe acted as Julie's godfather and he also managed to eat most of the christening cake! He also blew quite a number of Goon-type 'raspberries' much to the amusement of baby Julie!

Fortunately, family feuding was going through a relatively quiet period, so life was great! There was however, a small problem on the horizon. Ruby looked forward to giving Julie her last feed at night and tucking her into her cot. One night we arrived back and Edith had decided to give the baby the last feed before we arrived home. Ruby was anxious to take over from Edith but she was reluctant to hand the baby over to Ruby, but mother insisted. It didn't end there. On another occasion, we were about to depart for the theatre and Ruby turned to say goodbye to both the baby and the nanny. Edith said "Goodbye, we might not be here when you come back!" This careless remark stunned Ruby and she couldn't get it out of her mind. She felt that Edith was tending to cuddle the baby too often and the feeling grew that she was 'taking over' the role of mother, an unhealthy

RUBY—My Precious Gem!

situation. I too became concerned and tried to pacify Ruby by telling her that I was sure that Edith didn't mean any harm and was just being enthusiastic about her duties. It was clear a mother's concern for her baby is not something to be challenged in any way, so we had to consider what action to take.

Family members did attend the christening at the church, where Ruby and I were married, but it wasn't until later that another 'hiccup' occurred which was to prove to be another ugly episode. I made a statement that had serious repercussions within the Murray family. Because of Edith's tendency to be possessive with the baby and her continuous cuddling, I suggested that the baby should not be picked up every time she whimpered. Winnie seized on that remark as though it was aimed directly at her, which of course it wasn't. She even convinced Ruby that I was trying to prevent her from holding the baby. This was the first indication that Winnie was to use the children, and their welfare, as a means of getting at me and it was going to be an ongoing saga for years to come.

The fact that Edith was an ardent Ruby Murray fan made a resolution to the problem very difficult but an answer had to be found. Ruby was unhappy just leaving things as they were. She couldn't forget the unfortunate incident regarding Edith's careless remark about her and our baby that "We may not be here when you come back!" Although she was domestically very good, sadly it was 'goodbye' to Edith.

Ruby had made a promise to Marie Cunningham that she would do a tour of Irish dates for her when the timing was right. There happened to be a space after the summer season in Blackpool so the Irish tour was arranged. Paul Burnett was free along his wife Sally, which proved to be ideal. We took both of them on tour, with Sally acting as nanny to baby Julie. What a wonderful time it turned out to be, full of unforgettable experiences and a bundle of laughs.

In her capacity as a booking agent, Marie set up a string of dates, both in the North and the South of Ireland. The plan was that we booked into the Ormond Hotel, on the banks of the Liffey river in Dublin, and use it as a base. We would set off each day to wherever the venue happened to be and returned each night to the hotel after the performance. If the venue was too far away from Dublin, we would pack an overnight bag, stay at a local hotel and return to Dublin the next day. It was on an occasion such as this that we experienced the first of many highly amusing incidents. After packing in readiness for the trip, Paul offered to take some of the luggage down in the lift to the waiting car. Thanking him for his offer of help, I suggested that he went ahead of me carrying baby Julie, now about four or five months old, who was neatly tucked up in her carrycot. It must be pointed out here that Julie was a very bonnie baby, quite chubby in fact. We sometimes jokingly referred to her as the Michelin X Tyre man.

Paul set off with our bundle of joy and arrived at the spot where the car was conveniently parked at the curb side. There was, what we considered to be, a self-appointed car park attendant, a kind of Benny Hill character with a peaked hat worn on a skew and pulled towards his ear. His spectacles were almost dropping off the end of his nose. It was a mystery as to who, or how, he was employed but nonetheless he appeared a very astute business man. As far as we could establish there was no official car park but whenever we pulled up at the front of the hotel he would hastily appear and direct us to a space at the curb.

"I've saved this space especially for you sir," was his claim.

Somewhat confused about whether there was a charge I enquired "How much is it?"

RUBY—My Precious Gem!

Back came the saucy reply in a broad Irish accent and with a wry smile on his face: "Just your generosity sir!" together with a respectful touch to the peak of his official(?) hat.

When Paul duly arrived at the pavement with baby Julie, our friend the car park attendant arrived on the scene. Carefully placing the carrycot down at his feet, Paul became aware that our friend was gazing down into the carrycot with a puzzled look on his face.

"Good Lord… what a brute of a baby!" he remarked. Temporarily removing his hat and scratching his head, he enquired: "Is it a man or a woman?"

Paul, somewhat embarrassingly replied: "It's a little girl"

Presumably being a good catholic, he concluded: "Well,… it'll make a fine nurse for the rest of them!" as he strode off to find a convenient curbside space for the next unsuspecting 'customer'.

We came to realise, during the tour, what is meant by 'Irish miles'. As we journeyed through the beautiful Irish countryside we constantly kept our eyes open for sign posts to tell us how far it was to our destination. After we had established that we had another say10 miles to go, we would drive on for a while, keeping a careful watch for the next sign post, only to find that we now had 14 miles to go! It frequently happened, much to our amazement and amusement.

One of the venues that Ruby was to play was, surprisingly, a ballroom in the main street of a small village in the middle of nowhere. It was owned by a man who also happened to own the local cinema in the same street. We all looked around wondering where the people were coming from to attend the show that evening. It was such a tiny village and residents seemed to be few and far between. We consoled ourselves with the thought that the owner must obviously know what he is doing in running two such venues so far away from any apparent population. When we were escorted to the ballroom and ushered inside, we discovered that the owner was renovating his large boat and it was 'moored' right slap bang in the middle of the ballroom floor. Ruby, quick as a flash, came out with an aside that amused everyone: "I didn't know that we were going on a cruise".

You have to be adaptable in show business and this was one such occasion and Ruby coped with this hilarious, yet difficult situation.

The proprietor's abode was an apartment and, you've guessed it, it was above the ballroom and he invited us there for refreshments prior to the evening performance. He led us upstairs to a very attractive lounge that had obviously recently been decorated with a very expensive maroon flock patterned wallpaper. Much to our surprise and amusement, two wall lights had been fixed either side and above the fireplace. Whoever carried out the wiring chose to take the supply from a power point in the middle of a shelf and channelled both sides in a huge 'V' shape to the two wall lights. After completing the wiring the channels were roughly plastered over leaving this ugly scar on the expensive wallpaper. After we enjoyed the refreshments, my mind turned to show time and I glanced at the clock in the middle of the fireplace shelf. I was quite shocked and enquired whether that was the correct time. "Oh! No," he explained. "You see, when we switch off the wall lights the clock stops!" You may think that is taking Irish stories too far, but it's true!

We stayed over night in a small hotel in the village which, I believe, was also owned by this same wonderful character. Before setting off on the return journey to Dublin, we were once again invited back to the apartment for "A wee drink before you go!"

None of us were early morning drinkers but we politely accepted his hospitality. Out came a bottle of sherry and four large tumblers and he proceeded fill each to the top. When he came to Paul's glass he politely declined the sherry and explained that he didn't drink at all. The host insisted that Paul joined us but Paul still refused and placed his hand over the top of the glass. The host ignored the hand covering the glass and continued pouring through Paul's fingers!

RUBY—My Precious Gem!

When it was time for us to depart, the host gathered up three empty tumblers to take them into the kitchen. Paul felt that he should not appear to be rude by rejecting the host's sherry and quickly looked around for somewhere to dispose of the drink. A convenient plant pot hastily became the recipient of the said sherry, coupled with an apology to the plant from Paul saying: "I hope that it's not too early for you!"

We were never short of laughter on these tours. We later did another Irish tour. This time Ruby's accompanist was Geoff Sanders. On the itinerary was a small town called Carlow and the venue was to be an old cinema. There was just one way into the building through a main door straight off the pavement. As far as we could see it was the only door in the building which immediately posed the question—what happens in the event of a fire? We unloaded the car and I entered the foyer looking around for a dressing room, or somewhere for Ruby to change. I couldn't find a convenient place anywhere so I made enquiries to the man in charge, who led me back into the foyer and pointed to the ticket desk in the centre of the foyer. From waist level upward there was only glass panels. With a polite smile I diplomatically declined the offer and asked if there was somewhere a little more private. Unbelievably, we had to settle for the use of a front room in a house some 100 yards or so from the cinema. Whether or not some kind of deal was done with the resident of the terraced house I didn't ever find out but Ruby was asked if she would sing a couple of songs in the front room to the house owners. Assuming that it must have been some kind of exchange arrangement, Ruby decided that she would oblige, although I knew that Ruby didn't ever like the idea of impromptu singing. When show time came around Ruby arrived at the house to change. To her amazement she discovered that an old microphone had been placed in front of the window which had been opened wide to passers by on the outside pavement. Picture, if you can, Ruby, a big singing star, standing in the front room of a terraced house with the window wide open and a microphone placed in front of her so that she could sing to pedestrians walking by the terraced house. I kid you not, that is exactly what happened.

The following year a contract came through for Ruby to go to South Africa in the Spring of 1961. The tour was to include Cape Town, Pietermaritzburg, East London and Durban. The contract also called for a Musical Director to accompany Ruby and to travel with the show. Paul

Burnett was free, so we invited him to do the tour with us. We also enquired whether Sally his wife would care to join us again and be nanny to the baby. She was thrilled at the idea.

We set sail from Southampton on board the 'Pendennis Castle' in March for a voyage that was to last two weeks. I have always been a very bad sailor so I was full of trepidation about being sea-sick. The fact that we would be sailing through the Bay Of Biscay didn't help me one little bit so I decided to confine myself to our cabin, long before we reached the notorious bay. Even so the motion of the ship got to me. For three whole days I couldn't surface. I remained on the bed for most of that time, a horrible green colour! Once we approached the equator the stabilisers were deployed and life seemed to 'level out' and become more tolerable. Crossing the equator was great fun due to the fact that the crew always held a 'crossing the line' ritual, mostly for all the children on board, involving 'King Neptune' complete with his trident. Julie was coming up to 11 months old at the time, so she was inclined to be unaware of what was going on. However, we involved her in the frivolity anyway and took many photos of the ceremony. This included a certificate for each child, including Julie. Ruby and I took part in the various on board activities, including deck quoits, fancy dress parties and deck cricket. The participants in the deck cricket, which included myself, were delighted when they out scored and defeated the ship's team. Watching the flying fish as they leapt out of the water and sped through the air was quite fascinating to both of us, as did the porpoises who seemed to be able to keep up with the ship with consummate ease.

Our first sighting of Capetown was positively breathtaking. We had to rise at 5am in the morning to get the best view of it but it was well worth the early morning call. Our arrival coincided with the day that South Africa left the Commonwealth so celebrations were going on all around us. The impressario that had contracted Ruby for the tour, Michael Klisser, laid on marching bands, baton twirling majorettes, flags and bunting and a motorcade. Ruby loved every minute as she was driven through the crowds of cheering people lining the pavement waving flags whilst overhead there were banners declaring 'Welcome Ruby Murray'. It occurred to me that Ruby's management could take a few lessons from South Africa's Michael Klisser. He had also arranged a special reception which was attended by many local dignitaries.

RUBY—My Precious Gem!

Included in Ruby's contract was a clause stating that she only wanted to appear before mixed race audiences, not whites only. Only venues with a no colour bar policy were booked, so many Cape coloured people were in the audience. The hotel that was arranged for us was in Cliftonville, a suburb of Capetown. When we entered our room we found it to be festooned with multi coloured flowers, which thrilled Ruby. She was truly overcome by this display of kindness. Our balcony overlooked a beach of endless golden sand. We watched children each day happily playing games that we at home in England had long since forgotten.

Within hours of setting foot on South African soil, we were invited to meet members of the now new Republican government. One or two of the 'cabinet' members wished to be introduced to Ruby, thinking that she was from Southern Ireland and therefore a Republican herself. Fortunately the topic of conversation didn't venture into the realms of politics, so Ruby and I both breathed a sigh of relief. Before leaving Capetown we were taken on a trip to the top of Table Mountain, an unforgettable experience. However, I suffer with vertigo equally as much as I suffer with sea-sickness but, luckily, Ruby was not affected by either so she was able to enjoy the spectacular views unimpeded. Travelling up the mountain via the cable car was quite an ordeal for me but I kept a tight rein on my feelings as I had opted to carry the baby. Refreshments were available at the peak in a tiny café, which was perched on a rocky plateau providing great photographic opportunities.

After the scheduled performances in Capetown it was time to fly 'up country' along the coast to East London, Port Elizabeth, Pietermaritzburg and finally to Durban, and a heat wave! The penthouse in the Claridge Hotel was to be our base for the final part of the tour. It had panoramic views of the beach and the sea directly in front of the hotel, which was quite luxurious. We were both highly amused and entertained by the many rickshaws on the sea front pulled by very decoratively clad Zulu natives with their plumes, feathers and multi-coloured beads. They displayed their physical dexterity by leaping into the air as they transported their passengers along the promenade. Just how their passengers felt about being tipped backward until their heads were almost touching the ground is anybody's guess but neither Ruby nor I were anxious to personally experience their antics and acrobatics!

To our amazement the venue that Ruby was to appear in was an Ice-Drome, a new experience for her. The ice surface was well covered and seating was arranged on top of the ice, but it presented unforeseen difficulties. As soon as the audience arrived and began to take their seats, a white mist started to rise from the floor upward, presumably caused by body heat. It created an eerie scene.

The show continued uninterrupted and Ruby came out with a very funny line, much to the audience's amusement. When she made her entrance she addressed the audience with: "I know you're there, I can hear you breathing"

During the stay in Durban a local radio station asked Ruby for an interview. She was taken to the radio station where the interview was carried out by an 'ex pat' Bill Prince who had become a very successful broadcaster in South Africa.

We had time to go sightseeing to 'The Valley of a Thousand Hills' where a traditional Zulu Kraal was maintained, presumably for tourist purposes. At the approach to the native Kraal there was a carcass of a monkey hung on a branch of a tree, to keep evil spirits away we were told. Ruby's comment: "I hope they don't do that to all visitors when they arrive!"

The best of the photographs were of a crowd of the Zulus gathering around our portable tape recorder, which I had used to record their singing. Their faces were a picture as they listened to the 'playback' of their own vocal performance in sheer amazement. The Zulu singing fascinated us equally as much as our redheaded baby daughter fascinated them. In the evening we were treated to a group of harmony singers on the steps of the hotel, all very entertaining, especially for me, a harmony singer myself.

Just one blemish marred the tour for us. It was the way some of the Afrikaner residents treated the black people. We both found it very distressing. We, at one stage, considered bringing back a black girl, who had taken to our baby Julie, as her nanny. Her uniform was spotlessly white and extremely well pressed. The complications of bringing her back with

RUBY—My Precious Gem!

us were far too many. Not least of which could have been the dramatic culture change for a young girl who would be thousands of miles away from her native country. There were also the inevitable difficulties regarding paperwork which could have been long and drawn out. We considered the idea several times but didn't pursue it any further. Before leaving South Africa we were to witness a threatening ground swell of black unrest when we heard chants of 'Africa, Africa'. Nelson Mandela, although still imprisoned, was soon to make his mark in history. We left with slightly mixed feelings. Ruby had been given a wonderful welcome and the shows were received remarkably well but the undercurrent of racial tension was all too evident. The nation was decidedly restless.

Chapter 11
♪ 'Nice Work If You Can Get It' ♪

Our homeward bound journey from South Africa was to be by aeroplane instead of by boat due to the fact that Ruby was asked to deputise for Shirley Bassey on 'Sunday Night At The London Palladium'.

On this particular occasion the Palladium show was being staged at The Prince Of Wales Theatre, so it was to bring back happy memories for me. Ruby felt that this was a great opportunity to highlight the duet that we had rehearsed. I had devised a song and dance routine to a song that I had heard the McGuire Sisters sing called "Do You Remember?" It was perfect for a straw hat and cane routine, so I donned the straw hat, picked up my cane and Ruby purchased a wonderful parasol especially for the television appearance. Because it was to be a special occasion we purchased a special parasol for the routine. I'm delighted that the parasol is still a cherished piece of my memorabilia. I was thrilled that Ruby chose to do the routine. It proved that she could overcome her fear of dancing when we performed it together. When I stopped to think ... Ruby dancing? ... On television? ... 'Live'?—Wonderful! I adored Ruby, both as a person and as a trouper and looked forward to performing the routine with her on such a prestigious show.

It worked well, and the audience received it with enthusiastic applause. We had included the routine in Ruby's normal stage act but I had no visions of it becoming part of a complete double act. Although I thoroughly enjoyed performing with Ruby I certainly didn't want to give the

RUBY—My Precious Gem!

impression to Ruby's fans, or equally importantly, to Ruby's family, that I was 'muscling' in on Ruby's own act. That was the last thing that I wanted to happen.

Life was pretty good around this time but, out of the blue, we were given another nasty surprise by the tax man. Another huge tax demand fell onto our door mat. The actual figures quoted appeared to be completely wrong and needed to be challenged. Ruby was again dismayed. She had no head for figures and, up to this point, I had refrained from getting involved for two very good reasons. Firstly, because we had been told that her financial arrangements were being well looked after internally in the 'office', which of course turned out later to be a complete fallacy. Secondly, Ruby's family was ever present in my mind. If I were seen to be dealing or getting involved in any way with Ruby's finances, it would most definitely inflame an already disastrous situation.

The accountant that we had personally appointed, an ex-tax man himself, was ailing in health and was having to cut down on his work load, so we needed someone of quality to take his place. Fortunately, during our property discussions with Ruby's ex-pianist Geoff Sanders and Roy Castle, a firm of accountants was mentioned, Arnold Clayman & Co. I contacted them and a partner named Eric Farley came to see us. He turned out to be our saviour. Many years later, I heard that the same man had been so successful in property dealing he became the owner of a very large well known hotel in Blackpool. At last, the tax matters were being brought under control and there was less cause to fear other bombshells from the Inland Revenue.

Whilst visiting my family in Northampton, we saw a house for sale in an estate agent's window. It was a 17th century cottage on the outskirts of the town, approximately one and a half miles from the town centre. Its name was Rectory Cottage. It looked wonderful so we asked to be able to view it. Set in nearly half an acre of land, it was built of local stone and had four lawns on different levels, flower borders and a free standing garage at the end of a drive. It was also a 'listed' building. We both fell in love with it, despite the fact that it was in complete contrast to Oxshott with its big picture windows. I could see distinct advantages immediately. It was in central England, which would be geographically of great benefit when it came to travelling in different directions up and down the country. It would eliminate the escalating traffic problems around London, especially South of the Thames. I would be nearer to my father, who had severely restricted sight problems that were now permanent. I must also confess that it would be putting many more miles between the Murray family in North London and ourselves. It might just ease the on-going problems. Property in Northampton was far cheaper than in London and the Southern Counties so I could see ways of developing the property company that we had set up.

When I chatted to Ruby on the subject she agreed that the benefits were tenfold, so I laid out a plan to achieve all these advantages. We could start by selling the two properties that we owned in Surrey, our own house in Oxshott and the one in Croydon that we had turned into three flats. With the proceeds we could purchase Rectory Cottage, which was remarkably cheap at the time. It also would enable us to buy one or two other properties in, or around, Northampton that we could rent out. This would then become an income provider that could be expanded as we went along. I had great hopes of building up the property business to such an extent that eventually, when Ruby was ready to opt out of show business, I could carry on developing the rented house scheme and we could hopefully be quite comfortably placed financially.

We took the plunge. Instead of buying Rectory Cottage outright, we decided to take a 50% mortgage and used the balance to refurbish and make improvements, such as a modern kitchen and bathroom. I discovered a four storey terraced property situated in the business area of the town centre and ideal for flats. We bought the property and I set about the task of converting it into four flats. Then we purchased a three-bedroomed house on the other side of town and were lucky enough to find a secure let to Canadian government employees. Next we bought my father's modest house, which was adjacent to the property with the four flats. We transferred him to the ground-floor flat and then let his house. This gave us all another benefit. Because my father was residing in the ground-floor flat, he agreed to collect the rents from the other three, banking the money for us and finding other tenants when a flat became vacant. He further agreed to collect the rent from the house that he had vacated and he also carried out small maintenance tasks on all of the flats, which gave him an interest in his retirement. Because we had taken over my father's house for renting we allowed him to live rent free in his new flat.

RUBY—My Precious Gem!

Once all the renovations and alterations had been carried out, we had a flourishing business. We could continue to tour knowing that everything was being looked after. We hadn't however reckoned on Winnie. When she learned that my father was collecting rents and doing the banking, she was overheard saying that he was "stashing it away in his own account!".

I was speechless! What a cruel accusation to make about my father. Fortunately, I don't think he ever got to know about that wicked remark. Unfortunately, all the properties had to be sold when our divorce came about. Years later, purely as an interesting point of view and shortly before Ruby's passing, the total value of the combined properties was in excess of half a million pounds. I think that we could both have been proud of that but it wasn't to be.

Now that we owned Rectory Cottage, we set about the task of renovating the house in general and the modernisation of the bathroom and kitchen. With Ruby encouraging me all the way, I worked feverishly to transform the house into our dream home, one that we could be proud of.

The thought that sooner or later Ruby might decide to call it a day in show business and want to settle down with her family spurred me on to even greater efforts. In the meantime her career was to continue and an offer came along for another summer season again through the 'office'. We waited to see where it was going to be. When the contract eventually arrived it was a huge disappointment to both of us. It was for the

Bernie Burgess & Frank Bowles

Alexandra Gardens Theatre in Weymouth.

Let me swiftly clarify what the disappointment was about. Weymouth is a very pleasant summer resort but the Alexandra theatre, at that time, was an old, mostly wooden theatre and only approximately 200 yards away from a brand new theatre that had just been built.

Bernard Delfont had also been given the task of presenting a full production in the new theatre. That cast was to be headed by Harry Worth who was enjoying huge popularity through his television performances. This then meant that the new Pavilion Theatre was in opposition to Delfont's other show at the old Alexandra Theatre. Complicating the issue even further, the 'office' had decided to place another star name to top the bill over Ruby. I am reluctant to give that star's name but, with my past experience, I knew that the box office power of that name was negative. In fact I considered that it would have a decidedly detrimental effect on ticket sales. We also had the same dilemma that we experienced before about the timing of the contract. It had been sent when all other shows were fully booked and too late for us to secure an alternative engagement. The combined considerations weighed heavily on our minds. What should we do? I adopted a positive attitude to persuade Ruby to turn down the offer. She was in agreement and summoned up the courage to tell Keith Devon that she would not sign the contract and that it would be returned to the office. He had taken it for granted that Ruby would simply sign the contract without question and send it back. She had never questioned a contract before. By now of course he realized that it was my influence that had persuaded Ruby to decline the offer. He asked to speak to me.

I voiced my concerns about the 'star' name and the opposition theatre in close proximity. He didn't agree with me but I stood my ground. Next to come on the line was Billy Marsh, the number one booker in the office. He first tried with Ruby and then asked to speak to me. I repeated what I had said to Devon adding that I was amazed the 'office' had gone into opposition with itself. They knew they were not going to win, but they hadn't given up. Bernard Delfont was the next to call Ruby. His persuasion, coupled with the knowledge that it didn't pay dividends to place obstacles in his way, convinced Ruby to sign and return the contract.

RUBY—My Precious Gem!

As a family we moved down to Weymouth, found suitable accommodation and the show opened. There were some excellent artistes in the cast of the Weymouth summer season show, including a very fine comedy character called Wyn Calvin. He was a very well respected artiste within show business and he scored very well in the summer show that year. A member of the very famous Water Rats, he later received a medal from the Queen, an M.B.E. for his remarkable contributions to the entertainment world.

As I had predicted the box office receipts for the first four weeks were very poor, which brought Delfont onto the scene. He spoke to everyone in turn without divulging exactly what he had in mind. The following Monday morning a notice was placed on the backstage notice board telling the cast that, due to the poor box office figures, members of the cast will have to accept a 50% cut in their fees. Alternatively the show would have to close. There's that pistol to the head again!

Chapter 12
♪ 'Heigh-Ho, Heigh-Ho, It's Off to Work We Go!' ♪

Apart from the satisfaction of launching the property company, the year came to an end with more gratification when Ruby starred with Derek Roy in a box office record breaking pantomime 'Cinderella' at the Pavilion Theatre in Torquay. Derek Roy was recognised to be about the best 'Buttons' in the business so he was a perfect partner to play opposite Ruby as 'Cinders', the ideal role for her. The producer decided that a part should be written in for me, so I was cast as an Irish Leprechaun, of all things, a kind of go-between for 'Cinders' and her fairy godmother. I thought that the part was a bit incongruous in relation to the original story but seeing that I only had a few entrances to make, it went almost without notice, thankfully. Our great friend Paul Burnett, The Jones Boys ex-musical director, was in control musically. He was a very fine professional musician and a delight to work with, which pleased Ruby. It is always a great pleasure for any artiste

RUBY—My Precious Gem!

to be able to look down into the orchestra pit and see a confident musical director with a beaming smile on his face. Apart from Paul's wealth of talent, his sense of humour was enjoyed by everyone. The panto turned out to be a really happy show and, although I may be biased, I thought that Ruby excelled in her portrayal of Cinderella. This obviously made me a very proud and contented husband.

Turning the pages of history over quickly, we arrive at the summer season of 1962 in The Winter Gardens Theatre in Margate where Ruby was 'special guest star' in 'Hughie Green's Spectacular'. It was during this season that we first rehearsed a duo sequence of song and dance numbers to include in the middle of Ruby's act. I had built a portable cocktail bar which had flaps on top that unfolded to double its size. It could be easily handled and transported. The idea was that a set of tabs (curtains) should open, at a given cue, to reveal the bar with me sat on a bar stool with my back to the audience.

In show business terminology I was 'discovered on'. As Ruby went into 'Mr. Wonderful' she moved upstage, with a hand mike, to face me across the bar. At the end of the song she introduced me as her Mr. Wonderful and we commenced the duet routine we did on television 'Do You Remember'. I often wonder whatever became of that cocktail bar and stool.

During the season at Margate we found a new nanny for baby Julie. Her name was Jane. She fitted into the family scene very well and the baby seemed quite happy with the new arrangement in her life. Another development concerned information from Keith Devon that he had received an enquiry from an impresario in

Nottingham, a Mr. Woodward. He was proposing to put out a production of 'Snow White & The Seven Dwarfs' and wanted Ruby for the leading role along with me playing opposite Ruby as Prince Rupert. The idea was fascinating and it appealed to both of us so we asked for more details. Financially it really didn't appeal, but the fact that it was proposed to make an extensive nationwide tour in first class theatres was attractive. Details of a contract were negotiated between Keith Devon and Mr. Woodward but we were anxious to study them. As usual, try as we may, we couldn't get further information. We would have to wait!

Earlier in the year, Ruby had been very busy in the recording studios and I had been eagerly searching for suitable material for her to record. I became aware of a song called 'Pianissimo' (a musical term for 'softly'). In my mind it would have been a great publicity coup if Columbia had secured the song for Ruby. There was a natural publicity link with the two songs 'Pianissimo' and 'Softly, Softly'. I fully expected someone at her record company to pick up on the connection and to make sure that Ruby was given the song. Unfortunately for Ruby, Ken Dodd's recording company Decca beat everyone to the song and gave it to Ken to take into the studios. He made an excellent job of it and Ruby was delighted for him when it became a hit. Norrie did eventual get Ruby to record the song but by then Ken's version had enjoyed great popularity. We had missed out on a good song, which might have provided Ruby with another hit.

Another excellent song came along which Ruby fell in love with titled 'I Will Wait For You'. She heard the song whilst in the USA and on her return she enthused about it so much that I decided to track it down. I discovered that it was written by Michel LeGrande. We tried to get Norrie interested enough to bring Ruby into the Abbey Road studios to record it. For reasons that were never made clear to us, we failed to get Norrie excited enough with the song and therefore it passed Ruby by. Fortunately, the opportunity came along a second time when Ruby had changed record labels and it proved to be a superb recording.

Ruby didn't always sing 'Softly' in her act. She had sung it literally thousands of times and was anxious to give it a rest. She was also experiencing an ongoing problem with 'cracking up' on the first note of the song, due to a combination of the letter 'S' and the low note at the start. The result often turned out to be a separation between the 'S' and the 'o' in soft-

RUBY—My Precious Gem!

ly so that it became s - oftly. The more she worried about it, the more noticeable the cracking up became. Despite the fact that part of the great appeal of Ruby's voice was the huskiness, she continued to fret about certain notes in the lower register, especially those which emphasised her huskiness. Ruby always considered that she had a limited range with her voice yet she recorded 'Danny Boy' on an LP, which had quite a range. Strangely she sailed through the song without a problem.

When on a recording session, Ruby grew continually concerned by what she considered were 'blemishes' in her singing and they were beginning to play on her mind. They grew in proportion when surrounded by numbers of brilliant musicians and in particular any Musical Director with acute musical awareness. For her there was always concern that the flaws that she worried about, no matter how small, would be detected during a session. Her normal nervous disposition would be exacerbated by the thought that she might be letting herself down. Norrie picked up on this concern and at times he would complete the track instrumentally and allow Ruby to finish the vocal track on her own. He certainly knew how to bring the best out of her. By no means was Ruby alone when it came to certain frailties in a voice. A good recording manager would always know when to correct or disguise a note or phrase during the making of a track and he would have the technology at his disposal to eliminate the flaw.

After waiting for many weeks, the contract arrived for 'Snow White'. To say the details were sketchy would be an understatement even though there had been plenty of time during the summer show to hammer out all the minute details. The basic arrangements were in place, such as where the show would be produced, the producer's name, who the other members of the cast were and a list of the venues that had been booked up to that point. Strangely, there was no mention of music or when we would be running through the various songs in the show. There were no scripts available to learn either. Ted Rogers (Mr. Dusty Bin), another artiste that was represented by Keith Devon and the 'office', was cast in the show as the jester, although none of us had any idea where a jester fitted into the story of Snow White!

He too was concerned about the absence of a script and telephoned Ruby to find out whether she had received one. He was astonished to find that we were not only waiting for scripts but we had no music details either. We eventually got to know that there was only going to be one week's rehearsal and that it would be at The Kings Theatre, Southsea. For a show of this size, one week is frighteningly short, especially as none of us had been able to study words and/or music beforehand. With only a matter of days prior to commencement of the rehearsal week, the script arrived at long last. I opened the large envelope to discover a very dilapidated and torn pile of paper. I really thought that it was some kind of joke, but it was for real. Some of it was in type, some written in ink, various pencilled notes were scattered here and there—it was pathetic!

Despite numerous telephone calls seeking information, we remained in the dark right up to the day we were due to travel to Southsea to start rehearsals. Ruby and I discussed this serious dilemma and considered the possibility of withdrawing from the show, despite having signed a contract. We decided that if we did that, an emergency search would have to take place to find a replacement for Ruby at such short notice—no easy task. If nobody could be found then the whole cast would suffer by losing an extensive tour. We couldn't do that. Even when we were driving down to the coast, I was tempted to turn around and telephone Keith to ask how he had managed to get us into this ridiculous mess. We arrived at The Kings Theatre and walked in to a confused crowd of artistes who were all frantically asking questions of one another and looking extremely perplexed.

Then the bombshell exploded when we learned that there was to be no Walt Disney music—no 'Heigh Ho' and no 'Someday My Prince Will Come.' When I spoke to the lady producer about the songs Ruby and I would be singing she told me: "Anything from Ruby's repertoire that might be applicable." I was stunned, so was Ruby.

It was planned that the show would be based on the original Grimms' Fairy Tales. Apparently, the impresario Mr. Woodward had refused to pay the royalties for using the Walt Disney music. What a disaster! We all huddled together to try to make some kind of sense out of the script. Both Ruby and Ted found that there were even pages missing in their scripts. Now it was a deadly serious situation. The producer was asking for suggestions and ideas as we tried to piece it all together. We all realised that this was a case where we all would have to pull together and pool ideas to construct a show around ourselves. In the end we did exactly that and pro-

RUBY—My Precious Gem!

duced it between us. Coupling ideas and suggestions with improvisation, determination and professionalism we built a show from absolutely nothing. This was a very frightening example of how Keith and the 'office' had once again seriously mismanaged Ruby's affairs. How could they dare to place Ruby in such a chaotic and potentially career threatening position? The show could have been a total disaster resulting in cancellation and the obvious press fallout could have had serious consequences on Ruby's name and her career. Ted Rogers was furious with Keith Devon and let him know in no uncertain terms what he thought about the entire fiasco.

Tickets sales had been surprisingly good and the show opened to a full house. We were aware that without the Walt Disney music the public could, quite rightly, feel cheated, and we all dreaded what sort of reaction we would get from the press. Apart from one or two lukewarm comments, the show wasn't too badly criticised, which amazed us all.

Mr. Woodward put in an appearance on the opening night and the following day he was to make a suggestion to Ruby that she could be well served by a 'radio mike'. Very little was known about this type of sound system in those days. He was apparently the owner of a business dealing in sound systems—Pam Sound. Ruby was introduced to this piece of ingenuity which was to be clipped to the neckline of her stage costume and powered by a battery hidden under her skirt. As it was a new system, not all of the technicalities had apparently been ironed out. I must emphasise here that Ruby was to be the only artiste using this contraption on stage. All other artistes were not 'miked up'. We soon discovered the first of many problems. Ruby no longer needed to project her voice, whilst all the other artistes still needed to do so. When the artistes came close to Ruby their projected voices were picked up by Ruby's 'mike' and became deafening, which caused Ruby to place her hand over the microphone in an attempt to prevent blasting. This in turn caused oscillation and a scream from her 'mike.' When the artistes turned away from Ruby they had to remember to project their voices once again. Not everyone got the hang of this. Stay with me. It now becomes even more complicated! Whenever Ruby came off stage, the stage manager had to remember to switch Ruby's 'mike' off. If he didn't, Ruby was still 'on the air' and anything that she said backstage went straight through to the speakers in the auditorium. The moment this happened, I dashed to Ruby to disconnect her 'mike' by pulling the connector out of the battery causing oscillation and a scream again! The stage manager, on hearing the scream, then ran to switch off Ruby's 'mike'. When Ruby re-entered the scene he hadn't switched Ruby's 'mike' back to on, so Ruby had to project her voice. Realising his mistake he dashed to put the 'mike' on again. Ruby of course was now projecting her voice and became instantly too loud for the 'mike'. And so it went on. Talk about the Keystone Cops!

However, it didn't end there! The chaos and pandemonium was to be further complicated. Because the microphone was radio transmitting a signal, which was then sent through the amplifier to the speakers, the system was open for other transmissions that were in close proximity to the receiver. Amidst our dialogue, and from out of nowhere, came a very loud voice saying "Pick up Mrs. Robinson from number 11 Railway Cuttings … " —the voice of a taxi driver passing the theatre. This meant that we were wide open to transmission from police cars, ambulances and A.A. men. We had a complete farce on our hands. Imagine the scene the following week when we were booked to play The Empire Theatre, Liverpool. The theatre was adjacent to Lime Street Station and the Liverpool docks so, along with all the aforementioned 'intruders' such as taxis, police cars and AA men, all the shipping in the Mersey began to join in the chorus. Laughably, it

RUBY—My Precious Gem!

was possible for the reverse situation to take place. What a surprise it could have been for the captain of the Mersey Ferry, as he left the quayside en route for New Brighton, to listen to Snow White singing to the Seven Dwarfs!

The use of this contraption gradually escalated into a serious problem as the tour progressed.

Chapter 13
♪ 'King Of The Jungle' ♪

The ludicrous sound fiasco could not be allowed to continue. Not only was it causing Ruby unnecessary stress, the audiences, once they had realised what was happening, began to laugh in all the wrong places. I had hoped that someone of authority would take charge and do something about it, but that didn't happen. I decided to take the responsibility on my own shoulders to put an end to this ridiculous comedy of errors by suggesting to Ruby that she discard the offending apparatus and return to a normal vocal performance. After all the chaotic confusion, Ruby was only too pleased to agree. She shed the radio mike with great relief.

The moment Mr. Woodward became aware that his 'mike' was not being used, he came storming backstage to demand that it should be reinstated. I saw red and simply exploded. How could this man, regardless of who he was, allow the show to become a complete laughing stock? I stood there, in my white tights, lilac coloured tunic (fastened down the back) with pearl droplets and diamante adorning my chest, full chiffon sleeves and a sword slung from my waist, and I told Mr. (Pam Sound) Woodward, in no uncertain terms, where he could put his offending microphone. Adding, that until his system had been sorted out, it should stay there. IT DID!

The sword was to play a big part in my theatrical education during the long run of the show. I was involved in a scene which called for a clash of swords, à la Robin Hood ('Welcome to Sherwood my Lady!'). My protagonist was a huntsman played by an actor named Llewellyn Williams. At rehearsals we had devised a sword fight sequence to look as realistic as we

RUBY—My Precious Gem!

possibly could. Nightly we would leap around the stage, like Errol Flynn and the Sheriff of Nottingham until the 'goodie' had disarmed the 'baddie'. Lew acted his part with typical Welsh fervour which made it extremely difficult for me to win! Much to Ruby's amusement, I came off stage one night, dripping with sweat, and said to her: "I'm fighting for my life out there! One of these days he's going to kill me!" That tickled Ruby's sense of humour and, over the years, I listened to her relating that story a hundred or more times.

From time to time, artistes allow themselves to have a little by-play on stage, to help combat the inevitable monotony of delivering the same lines of dialogue night after night. One such occasion took place during a scene involving Ruby (Snow White) and the Dwarfs. The story calls for Snow White to take a single bite of a poisoned apple, which makes her tired and then lies down on a couch, which has curtains around it. Snow White pulls the curtains shut. The Dwarfs become alarmed when they can't find Snow White and start a frantic search. One dwarf would draw back the curtain during the search and revealed Snow White holding the poisoned apple on her chest, usually with one bite missing from it. On this occasion Ruby had jokingly eaten the entire apple leaving just the core, which she held up prominently for them to see. The Dwarfs really appreciated Ruby's sense of humour.

The tour of 'Snow White' was interrupted for a period whilst Ruby undertook a previous contractual commitment for 'Puss in Boots' a pantomime at The Royalty Theatre in Chester. Ruby was to play Princess Valentine and yours truly to play 'Jack' the Miller's son. Peter Goodwright and Alex Munro took care of the comedy roles and Daphne Lacey (a relative of George Lacey the famous pantomime dame) played the role of Puss. The manager of the Royalty Theatre, and also the producer of the panto, was a man who had a wealth of theatrical knowledge and show business history – Denis Critchley. I first met Denis when we were both ASMs (Assistant Stage Managers). I was resident at the New Theatre in Northampton when a touring revue, with Dennis as ASM, visited the theatre with Nat Mills and Bobby starring. Denis really knew what he was doing when it came to entertainment and the production of shows. At one time he nurtured and schooled a comedy show group that he considered would have a great career in the business, namely The Black Abbotts. They featured Russ Abbott later to become a huge star with his own T.V. shows. The wardrobe department was underneath the stage at the Royalty and the wardrobe mistress toiled feverishly without seeing daylight during her working periods. Her son obvious had great hopes of one day becoming a performer and played happily with a ventriloquist doll. He succeeded in his dream, as he became a big star. His name—Keith Harris and his doll, Orville the Duck.

Our small daughter, Julie, made her debut in the panto when Peter Goodwright spotted her in the audience during the pantomime's favourite spot for children—the song sheet. I made a record of this historic event by filming it with my cine camera. Sadly the film of her appearance went mysteriously 'missing' later on, along with other items belonging to me.

With the completion of 'Puss In Boots' in Chester, we returned to the touring production of 'Snow White'. Ted Rogers had decided not to come back to the show and he moved on to pastures new. Before I leave the subject of Snow White there is another point of interest about this production. Ruby's publicity agent, Eric Braun, had achieved quite a remarkable feat. He was a keen fitness man and cycled everywhere, not allowing himself the luxury of travelling anywhere by train or coach.. He carried out an advance publicity tour of the complete list of booked venues for Snow White on his cycle, a total of somewhere in the region of 3000 miles. He cycled through every kind of weather, including snow and ice, to venues as far apart as Southsea and Aberdeen. That's dedication!

I must be perfectly honest and say that we were glad to leave Snow White. We did have some interesting experiences, but that was all that could be said about a show that we couldn't truthfully look back on with pride. However, we could return to a home that we could justifiably be proud of, Rectory Cottage. Some friends from the show, Jean and Peter Barbour (a stilt walking act) came to stay at our home with us. We first met the couple in the 1958 Great Yarmouth season in the summer show. They were currently having to live 'out of a suitcase' and were on the lookout for a permanent home of their own. Ruby extended a hand of friendship by offering them accommodation until a suitable home came along. They stayed with us at Rectory Cottage for a whole year before they found

RUBY—My Precious Gem!

a home which was only 200 yards from us. Ruby assisted them by standing guarantor when they applied for the lease on a property owned by Northampton Borough Council. I was eventually to have extreme difficulties with this situation when our personal problems started to develop.

Back home and ensconced in our beautiful cottage, Ruby was able to catch up on a backlog of things that she wanted to do in the house. It was around this time that some worrying signs appeared in our lives. There was quite a spate of recording sessions on the agenda. An L.P. was in the making, and Ruby was still worrying about her voice. During one session at Abbey Road, Ruby was trying to cope with what she told me was a dry throat. Halfway through the recording session we took a break and went for lunch at a restaurant just across the road from the studios and Norrie ordered a very pleasant drink with the meal. Its name, I think, was Grappilon—a pure grape juice. We all indulged in this very pleasant drink. On our return to the studios, Ruby was relieved to find that the dryness that was causing her concern had eased quite considerably and immediately put it down to the bottle of Grappilon.

During the next recording session, she asked me to buy a bottle of the same drink that had so easily solved her throat problem. I dutifully went to the restaurant but it was closed. I told Ruby that I had been unsuccessful but she was anxious to have something by her. I remembered that someone had told me that Port soothed the throat so I found an off-licence and bought a small bottle. During the two hour session Ruby had consumed most of it and was a trifle merry on our way home. However, I thought nothing of it at that time.

There were other sessions booked to complete the album and Ruby was looking to me to bring either Port or Sherry to see her through. My concern turned to anxiety! Now I was trying to find a diplomatic way of telling her to stop asking for more. There was a distinct possibility that someone in the studio would detect the need to drink during a session. It was also beginning to become quite noticeable that Ruby became very insistent. If I didn't comply she became agitated, in fact quite angry, very unlike my gentle Ruby. This was her first real encounter with any form of alcohol and I was beginning to think that I had caused the situation. Looking back, I suppose we were both considered to be a perfectly normal couple, who enjoyed normal social drinking but never indulged in drinking for the sake of it. We had now arrived at a situation where Ruby not only wanted 'something to soothe her throat' at recording sessions, but whenever she appeared on television, in the theatre or on any occasion when some form of stress was involved.

A significant date comes to mind, the day that President Kennedy was assassinated. It was reason enough for Ruby to look for something to comfort her, something to mask the pain, something to ease the sorrow. It was the day that I saw a distinct change in Ruby's personality when she had taken a couple of drinks. I have since tried to find other examples around that period and I checked with friends who may have noticed the changes that I had seen. Her friend Marie remembered when they were in America carrying out an engagement the news came through that Alma Cogan had sadly passed away. Upon hearing of her untimely death, and at such a very young age, Ruby wept, openly and needed something to take the pain away. When she drank a little too much Marie was surprised by the way Ruby changed by becoming so aggressive. Marie had never known Ruby to be anything other than a sweet natured person with a loveable nature. It was very difficult for her to understand the sudden change.

In truth, Ruby and Alma were never the best of friends. I remember being with Ruby at a theatrical party in Blackpool where a number of show folk had assembled for some kind of celebration. A suggestion was put forward that Ruby and Alma might like to do a duet, not an easy plight for Ruby to stand on stage impromptu with no form of backing and with no preparation. They were amongst fellow artistes so Ruby was put under pressure to oblige. During the rendition of their duet, Alma began to ape Ruby, but not in a friendly way and Ruby became aware of what Alma was doing behind her back and was thoroughly embarrassed and noticeably upset. I was standing with Tommy Steel, watching the incident and witnessed the unkind gestures and innuendoes from Alma. I felt that she was not just being unkind. She was being cruel. Despite this Ruby didn't hold anything against Alma and Ruby was deeply moved by the news of her death. She looked for solace at the bottom of a glass.

Towards the end of 1963, another opportunity came along to tour foreign lands when a request came through for Ruby to entertain the British Forces again, this time in Nairobi and the Middle East. We hesitated as it meant that we would be parted from our baby daughter Julie for three

RUBY—My Precious Gem!

weeks. She was then three and a half years old. This bothered both of us. I was never comfortable with the idea of children being left by their parents, no matter what period of time was involved. That applied also to children being sent to boarding school, which was to become a bone of contention with Winnie later on.

Studying the situation carefully, our nanny Jane had been with us for quite a long time and Julie was very attached to her. As Jean and Peter Barbour were still our guests at Rectory Cottage we decided, with mixed feelings, to accept the invitation.

We had a good cast on tour. It included Don Crockett, my favourite entertainer of all time, Frankie Desmond a Welsh pianist/comedy act, Jessie Caron a contortionist and Colin Keyes on piano. Colin was outstanding musically. He had played piano for many star names in the profession including Matt Monro, Bruce Forsyth and Des O'Connor. He had become very well known on television through being featured by Bruce and Des as a silent deadpan white-faced character. We set off with the knowledge that, should there be any emergency back at Rectory Cottage, the War Office (the government department responsible for arranging Forces entertainment) would immediately fly us back home to England. The show knitted together well. We had all worked with each other within the profession and were a happy bunch of artistes who all had a good sense of humour and enjoyed each others' company.

The recognised format for most of the C.S.E. tours was to entertain the Officers, NCOs and other ranks in their respective messes and to be invited after the show to have refreshments and to socialise. Afterwards we were taken back to our 'billets' and then flew on to the next port of call the following morning. On arrival at the next station our time was our own until the evening show so it provided us with the opportunity to go on sightseeing trips to the various places of interest.

We flew from RAF Lyneham in Wiltshire to Nairobi via a refuelling stop in Tripoli. Our accommodation was in the luxurious Royal Norfolk Hotel in central Nairobi. There were five or six stations on the Nairobi itinerary so we were due to remain in the hotel for some time, travelling to and from each station and returning each night. We soon discovered that there was a huge game reserve close to Nairobi and that an early morning guided tour had been previously planned for us. It was essential to have a very early morning call on the day of the trip to enable us to catch sight of the various animals on their dawn patrol in the park. Right on schedule, an extremely smart Camba tribesman, immaculately dressed in a crisp safari suit, arrived at the entrance of the hotel to pick us up. He spoke fluent English and told us that, with luck, we might catch sight of some lions in their natural habitat and to make sure that we all had our cameras at the ready. Once loaded on board the small coach, we set off for what we hoped would be a thrilling experience. We were not disappointed!

We trundled our way through the game reserve until our driver-cum-guide spotted a type of gamekeeper. He was a Kikuyu tribesman wearing, above all things, a British Army overcoat and a green coloured Foreign Legion style hat. It had a sunshade flap at the back of his neck and he carried a panga knife, or machete, glistening in his hand. As is customary with most Kikuyu, his ear lobes had been opened and were swinging freely back and forth as he walked along. Our guide, obviously multi lingual, asked him if he had spotted any lions and if so, could he indicate their whereabouts. He jabbered away and indicated with his machete, apparently his only means of defence, and then continued on his way. The 'ad libs' coming from us passengers on the bus were hilarious as we watched him departing with his trusty weapon. One remark was: "I wonder who is having who for breakfast!" whilst Ruby added a caption to the picture of the lone game keeper on solitary patrol wielding a machete saying: "I'll kill that cat when I find him".

Our luck was in. We came across a pride of lions, several lionesses and a solitary male who had draped himself lazily on a small mound and was surveying the scene as we approached. Windows were tentatively lowered and cameras clicked frantically but the King of the Jungle didn't bat an eyelid. He simply yawned as though he was bored with the sight of yet more camera happy tourists.

There was an abundance of wildebeest and gazelles, the occasional giraffe and a few secretary birds, but our guide thought that the hippo pool would provide us with even better photography. As we drove off toward the hollow our guide informed us that we would need to alight from the bus and walk down to the spot where he knew the pool would be. The two girls, Ruby and Jesse, debated as to whether the idea of getting off

RUBY—My Precious Gem!

the bus really appealed them, considering we had just been filming lions. They both decided to diplomatically decline the invitation. Ruby summed up her feelings by saying: "No Hip Hip Hipporays for me today!"

Don thought that it would be 'advisable' if a man stayed on the bus with the girls. Well, that was his excuse anyway. The rest of us disembarked and made our way to the pool to take photographs of the hippos. The girls remained on board and unwrapped the freshly made sandwiches in readiness for our return. Unbeknown to us, a rather large baboon arrive in the vicinity of the bus. He was obviously on the lookout for food in any shape or form. Ruby and Jesse were sitting in the front seats facing forward and Don had his rear end parked on the steering wheel facing the two girls. The inquisitive baboon found the ladder at the back of the bus that was used to stow baggage. As he scaled the ladder, Don caught sight of him through the rear window. His mouth dropped open with a sharp intake of breath. The girls turned around to see what had scared Don but by then the baboon was on top of the bus and out of sight. However, they then heard the padding of his feet as he walked the length of the bus towards the front window. There was a mad panic as Don called for all the windows to be closed. When he reached the front the baboon leaned down, head first, to peer through the window. Don made a dash for the motor horn and blasted away furiously on it hoping to get reinforcements.

I pause here to point out that before departing we had all been told that if we ever came across any form of primate, we should not show our teeth as it was a form of aggression. At the sight of the upside down baboon looking through the front window, both girls screamed. Ruby yelled: "Don't show him your teeth" and all three clamped their hands over their mouths whilst Don blasted another clarion call on the horn. Hearing the commotion, we hurried back towards the bus. By the time we had retraced our steps all three passengers had partially opened one window and were desperately throwing sandwiches out in the hope of distracting the baboon so we could get on board. The other men clambered on board but I wanted some film of this scavenging creature who was now cramming our food into his rather large mouth. Ruby once again spread her lips to cover her teeth and shouted to me: "Whatever you do, don't show him your teeth!" The last items thrown were small cold potatoes, which lured him far enough away from the bus door to enable me to get to safety. Everyone breathed a sigh of relief and Ruby said to me: "It's a good thing he was grateful for small 'Murphies!'"

Don was a man of immense talent. As a comedian/impressionist he was in his element on this tour. There was so much in the way of potential material that he could use. He treated all of us to life-like impressions and realistic sounds that were quite fascinating.

A succession of misfortunes came Don's way. He frequently missed meal times. He often had to make do with a makeshift meal replacing the one that he should have had if he had been on time. He lost his bow tie. He cracked his shin. The lock on his suitcase became jammed. It became a running joke with the rest of us. The final indignation for Don came when we were all receiving a meal on a plane. Each person had a plastic tray placed on their lap with a lid that slid open to reveal the food. Don was kept waiting and when it finally arrived, he pushed the sliding lid back only to find the tray was completely empty. Up chirped Ruby with: "Don't make a meal of it, Don!"

Chapter 14
♪ 'Around the World' ♪

During our stay in Nairobi, Ruby was asked if she would agree to visit a British Forces Broadcasting studio with a view to being interviewed. She was delighted. The DJ/presenter meticulously did his homework researching data on Ruby's recording career and did a wonderful job with the interview. We were to meet up with him again a few years later back in England when he contacted us at a time when he was 'illegally' working on a boat offshore called 'Radio Caroline.' His name was Keith Skues. In later years his professionalism eventually came to the attention of the BBC and as a result he became nationally well known. We remained friendly with Keith for many years and appreciated his talent. I still keep in touch with him from time to time.

The Royal Norfolk Hotel was quite close to another first class hotel in Nairobi, The Stanley Hotel. Don Crocket soon heard that one of his film star heroes, Robert Mitchum, was staying at that hotel. He made it his business to visit there several times in the hope that he might just be able to catch even a glimpse of the super star that he admired so much. Of course, Mitchum was always a featured impression of his, one of a whole host of film stars in Don's highly talented and entertaining act. He had a wonderful knack of picking the right lines of dialogue that suited each of his characters. For Mitchum he put on a Stetson, which he pushed to the back of his head with his thumb, lit up a cigarette which he allowed to hang from his bottom lip and said (to his leading lady) "Hey! honey,.. put some lipstick on,.. I need a target!"

Bernie Burgess & Frank Bowles

His Walter Brennan impression was hilarious and again he chose just the right lines of dialogue. Changing to a battered old cowboy hat, he muttered in Walter's creaky old voice: "Went out west in 1870, me and the wife in a covered wagon and, if you've seen the wife you'd have know'd why I covered the wagon!"

Going way back in Hollywood history Don chose a very unusual impression, that of Dan Dureya the surly, cunning 'baddie' character that everyone loved to hate. This time using a trilby hat, his dialogue for Dan was: "Hello lazy legs! Say honey, you have face like a million dollars, all green and crinkled!"

For Edward G. Robinson his lines were: "They call me the Little Caesar see….You too can have a mouth like mine by eating a banana sideways!"

Chilling lines were attached to Peter Lorre which were coupled to a maniacal laugh. His lines were: "As a child, I killed my mother and father. I wanted to go to the orphan's picnic!"

To introduce Boris Karloff, Don used his noise impressions to great effect. A knocking sound preceded the opening of an imaginary castle door which creaked and groaned as it slowly revealed a wide eyed old character who greets the caller with: "Welcome to my humble abode. Let me take your hat and throat. Everyone thinks that my wife is peculiar, just because she sits on the Brooklyn Bridge and dangles her feet in the water!"

After several happy days in the Kenyon capital, we were flown northwards to Aden. Local feelings were on a high when we arrived due to the fact that Aden was about to shed its connection with the UK to become independent. We were booked to stay at The Eden Rock Hotel and the moment we had settled in there was a message from another Forces Radio station. The person asking for an interview this time surprised us when he announced himself as Paul Burnett. When he turned up at the hotel to carry out his interview, we discovered that he was the son of 'our' Paul, the musical director that had played for both The Jones Boys and Ruby. He too was taken on by the BBC when he came home to England and Paul Jnr. became extremely popular and successful as his broadcasting career progressed.

RUBY—My Precious Gem!

Our stay in Aden was to be a very short one. We were only called upon to do a couple of shows. Ruby's brother Jack came to see us. He was stationed in Aden but was about to be transferred to Cyprus. Our itinerary then took us on a 'whistle stop' tour around the various desert stations in the Persian Gulf and it turned out to be the most thrilling part of the tour. The full compliment of personnel at one of these isolated stations was surprising only 39 servicemen. It was difficult to imagine how they could endure such a solitary posting, which in some cases could last between six and 12 months.

Our nerves were tested to the full when flying in to one station that was situated right on the Yemeni border, supposedly hostile territory. The approach from the air was hair raising. We were flying through very low cloud, uncomfortably close to what was high ground, and it gave the impression that the pilot was almost reaching down to feel for the roughly constructed runway. For the whole of this hazardous and unnerving experience, Ruby sat next to me with her eyes tightly closed and with white knuckles as she clutched the arm of her seat with one hand and my hand with the other. I've still got the scars on my arm! We taxied and came to a halt close to a 'mock up' platform, which turned out to be our stage. This was going to be alfresco entertaining in its most raw state. A mere 200 yards away, or perhaps less, was the border with Yemen, which was being patrolled by armed guards on both sides. On the other side of the border was another runway in close proximity, presumably belonging to the Yemen. Our luggage was unloaded and the piano was manhandled from the aircraft by the very willing servicemen who had been eagerly awaiting the arrival of us troupers. The whole scene was perfect for taking photographs so my camera was near to hand. The wearing of stage clothes was completely out of the question so we all decided to appear in 'civvies' adding to the informalities of this unique setting. During the actual performance, an Aden Airways Dakota aeroplane roared up the runway for take off. Most inconsiderate and not something that one would expect to happen when entertaining an audience!

It had been pre-arranged that we didn't stay over night at that station. Perhaps the security risk would have been too great and we were not sorry to leave. One station that we played had a fortress style building within the compound which gave Don a perfect setting for a photographic session. He had managed to acquire two Arabian headdresses, one a Trucial Oman

Scout's headdress and the other was identical to the one worn by Peter O'Toole in the epic film 'Lawrence of Arabia'. Firing his imaginary rifle through the slits in the wall of the fortress he called out in his best Anthony Quinn voice for "El Lawrence." He collected many such 'props' so that when he retuned to England he could rehearse routines using the various headgear. For example, a Foreign Legionnaire's hat for his impression of Gary Cooper in the old Hollywood classic 'Beau Geste.' Despite the fact that the film was made lights years previously, Don's audiences couldn't mistake Gary's unmistakable voice saying—"Yep!"

The tour came to an end after we played in Bahrain and we had shed our personal aircraft. The crew said farewell to us by carrying out an extremely low fly past as we waved goodbye from the runway. It had been a remarkable tour and all the members of the show had enjoyed every minute of it. We boarded a much larger aircraft for the return flight back to the U.K. which had a rear entrance at the back of the fuselage and a flight of steps which was lowered from the belly of the 'plane to the tarmac. It had been stressed upon us, by the War Office before we left England, that some of the aircraft that we would be flying in were not as effectively pressurised as civilian aircraft. It was not advisable therefore to carry in our luggage any aerosol spray cans, such as deodorants and hairsprays, as there was a danger that they might explode or implode, whichever the case maybe. We boarded the RAF 'plane and were 'belting up' for take off when one of the girls let out a yell crying that she had unwittingly brought a canister of hair spray on board in her hand luggage. She hastily removed it from the bag and was juggling with it in a panic. It was then thrown from one person to another as though it was a hand grenade with the pin out! I grabbed the threatening canister and made my way to the back of the 'plane where the rear entrance door was about to close. Leaning down, I peered through the rear entrance door and caught sight of someone's legs as they stood on the tarmac so I reached out and handed over the offending canister. Contented that I had removed all the possible danger, I returned to my seat for take off. The aircraft taxied to the end of the runway but before the anticipated roar of the engines, a member of the crew walked up the aisle and enquired: "Has anyone left this canister of hairspray behind?"

We quickly winged our way into the clear, blue sky. There was hardly a cloud to be seen and we were on our way back to England but with mixed

RUBY—My Precious Gem!

feelings. Ruby and I had missed Julie very much and looked forward to seeing her but at the same time the thought of returning to family squabbles and the constant 'phone calls were a daunting prospect. In truth, the Murray family was in complete disarray. Dan was in Belfast, living with another woman and still drinking. Winnie was living in a flat in North London, close to Patsy and her new partner Henry and their drinking bouts were all too frequent and very troublesome.

Lilian had returned to Canada with her small child, Janice, still struggling with her drinking problem, whilst Jack and his wife wee Ruby and their children were still abroad. Relations between all of them were strained to say the least. I also knew that the moment we arrived back at Rectory Cottage the telephone calls would recommence and Winnie would be crying on the 'phone asking, no—telling Ruby to come to London at once! I had estimated that, at one stage, Winnie was making on average of five calls a day to Ruby and because of the nature of those calls it was putting our marriage under a great strain. She of course knew exactly what she was doing and had no intention of giving up. Her hostile attitude towards me never wavered. No marriage can withstand such a barrage of emotional crossfire without becoming in danger of falling apart.

Making matters even worse our children (when our son Tim arrived) were to become pawns being used by the family, especially Winnie. Whenever she came to Wootton she would arrive loaded down with chocolates and sweets. I accept readily that it is quite natural for a grandmother to spoil her grandchildren but the sheer volume and her insistence on giving them before meals was so annoying. I dared to suggest that the chocolate and sweets should be consumed after their meals. That really put the cat amongst the pigeons and prompted Winnie to complain to Ruby that I had 'banned' them purely because she had bought them. Then, to rub salt into the open wound, she underlined and inflamed the situation by saying to the children: "Who bought those for you then—Nanny did, didn't she?"

This may appear to be a trivial remark, made by a doting grandmother, but it was done purposely to give the children the impression that I was an ogre who was bent on depriving them of their 'goodies'. The frighten ing part about it was that Ruby gradually became blind to what was happening and could not see how Winnie was manipulating the children against me and doing untold damage to our marriage.

It was a well known fact that I took pride with my hair and was style conscious. I went to great lengths to find an award winning hairdresser who would be capable of sculpting the particular styles that I wanted. When Tim came along, and was old enough, I took the same pride with his hair and would take him with me to my hair stylist. He looked great! On one occasion Ruby took the children with her to London. Winnie decided to take Tim to the market and took it upon herself to take him to the hairdressers. In full knowledge of the pride I took with Tim's hair, this vindictive woman ordered the hairdresser to give him a 'short back and sides' The style that I had so carefully nurtured was totally wrecked by a butcher of a hairdresser who left steps all over his head. I was devastated. She had found yet another way to get at me via the children. Then Julie was brought into the picture. Again on a visit to the London street market Winnie purchased a pair of trousers from a market stall for Julie. She couldn't have found a worse fitting pair of trousers. They were a disaster! They simply hung on her, a total misfit. Winnie got to know that I had the temerity to pass the comment that they looked dreadful and she instantly told Ruby that I only said that because she had bought them. Forever after it became: "Bernie has a thing about women wearing trousers" a remark that is totally untrue. I had bought slacks for Ruby. She had several pairs and looked fantastic in them. In an attempt to erase this wild claim, I bought Julie a very smart, expensive trouser suit that fitted perfectly. I then requested that the claim about me not liking women in trousers could now be forgotten. It never was.

It became so ingrained in their minds that Julie came to believe it, Ruby believed it and later on so did a nanny, who was actually quoted in an earlier biography as saying: "I had to make sure that Julie wasn't wearing trousers when Bernie was around." I simply couldn't believe how Winnie was able to weave her influence so easily over so many people. Once again, it all looks and sounds like a triviality, but putting all the pieces together it formed a large part of a mischief making scheme. Come what may she was adamant that she would succeed in driving a wedge between us – husband and wife.

RUBY—My

In the summer of 1964, Ruby was booked as 'special guest star' at the ABC Cinema (Theatre) in Great Yarmouth in a big musical extravaganza with The Shadows.

At the time I had entered the agency and management side of the profession. I ran this business from an office in our home at Rectory Cottage, Wootton. Julie had started at a Preparatory School in Northampton. It required me to drive her back and forth daily to school, some two to three miles from our home. Between us, Ruby and I decided on a plan of campaign for the summer. I had rented a house in a suburb of Great Yarmouth for us to use during the run of the summer show. I would take Ruby to Yarmouth to commence her season, come home to attend to the new agency business and take care of Julie's transportation needs from Monday to Friday. Every Friday afternoon, at school leaving time, I would pick her up and drive back to Great Yarmouth so that we could all be together for the weekend. I would then make the return trip on Sunday evening back to Wootton in readiness for Julie's school on Monday morning.

One difficulty remained, Ruby's means of getting to and from the theatre each night.

My only way of taking care of Julie's needs, and those of the business, was by using the car, which left Ruby without transport. The difficulty was resolved when Ruby assured me that I needed the car to enable us to be together each weekend. She said: "It will not be a problem." She offered to get taxis or "there is a bus that stops outside the house and goes directly into the town." I wasn't all that comfortable with the arrangement but there seemed to be no other answer, other than to buy a second car. With Ruby's assurance that she would be fine we put the plan into operation.

However, I hadn't reckoned on Winnie! When she heard about the arrangement she managed to twist it into a sinister charade.

"There he is, lording it up, with your car in Northampton and leaving you to catch buses, of all things!" she cleverly exclaimed. Of course this was not the true situation at all, but with Winnie's powers of persuasion, Ruby began to believe it too. I was totally amazed at this about-turn in Ruby's thinking.

Late in July it was confirmed that Ruby was in the early stages of pregnancy and that our second baby would be born in February the following year. We were excited by the news and we engaged ourselves, as all families do, in choosing a name. I put forward the idea that we should think carefully before deciding on a name that could be abbreviated and used by playmates when at school. Julie's name was shortened to 'Ju', but due to her red hair she was more often called 'Ginge' Of all the boys names that we considered, Timothy seemed to be the favourite as is could only be shortened to Tim and that sounded good to us. It slightly backfired somewhat when Tim grew up. He didn't want anyone to use his full name. He preferred the abbreviation!

One weekend, when we were all together as a family in Yarmouth, Winnie arrived for another visit and I braced myself in anticipation of her evil doings! I didn't have too long to wait. Her niggling gave way to arguments. I tried to curtail one outburst by suggesting that it was time to retire and Ruby and I left for the bedroom. We had both climbed into bed when suddenly, without prior warning, Winnie burst into the bedroom to announce that she was leaving immediately. Her packed case was in her hand. Off she went into the night. Ruby obviously wanted me to chase after her to bring her back, which in my mind was exactly what she wanted to happen. I dressed rapidly and went downstairs to go after her. It was perhaps two miles, or thereabouts, to the centre of Great Yarmouth and without transport I knew that she couldn't have gone very far. I searched high and low but could find no sign of her at all. It didn't seem possible for her not to be in sight. I decided to return to the house to pick up the car so that I could use headlights to search side roads in case she had got

RUBY—My Precious Gem!

lost. I drove like fury through darkened back streets without success. I was bewildered and returned to the house to discuss with Ruby what we should do next. When I emerged from the garage, I heard a noise. I walked around the house to find her sitting on her case at the back door. She had managed to create mayhem and an atmosphere of disharmony. This was her way of protesting against my presence and she had become very adept in disrupting our lives on a regular basis. Eventually Ruby and I began to have occasional differences about trivial things, almost inevitably concerning Winnie.

The summer season was a short one and long before the autumn leaves started to fall we were back home in our cottage. Any hope of being able to repair whatever rifts had appeared in our relationship during the season in Yarmouth, were soon shattered by the re-emergence of telephone calls, crocodile tears and pleas from London. Much to my great concern spates of drinking also re-commenced. I began to look back over the years trying to find what reasons Ruby might have had that made her look for solace in drink. I knew that we both loved each other very much so, why? Although I didn't realise it at the time, the overdose of tablets at Oxshott should have been a sign of trouble to come. However, I failed to recognise it. As time progressed a clearer picture came to light. Ruby without drink was her gentle sweet self but after a few drinks a different person came to the fore. One side of her personality craved for drink and became aggressive whilst the other was repentant and full of promises that "It won't happen again".

Christmas was on its way, but with the baby due in the new year, pantomime was out of the question. Mr. Watson, the gynaecologist, had decided that another caesarean operation would be needed but Ruby had great faith in his ability as a surgeon. Tim, our son, was born on February 3rd. 1965 at the Barratt Maternity Home, the same hospital where Julie was born. There were one or two minor complications, one of which was a lazy heart valve that didn't close when it should have. We were re-assured that everything was fine and that there was no cause for concern. He was a good baby, handsome like his father! He slept most of the time and had to be woken up to take his feed. Julie, on the other hand, was a difficult baby, crying most of the time and giving us many sleepless nights. I still can visualise the bottle warmer by the side of the bed and having to switch it on to warm the milk, so that she could have a 'wee' drop more in the hope that it would pacify her and send her to sleep. Strangely, in another publication, Ruby was reported as stating the complete opposite about the two babies. She had got it wrong, as were so many of the facts in that book.

Prior to her next summer season, Ruby was booked in cabaret. This was her first ever attempt, after stardom, to perform in this environment and the transition from variety theatre to clubland was a huge step to take. To entertain a seated captive audience in a theatre setting was one thing, but attempting to hold an audience in a nightspot is entirely different. Meals are usually served and waiters with trays of clinking glasses are frequently passing in front of the artiste with the result that a performance can easily be disrupted and sometimes ruined. The performer is constantly struggling to gain the attention of drink affected patrons who at the same time are eating meals throughout the act. Add to this the fact that television was now a part of every day life and one could hold a conversation whilst a programme was on, so why not during the cabaret performance? Times were changing, but not always for the better!

Chapter 15
♪ 'My Melancholy Baby!' ♪

Juggling family arrangements around to cover all eventualities was no easy task. Now that we had a new baby, as well as five year old Julie at school, life was going to be more complicated. Ruby was contracted to play a season at the Spa Pavilion, Bridlington. Members of the cast included Joe 'Mr' Piano Henderson, Vince Hill, Johnny Hackett and a double comedy act Edmundson & Elliott. I drove Ruby, Jane the Nanny, Julie and baby Timothy to Bridlington and managed to stay for the weekend. During this time we had a very distressing incident with Timothy. Jane made him clean, tidy and comfortable and left him just outside the back door in a carrycot. The weather was glorious and the fresh air was going to do the baby a power of good. He had only been left for a few minutes but an ever anxious and caring mother wanted to check on him. I heard Ruby scream. The baby had taken the corner of the blanket into his mouth and, presumably, started to suck the blanket. As he continued to suck it was gradually being drawn into his mouth until it was entering his throat. Ruby discovered him when his face was turning blue. She immediately removed the blanket but wasn't sure whether the baby was breathing. My first thought was to get Tim to a hospital so I raced to get the car and bundled mother and baby into the back hoping to quickly find a hospital. I broke every rule of the road, in some cases even the law, by mounting pavements to avoid being held up. I was fortunate enough to pick up a sign and got to a hospital very quickly. Ruby desperately tried to explain what had happened, but as she was doing so the doctors and nursing staff had taken charge of the baby and was thoroughly examining him. My thoughts went back to the problem at his birth, when the heart valve had not closed as it should and I hurriedly tried to explain to the doctors about his problem. Ruby was trembling with fright and I tried to calm her down, but I was just as shaken as she was. After a matter of minutes a nurse handed baby Timothy to Ruby and the doctor's diagnosis was: "I think we had better treat the parents! The baby is perfectly alright!"

Sunday afternoon came and it was time for me to return with Julie to Wootton. She had to be at school in the morning. This particular departure was more than difficult for me and was very worrying. I was aware that Ruby was beginning to drink more than she ought to, but with a new baby I hoped that her mind would be concentrated on him, and hopefully curb her drinking. Jane was a very good nanny and I knew that she would not hesitate to contact me if she had worries of any kind. Ruby was aware about my concern and was quoted as saying: "Bernie wouldn't approve".

Of course I didn't. Would any husband who loved his wife?

Late night drinking made her melancholy and was invariably accompanied by sad music, yet another cause for concern. She was beginning to look for something, or someone, to blame for her drinking. I was soon to learn that it is usually the person nearest and dearest that is the chosen one. I had to leave her during the week but returned every weekend to be with her and the new baby. Was that enough?

As soon as Julie's summer holiday came around, I gathered her up, packed a suitcase and set off for Bridlington. Peace reigned for a while and, as we were hundreds of miles from the capital, there was no possibility of a call asking Ruby to come to London. I even managed to accompany Vince for a little fishing. It was quite therapeutic. The season ended early that year, so we were soon on our way back home. I had hoped that Ruby and I could enjoy sometime on our own, quietly and peacefully as a family, but it wasn't to be. Because Ruby had been away for a season, the moment she returned home Winnie, Patsy, Henry and their small son David arrived for the weekend. This time, I was not alone when it came to her non-stop criticism. The cottage was also in the firing line! "I don't like the windows," she said. "They're far too small" followed by "I don't like the Woottonites (local residents) either. It's not like living in London. I certainly couldn't live here!" I wondered why she said that. Could it be a little indoctrination? I wanted to correct her on the name that she gave the local

RUBY—My Precious Gem!

village residents. I much preferred us to be called Woottonians! This was far more refined, I thought. I refrained, as I knew that I would be playing with fire. According to Winnie: "Oxshott was far better for Ruby and the children" and "the people there are much nicer, not like these horrible 'Woottonites." Perhaps the length of the journey came into her calculations. Oxshott was a mere 30 minutes away whereas Northampton was more tedious with two journeys, one into Euston and the other to Northampton. It took more than two hours by train but by car it was a little quicker.

There was more to come. Somehow or other, Winnie discovered my political leanings, perhaps unwittingly through Ruby, so I became a 'Labourite.' It was said as if I was a leper! By now she had accumulated sufficient reasons why Ruby shouldn't be living in such a dreadful place and socialising with heathens (like me?).

Surprisingly, it wasn't too long before Ruby adopted a similar tone regarding the village folk and spoke detrimentally about them although, in reality, the only locals she ever conversed with were our domestic help and the old gardener. It was a strange, almost a surrealistic thing that was happening and I could do nothing about it. In the previous biography, Ruby is quoted as saying she was convinced that the village people did not like her yet we didn't ever meet or socialise with them as we were always away.

The Murrays idea of enjoyment at the weekend, wherever they may be, was to go to a 'pub' or club for a night of heavy drinking. The night was not complete unless they became thoroughly inebriated which, in turn, created big problems. This particular weekend was no exception. Drink had flowed freely in the house prior to them departing to go to the local 'pub' in the village. It was taken for granted that I would not be accompanying them so I received no invitation thankfully! I had hoped that Ruby would stay with the children and me but to suggest that would have widened the growing rift between us. They stayed very late in the pub, way beyond closing time. My fears regarding the homecoming were not unfounded. Already there was antagonism between Patsy and her husband Henry and heated words were being exchanged in front of David, their bewildered son. To my dismay, Ruby had consumed far more than she should have and felt the need to go to bed. Winnie also retired straight away. I didn't even see her departure. There was an urgent need for me to attend to Ruby as she was feeling unwell, so I gave her all my attention. Downstairs the scene had become decidedly ugly and soon Henry became physically violent towards his wife Patsy. David, their terrified child, came running upstairs to appeal for help as his mother was being beaten. I had a choice to make, attending to Ruby or assisting Patsy. David was hysterical so I tried to attend to both. I laid Ruby on her side and placed pillows in her back, as I had done previously with Lilian, and ran downstairs to try to quell the fighting. I called to Henry to stop but his reply to me was unrepeatable. Fortunately, my arrival had caused sufficient distraction for Patsy to get up and run out of the house into the garden. Henry followed in close pursuit as well as their son. During the scuffle in the garden, Patsy lost her glasses and couldn't find them in the dark. When the fracas eventually subsided Henry announced that he was going to drive back to London, taking David with him. A distraught Patsy pleaded with me to stop him. He was obviously in no condition to drive. I managed to persuade Henry that it would be better to sleep on it and then go back to London in the morning. I succeeded and everyone went to their rooms to 'sleep it off.'

In the morning, nobody rose early except me. I decided to let Ruby sleep on. I knew that there would be sore heads for everyone and considered it best for me to keep a low profile. I had plenty of work to do in the garden so I set to, to be out of the way. By the time I had completed the weeding of one flower bed, I heard voices from inside the house. Later, Ruby appeared at the door, saw me and came over to talk. She wanted to know why I was not socialising with the family and that Winnie had taken exception to the fact that I was ignoring them. Obviously, Ruby had no idea of the extent of the rumpus that had taken place the previous evening or of the threatening behaviour from brother-in-law Henry. I was most grateful when they eventually made their departure.

Our show business friends living across the village green, Jean and Peter Barbour, were about to play a permanent part in the scene. Whenever we paid them a visit, more often than not for elevenses, they displayed great hospitality, which inevitable included the offer of a drink. I invariably declined their kind offer and politely suggested to Ruby that perhaps it was a little too early in the day. I soon realised that I had reached a stage where I was constantly trying to keep Ruby away from alcohol. Morning coffee was part of life for show people so the invitation was to be repeated from time to time. I have already mentioned that the 'disease' had a cunning side to it. It was now apparent that Ruby had made a mental note of the fact that if alcohol was being denied at home, there was always another source that could be tapped. Ruby now knew that by walking a hundred yards or so across the village green she could find solace in drink at the Barbours' place. Another symptom of the disease is deceit. From then on she would frequently return home having sampled their 'hospitality' and then, to my utter amazement, would show aggression towards me. Before I depart from this unpleasant subject, let me point out a few facts. A person that is becoming addicted to alcohol thinks, schemes and lies to get what they want. As the problem escalates, they will cheat and be untruthful to the very person who is closest to them. I was trying to save Ruby from what threatened to become a terrible fate not only for herself but for her immediate family. I loved her very much but I could see there was a danger that our marriage and our wonderful life together could be gradually falling apart.

It is vital for me to make it totally clear, yet again, that I have no desire to criticise or blame Ruby in any way. I am describing an illness, one that was consuming my loveable wife. I am telling the story as is was, a story of a lovely lady who became its victim. She was to suffer a great deal and it broke my heart to see it happening and to be powerless to stop it. My story may sound familiar to many others who hopefully will read this book. Drink can cause a dreadful malady in some people and those closest to them cannot always find a solution. They in turn suffer extreme pain and heartache followed by pangs of guilt themselves. Why didn't I do something about it earlier? Why didn't I get help sooner? Why? Why? Why?

As I have said before, the disease is insidious. It creeps up on its victim unnoticed and neither the sufferer nor those around them realise that there is a major problem looming until it's gone past the point of no return. It's at this point that the victim cannot go back to normality and able to drink socially. They have lost control. The onlooker is incapable of offering any kind of help, and even if they did, the sufferer immediately denies that there is a problem.

"How dare you suggest that I have a drink problem"—is their attitude. To this day, I have a solicitor's letter stating that his client (Ruby) tells him that there is no such problem and that I must desist in insisting that she has one. I asked myself, had Ruby convinced her solicitor, or was he choosing to ignore the fact by getting on with representing his client knowing full well that there was a problem?

I cannot believe that highly intelligent people in the legal profession readily accept the word of their client telling them that drink is not a problem in their life when all the facts are staring them in the face. Maybe the cheque book looms large quite early on in the case that they are pursuing?

Ruby's engagement diary was not getting much attention from Keith Devon and the Delfont office, so I began to fill some of the dates in through my agency/management office. I did so with more than a little concern. I didn't want to upset the 'office' so whenever I came up with an engagement for Ruby, I handed it over to them so that they could issue a contract and take the appropriate commission. With constant fears at the back of my mind, I was beginning to wonder whether I should suggest to Ruby about the possibility of her retiring and for me to make every effort to expand my business. Apart from the children growing up and needing more care and attention, along with the constant family problems, her need to drink had to come into the equation. How long, I wondered, would it be before her drinking was noticed by those who provided engagements and those who paid to see her perform?

We discussed at length whether or not she should continue with her career, but I took great care to make sure she realised that she was being asked and not told. Oops! I touched a nerve and from then on I steered clear of the subject and it was never raised again. Singing was life itself to Ruby. It meant so much to her. She didn't want to discuss the retirement with me, so I continued to seek engagements for her, but at the back of my mind I repeatedly asked myself the question: 'Am I really doing the right thing?'

Winnie again entered the arena! "Why doesn't he get himself a proper job?"

She chose to ignore the facts. In the first instance, I had given up a very successful and lucrative career with The Jones Boys to concentrate my efforts on Ruby. At the same time I had found an income via the properties and I was building up an agency business with Ruby's approval. I was helping to fill her date sheet. Winnie knew nothing about show business

RUBY—My Precious Gem!

but she certainly knew how to undermine a marriage. This enraged me, but gradually Ruby was being swayed by her mother, very much to my dismay.

It had to be accepted during this period that ballad singers of the fifties were being overshadowed by the arrival of rock n' roll and 'beat groups'. The rock era took over completely and sentimental ballad singers were no longer the flavour of the month! The 'office' certainly didn't know how to counteract it. They didn't even try and I found myself alone with the datesheet. I was

incensed when I read quotes from Keith Devon's biography. In one such quote he said: "If Ruby had been handled properly she could have been one of the biggest stars ever." That remark was a travesty as, up to this point, he was supposed to be handling her career not me. I was having to find Ruby's engagements as he wasn't capable of doing so!

Another quote: "She turned down several important engagements soon after she married Bernie!" That was sheer nonsense and totally untrue. How could a man who had been responsible for the Pattie Page fiasco in the States, the disasters with 'Snow White' and the summer season at Weymouth plus the definite lack of contracts coming in, have the temerity to say such things. The truth was, I didn't start looking for dates until the 'office' stopped coming through with engagements and then I passed them over to allow them their cut! He was blatantly lying and totally out of order with those statements. The blame for any of Ruby's mismanagement must be laid well and truly at the door of the 'office'. In brief, they moved in to take over a star that had already been born through massive recording and television success that they had not arranged. They exploited her shamelessly and when her box office power started to dwindle they simply abandoned her. They tried to use me as a scapegoat to hide their own guilt and inadequacies.

I digress! Returning to the story, 1966 brought a return to Great Yarmouth for Ruby. The venue was The Tower Ballroom, a brand new complex. It was to be a floor show presented by Bertie Green of London's Astor Club fame. Once more the juggling had to be done to cover all the ongoing factors. This included Ruby's needs to carry out the engagement, the two children, Julie's schooling and the development of the agency office. Keeping all of the balls in the air at the same time wasn't going to be easy!

Chapter 16
♪ 'Little White Lies' ♪

A new nanny was about to join the family, another ardent Ruby Murray fan. She was to be one more in a long list of nannies that presented us with problems. Finding a good nanny is a very difficult task. The mere fact that we had such a long list confirms that point. Looking back, we certainly had a mixed bag of nannies over the years. Each one seemed to develop a particular idiosyncrasy, which was to manifest itself in a short space of time.

For example, the first one we engaged in Blackpool scared Ruby with her possessive nature towards Julie, our first born and her sick joke when she said: "We may not be here when you get back!"

Another proved that she could not be left alone in the house with a man. A third who concealed the fact that she was receiving treatment in a local rehabilitation centre following a drink problem. The one from Belfast didn't stay too long followed, believe it or not, by a three-week stint by Ruby's mother Winnie. Despite all her claims about her dislike for Wootton and its inhabitants and the small windows in the cottage! It certainly demolished her claim that I wouldn't allow her to cuddle the children. Finally, the pull of London was too great for her, plus the fact that she had let herself down when she had drunk too much and left me with the unenviable task of cleaning up after her in the bathroom.

The next nanny preferred Ruby's company to that of the children. She once took the two kids into Northampton town centre to the local swimming baths, a ten minute drive away. She then left Julie and Tim unattended whilst she drove back to Wootton to try to persuade Ruby to come into town to join them. I was furious and quickly dispatched her back into town to pick up the children and to bring them back home.

The constant chopping and changing of nannies certainly had an unsettling effect on the children. My aim had always been to provide a stable home for them and to make sure that one parent was with them at all times. I felt that it was important to have an anchor to stabilise their lives and their upbringing. Despite all my efforts to achieve this, I feel that the constant disruption must have affected them to some degree.

Ruby was offered another summer show again in Great Yarmouth. This time it was to be at The Windmill Theatre with a blend of comedy and singers. Ruby co-starred with Freddie and The Dreamers, Toni Dalli, Joe Baker, Dev Shaun, and The Tornados. I found accommodation for her in a holiday village with very smart chalets where some of the cast were also staying. The area was great for the two children. It had a playground with the usual swings and slides. However the slide was to prove to be a disaster for Julie! She fell off it and broke her arm. It's amazing how young children manage to recover so very quickly. Julie was back on the swings and slides in no time at all.

There was another down side to the holiday village set-up. It provided members of the cast with an ideal way of socialising together after the nightly show and that meant of course that there would be liquid refreshment flowing freely!

There were plenty of quotes in the press in relation to this particular scene. One amazing story was attributed to Ruby where she states that on one occasion she slipped sleeping tablets into my tea and when I was asleep she 'escaped' through the window to join the drinking party. No such incident in connection with sleeping tablets ever happened to me. This story was linked to others where Ruby claimed that our marriage was suffering because of the constant bickering. The cunning element carefully detracted from the real cause of our differences, that of trying to keep Ruby away from 'the problem.'

The cat very nearly got out of the bag when she supposedly told her friends that she needed the laughs and frivolity of the late night binges because she 'hadn't been sleeping too well'. In fact, the contrary was the

RUBY—My Precious Gem!

real truth. Ruby could have slept for England! Throughout our marriage, Ruby invariably slept until lunchtime and after lunch could nod off in the armchair, so she had no problem with sleep. At one point I was getting quite concerned by the fact that Ruby slept far too much, a trait that was to show up in Tim's life later on.

I can itemise a whole list of published quotes, which epitomises how the nearest and dearest comes in for severe criticism from a problem drinker.

"These get-togethers kept me sane when our marriage was going sour. I knew parties and drinking were not the answer but Bernie was not there most of the time and I got into the habit of going out after the show."

My reply to this statement was that I was doing the usual school runs to and from home with Julie but was there every week-end and for the summer holidays. Our marriage was suffering because of the 'drinking' and the fact that I tried so hard to keep Ruby away from it. As I said earlier, the person standing between the drink and the sufferer is the enemy.

Another Ruby quote: "I never did leave the children alone. Maureen, our nanny, was marvellous and always knew where I was in case of an emergency."

My reply to this, one can see the guilt in that statement but she had to find a reason in case the one about me didn't hold water.

There was an endless list of press quotes that needed to be corrected but I think I have made me point.

I frequently asked myself the question—how many other female entertainers need their husbands to be permanently at their side, with or without children? Not many I suspect. I tried to achieve everything at the same time. I was taking care of Ruby's engagement date-sheet, finding accommodation, finding pianists, attending to the children's' schooling and building a business that I hoped would enable Ruby to stop travelling up and down the country without financial problems. With the income coming in from the properties and the agency that I was building up we were well on the way for Ruby to retire if she so desired! But did she?

Bernie Burgess & Frank Bowles

At the end of the season in Yarmouth, Ruby was asked to do a short tour to Canada with David Whitfield. I knew already that David enjoyed his tipple and that came to light quite glaringly when he stayed with us at Rectory Cottage. I was quite concerned about the tour because I would not be there to keep an eye on things. I stayed in Wootton with the children and my growing agency business. Other offers came in from countries abroad, amongst them was a trip to Nigeria to do a week's cabaret engagement in an hotel in Lagos. I arranged for a pianist called Bob Francis to accompany Ruby on the trip. They had a strange, yet rather amusing experience when passing through customs on their arrival in Lagos. The customs official indicated that he wanted the case holding Ruby's band parts to be opened. He was not happy about the pile of music and for some unknown reason he was not going to let them through. Bob took control of the situation and after an exchange of words, he took Ruby to one side and suggested that he had picked up a hint from the official that there might be a way around the problem. Ruby remained perplexed but Bob had taken the 'hint' and after a discreet back-hander the obstacle to their entry miraculously disappeared.

My agency/management business was building up very well and I was beginning to accumulate a healthy list of clients throughout the Midlands who needed to book entertainment. Don Crockett asked me to become his manager and to hold his datesheet so, coupled with everything else that I was handling in the office, I was confident that I had the means of providing a good income for the whole family. Amongst some of the cabaret club engagements that I secured for Don was a week's contract at a cabaret club in Manchester that was owned by a wrestling star Man 'Mountain' Benny. I attended his opening night and I was joined at my table by Freddie Starr who was appearing at another venue nearby. He was a great admirer of Don's talent and we chatted for quite some time about Don's attention to detail in every one of his impressions. He was particularly impressed with the way Don used props in his act. Unquestionably Don's greatest admirer was Ruby. As families, the Burgesses and the Crocketts enjoyed each others company immensely and when Don and Ruby got together, fun and laughter was in abundance.

Chapter 17
♪ 'Summer Holiday' ♪

We had all worked very hard over the past few months so felt that we deserved a break somewhere in the sun, so Don and his wife Moira suggested that both families should go on a joint holiday to Ibiza.

Ruby and I had not visited that beautiful island and we were very happy with the suggestion. Both families took two children each and our happy band set off for the airport to fly through the night. On reflection, night flying is not a good idea when travelling with young children. Not that our four children misbehaved, but the younger ones on board showed that they were tired and became a little fractious. The early hours of the morning, with a plane full of passengers all trying to sleep, was not the right time for Don to engage in humour, so he wrestled with trying to get comfortable enough to get a little 'shut-eye'.

After the initial spate of hand squeezing on take off, Ruby slumbered for most of the flight. Both Julie and Tim were well behaved although the excitement of the holiday prevented them from getting much sleep. We were due to land in Ibiza around 5-30am. Transport was arranged to take us to a newly built hotel. The night staff attended to our luggage and then we were shown to our respective rooms. Although the children were anxious to get a sight of the sea and the sandy beach, we persuaded them that we should all try to get a little sleep first and then the fun would commence!

They allowed us to have only a couple of hours rest before they pulled us out of bed, wanting to go to the beach right now. Bleary eyed and bedraggled, the four parents headed towards the restaurant for breakfast, but the kiddies were having none of that! There were more important things on their minds. Ruby and Moira managed to hastily wrap a few items of food in serviettes to take with us, and then both had their sleeves tugged to hurry their exit from the hotel to the most important part of the holiday, the beach.

Beach towels were neatly laid out for each family and the bottles of sun tan lotion were unloaded from the girls' beach bags. In the meantime all four children excitedly made off towards the edge of the sea to paddle. The parents looked forward to some relaxation as we all sprawled ourselves out onto the waiting beach towels and creamed ourselves well in preparation for some well earned sun bathing. Only a matter of minutes passed when we were disturbed by the children scuffing their feet causing some of the sand to spread itself over our sun-creamed bodies. "We're bored.....," they cried....unbelievable!

Perhaps it will come as no surprise to readers to learn that Don was a very heavy drinker, although on this holiday, fun and laughter were the predominant features. Ruby played a leading role in providing the laughs. I only wish that I had taken my movie camera to put it all on record. Being away from outside influences Ruby was much more relaxed. The Burgess quartet treated the Crockett family to a sample of our harmony singing. It was something that we always enjoyed whilst on long car journeys. Tim and Julie sang the melody lines and Ruby and myself took care of the harmonies. Our repertoire included 'Soon It's Gonna Rain' 'Lemon Tree' and 'Tom Dooley.' Alas, I failed to get our family to record. It's a pity really, because family recordings were quite a novelty then. Remember, in the years to come the Osmonds made it big.

I was to work with Don as his agent/manager for a number of years before he left for Australia where he rubbed shoulders with his idol and arguably the greatest impressionist of all time—Frank Gorshin. When he came back to England, I was to learn that Don's health was causing concern. I later found out that he had suffered either a mild stroke or a heart attack in Australia but he wouldn't tell anyone about it. He had asked me to book him some dates for when he came back home, but when I went to

RUBY—My Precious Gem!

see him work it was obvious to me that he was not his usual self. He then decided to leave show business and took on a training course in pub management. In the first few days of the course he was asked to go down into a cellar to bottle up and collect crates of beer. When he didn't return the manager went to look for him and found him slumped at the foot of the stairs. He was rushed to hospital. Moira telephoned me and I took off in my car at great speed to see him but I didn't quite make it. He had passed away. It was revealed that the main cause of his death was alcohol. I knew from the stories Don had told me that his father had died in exactly the same way. This was yet another pointer to the fact that illnesses can be hereditary. I managed to stage a charity show to raise funds for Moira and his family. I was grateful to all those artistes and musicians who gave their services to the cause, in particular to Syd Little & Eddie Large. I compered the show and when I introduced 'Little and Large' Eddie took the microphone from me, looked upward and said aloud: "This one's for you Don!" I was choked.

A second engagement in Rhodesia came Ruby's way and to her great delight her friend Marie was able to go along to accompany her. It was for a three-week stint at the Celebrity Club that was owned by an Egyptian businessman but had been leased by an English artiste named Chris Shaw. Accompanying musicians can vary in their musical ability in most parts of the world but when Ruby and Marie listened to local Rhodesian musicians it was quite an experience. Marie had struggled to rehearse them playing 'When Irish Eyes Are Smiling' but came good in the end. By the look on their faces in the photos that Ruby brought back, they really enjoyed playing for her with smiles all round.

A surprise invitation arrived at the club for the girls to join the Prime Minister, Mr. Ian Smith and his wife for tea. Ruby was by no means politically minded, neither was Marie, but they were delighted to accept the kind offer. A typical English tea and sandwiches were served and the conversation flowed freely without bordering on politics. To their amazement, Mrs. Smith was very knowledgeable on the popular music scene and was aware of Ruby's recording success. Before they departed for England a note arrived from Mrs. Smith thanking them for their visit and wishing then a safe journey home.

Bernie Burgess & Frank Bowles

Around 1967, Ruby's recording career took a different direction when she was asked to join the Philips-Fontana label. She was to make two albums 'The Spinning Wheel' and 'This is Ireland' plus two singles 'I Can't Get You Out Of My Heart' and 'Sooner Or Later' all under the direction of Terry Brown. The latter of the two singles was a rare excursion into country flavoured music and an extremely good track it turned out to be too. I often wondered why this avenue wasn't explored before. Ruby would have taken to the country music scene quite easily. Moving on to 1970, President Records made an approach and as a result Ruby came within a whisker of getting back into the hit parade with a song called 'Change Your Mind'. It entered the Radio Luxemburg charts at No.23. This prompted President to get Ruby to make an album of the same name.

On the domestic scene our problems had not gone away. Fewer and fewer bookings were coming in via the Delfont office so I redoubled my efforts to find my own engagements for Ruby. The entertainment scene was changing at quite a dramatic rate. Theatres were either closed or closing and 'live' entertainment was moving more and more into the cabaret market. Social clubs were flourishing and the function scene became more prominent. Bill Haley and the whole Rock 'n Roll scene had overshadowed everything and everybody in the entertainment world. Elvis was King and The Beatles were on their way to the top of the world. For a gentle, predominantly ballad singing star like Ruby, working in social clubs was difficult to say the least, but she had to adjust. I really didn't cherish the thought of Ruby being exposed to this new rumbustious type of audience and I seriously considered making another delicate approach to her to see if she might consider giving up her career. Even though I knew that she lived for singing and so easily related to show people, I wanted to lessen the stress and by doing so perhaps reduce the need for her to look for relief elsewhere. I still hoped!

Chapter 18
♪ 'That's Entertainment' ♪

From out of the blue I had a message from the manager of the local pub in Wootton to call in for a chat. He told me that his immediate boss at the brewery, Mr. Saunders the General Manager of Managed Houses, wanted to speak to me about entertainment. I made an appointment and went along the following day to meet him. We chatted for a while but then I became aware that he was probing into my show business knowledge. He eventually divulged that the brewery, Watney Mann (Midland) Ltd, had taken over the lease of a social club called the Cresta Bingo & Social Club in Solihull. As an entertainment venue it was struggling to survive. I knew most entertainment venues throughout the country and I was very familiar with this club. He asked me for my opinion about the place and why was it doing so badly? I had nothing to lose, so I pulled no punches and told him bluntly. The policy was wrong and the atmosphere was non-existent. Somewhat taken aback by my bluntness he asked me to expand on my views so I did. I explained that the name Cresta Bingo & Social Club did nothing at all for such a venue, the cabaret policy was abysmal, the decor was unsightly and the atmosphere was a disaster. He then enquired as to how things could be put right. I pointed out that Cabaret Restaurants were springing up all over the country and that this venue was just right to be converted to such a night spot. Its geographical location was ideal being so close to Birmingham and Coventry. The major motorways in the vicinity were also in place to draw on a massive catchment area for miles around.

It should offer a very bold policy of a 'Top of the Bill' star name with supporting acts and a resident 'live' band for dancing and should open seven nights a week. He smiled in agreement with everything I had said and then took me completely by surprise! He asked me if I would consider taking the venue over as General Manager? This stunned me and I was almost speechless but gabbled that I needed time to think. I asked him if I could have a day or so to talk it over with my wife. We agreed to meet two days later.

On the way back to Rectory Cottage I thought deeply about how this would affect both Ruby's life as well as my own and the children? Just how would Ruby react to this proposition? Here was an opportunity to be able to solve quite a few problems all at the same time, but it could have huge repercussions. I studied the matter very deeply then carefully talked it over with Ruby. I laid out the entire picture in detail to her. There was a very big plus in the advantage column. It would solve the alternative income question and provide the financial means to relieve the pressures on her. It would mean that Ruby could either give up working altogether or maybe pick and choose occasional engagements.

Part of the deal I required with Watney Mann was to maintain my agency/management business. This would enable me to book all the artistes for the Cabaret Restaurant giving me an 'ace in the hole' when it came to booking dates for Ruby, when and if she still wanted to work. An odd night here or there would be easy to cover domestically and I could book driving pianists to take her to each engagement, and the nanny was in the house looking after the children. Taking over a failing business and resurrecting it would be a massive undertaking. It was quite big in size, capable of seating 750 people, and represented a huge investment for the brewery. Another huge tick in the advantage column would be that Winnie's cry of: "Why doesn't he get himself a proper job" would be squashed. We could get a second car for Ruby's personal use and the nanny had her own car which she used to take the children back and forth to school. We went over the details many times and finally we both decided for me to accept the deal. There was of course the small matter of the venue being 50 plus miles from our home and I would have to commute seven days a week. However, being an experienced travelling professional all my adult life, the journey to and from didn't bother me one iota.

RUBY—My Precious Gem!

I completed negotiations with the brewery, which included my retention of the agency, as planned. I would be solely in charge of the entire operation and would be answerable to only one man at the brewery. I did not want duty directors visiting the venue and interfering with things. I started the project with high hopes. I installed a policy that I considered to be a winner—a top of the bill, three supporting acts, a resident band and myself as compere seven nights a week. I had no experience on the restaurant and bar side of the business but I knew of a fine Assistant Manager who had an enormous amount of experience in that field. I engaged him right away. A financial meeting took place and I was given in excess of £10,000 to transform the club into a Cabaret Restaurant. Everything went smoothly and we were soon ready to open.

For the opening week I made a big splash by putting in three big names. Apart from Ruby I booked David Nixon and Ken Platt. Ruby was the crowning glory to the new venue, she looked stunning.

We played to packed houses all week and had rave reviews. However, I anticipated that there would be a surge of inquisitive patrons to begin with followed by a lull. The struggle to bury the previous image of a bingo and social

club was long and hard. I was rescuing a doomed venue and transforming it into a first class Cabaret Restaurant. I can state with pride that I eventually managed to create a highly successful venue, where every artiste in show business wanted to perform. My backstage knowledge from my younger days paid huge dividends enabling me to arrange stage and lighting arrangements that would enhance the whole presentation. After the initial struggle the crowds gradually began to swell until we reached a stage whereby we were bursting at the seams. Business was booming! I had a winner. I managed to convert the trading deficit that existed on takeover into a healthy £10,000 profit in the first year. Over the next year or so it continued to grow and grow.

As time passed by my domestic life began to fall apart dramatically. Ruby simply could not cope with the changes that had taken place and far from easing the pressures on her that caused her to drink, the new situation brought about an acceleration in her condition. I began to realise that I had made an enormous blunder, but by now I had a tiger by the tail and I couldn't let go. My assistant stayed with me through the early stages but then decided he wanted to work for himself and move on. I had nobody to whom I could delegate. A domestic nightmare was descending upon me.

To add to the drama 'Big' Dan went into hospital, soon to pass away. Ruby needed to fly to Belfast so I drove her to Birmingham Airport, which was close to my office. With no one to take responsibility from me I was unable to go with her to attend the funeral. My in-laws had a field day with that one! Bernie had snubbed 'Big' Dan and didn't go to his funeral. There was no way that I could win. I had a very good position, a good income, the Cabaret Restaurant was fully booked, but despite having a staff of over 50 people there was nobody who could take control of the operation in my absence. Now all the success that I had worked so hard for was utterly meaningless. My marriage was falling apart.

At the same time my own health began to buckle under the strain. Fortunately, one of my patrons was a consultant surgeon at the Solihull Hospital. I had befriended him when he was going through a difficult divorce situation and I gave him an open invitation to the Cabaret Restaurant. In return he invited me to call on his professional services if at any time I was in need. The heavy strain, the lack of sleep and the endless

RUBY—My Precious Gem!

anxiety had taken their toll. I was sitting in my office when I suddenly burst into a floods of tears. Remembering the surgeon's offer I rang, tried to talk to him but was unable to conceal the sobbing. He knew I was in my office and told me to stay right there. Within minutes he arrived and, without hesitation, took me to the hospital. After a thorough examination he told me that my colon had gone into spasm due to the extreme stress I had suffered and that I would need to relinquish my position. If I didn't I would be hospitalised for a very long time. He made it quite clear by saying: "Quit now, otherwise I will write you out of your job!" There was no alternative. I had to heed his warning so I informed the brewery that they would have to find a replacement for me immediately.

Fortunately, I was able to negotiate a position whereby I could maintain the booking of the artistes, which would provide a good income and a bargaining position for other bookings too. I started working from home and had a very healthy business, which was now boosted by the commissions from the artistes that I booked for the restaurant. I was soon to make a disturbing discovery. Unbeknown to me, while I was working each night, Ray Lamar had been making telephone calls and paying visits to Rectory Cottage to see Ruby. But why and for how long? The inescapable fact was that Ray had come back onto the scene. Ironically, I had achieved the aim of finding an alternative to the dreadful situation that was causing Ruby to rely on alcohol. Now I was about to be confronted by the possibility of a divorce that I certainly didn't seek.

I made other disturbing discoveries. I began to find empty bottles in various hidden places around the house. It was also significant when I noticed that there had been a change in the kind of drink she was consuming. Now it was vodka, a drink that is odourless. The cunning side of the disease also extended to using mouthwash to mask the smell on her breath. The reality of using these disguises was that their use clearly indicated what the 'sufferer' was trying to hide. I was in despair! My wife was suffering badly from alcoholism. She completely denied that she had a problem with drink and she objected very strongly when I told her that she had a problem. I was unable to stop her drinking. There was nothing that I could do to help her. I was powerless.

Chapter 19
♪ 'One Day At A Time' ♪

During my time at the cabaret restaurant, Ruby was booked to do a very short season at the Festival Theatre in Paignton. It was an Olde Tyme Music Hall production and one of the last contracts that Ruby fulfilled for the Delfont office. Her co-stars included the brilliant comedy star Max Wall and the Dorset country yokel Billy Burden. Max was experiencing matrimonial difficulties himself so between them they had both found a shoulder to cry on as well as a buddy to accompany them for the usual after-the-show laughs plus drinks!

Ray Lamar was only a few miles away in Torquay looking after Delfont's interests at the Princess Theatre. I wasn't blind to the fact that he could well call into the Paignton Theatre to see Ruby and, just like the 'phone calls and visits to Rectory Cottage, I soon realised the magnitude of the situation. Years after our divorce, I read in the newspapers that Lamar was quoted as saying: "We fell in love with each other all over again". It was also in print that they cried on each others' shoulders because they both had tried to make a go of their marriages but without success. The real truth of the matter was Ruby had found that elusive person who did not consider drinking a problem. Every 'problem' drinker searches high and low for such a friend.

Lamar, of course, was a heavy 'boozer', which is entirely different to a 'problem' drinker. He would be prepared to drink all day and all night, so he was the ideal partner for her craving. History was to prove, quite conclusively, that Lamar was the very last person that should have teamed up with Ruby. He was lethal for her.

RUBY—My Precious Gem!

Shortly after returning from Paignton, Ruby received a telephone call from a certain Freddie Clayton. Neither of us had met him before but he told us he was an ex-session musician and wanted to meet us, so we invited him to Rectory Cottage. It turned out that during his recording session days he fell victim to drink and had written a book on the subject called: 'Stop Drinking and Start Living'. He eventually become 'dry' and confirmed everything that I had discovered. The sufferer normally seeks someone who will sympathise and become a drinking buddy.

Just how Freddie Clayton got to know about Ruby having a drink problem bothered me greatly. He chatted and asked probing questions as he really tried hard to reach out to her. He told his own story about how he had fallen to the bottom of the well and with the aid of his devoted wife had managed to climb back out. He related about his own experience and how he had spent years wrestling with his addiction. To eventually become a 'dry' alcoholic was a tribute to his courage and tenacity. Unfortunately Freddy is no longer around.

His story, which reminded me of our problem, started with a situation that could happen to anybody. During a recording session he was confronted by a particularly difficult passage of music to read and to play. When he came to this particular passage, he fluffed it! The musical director called for another 'take' and Freddie fluffed it again. He naturally tensed up, not believing that he could make such a silly error. Although it was an intricate passage, it was straight forward enough and shouldn't have presented him with a problem. After failing for a third time the musical director, who had heard each mistake and knew who was responsible, diplomatically called for a break.

Freddie was just one in a whole host of brilliant session musicians and he knew that every one of them would be aware that he was making simple errors and why the break was called. The trumpet player sitting next to him sympathised with him and suggested that he went for a drink instead of the usual cup of tea. He bought him a large whisky and encouraged him to loosen up a bit and not be so tense. They returned to the session and Freddie sailed straight through the troublesome musical passage without difficulty. At the next session, Freddie decided not to let a similar incident embarrass him again, so he took a large whisky before he went into the studio followed by another during the break.

One soon became two, which started him on the slippery slope to oblivion. Before he realised he was hooked and it had major repercussions on his trumpet-playing career. He became unreliable and as a consequence he was unbookable. Treatment in various clinics throughout the U.K. followed after he had left a trail of lying, cheating and deceiving. As he related his stories to Ruby it became unsettling to her. Practically every day of his 'lost' period he would find himself in some kind of predicament. There were times when he would wake up not knowing where he was. On one such occasion, he found himself in a telephone box without knowing where it was and called his wife to come and fetch him. She pleaded with him to let her know where he was but he had no idea! Eventually he crawled back home full of apologies and remorse, which was an all too familiar story.

After another night of 'bingeing' he arrived home in the early hours of the morning and the cunning side of his illness told him to hide the bottle he was carrying. There was a litter bin attached to a lamp-post across the road from the house. He lifted some of its contents and slipped the bottle underneath the rubbish. The following morning he returned to the lamp-post and retrieved the bottle. He confessed openly that he had taken his long-suffering wife to hell… and back. However, she continued to stand by him by being there to pick up the pieces. Finally he discovered Alcoholics Anonymous, that much maligned organisation, and after several lapses from the straight and narrow managed to reach out and hold on to sobriety.

Following Freddie's meeting with Ruby, he came to the conclusion that Ruby was not yet ready to admit she had a problem. She certainly had one but until such time as she was prepared to admit it and seek help, she would continue to suffer badly. He repeated the analogy of the well. A person with the 'Big Problem' can be compared to someone falling down a well. At the top someone else attempts to save them by throwing down a rope so that the victim can be rescued. That person is in free fall and cannot grasp the rope. It is not until he or she hits the bottom of the well that the rope can hopefully be grasped and the rescue can then take place. Ruby, he told me, was in 'free fall' and had not yet reached the bottom of the well. Until she did there was no hope of saving her. Come what may, I wanted more than anything to be the person at the top of the well throwing down the rope. Before Freddie Clayton left our house, he surrepti-

RUBY—My Precious Gem!

tiously suggested to Ruby, in the nicest possible way, that she should make contact with Alcoholics Anonymous. Her family, especially Winnie, were appalled at this suggestion which helped to turn Ruby against the idea. In their eyes this so called 'treatment' was for tramps, vagabonds and social drop-outs but definitely not for Ruby, a star in show business. How little they knew! The 'illness' knows no barriers in society, culture or creed. Whilst in denial, Ruby claimed that she never took a drink before going on stage. Within that remark there appears to be a confession about drinking, although it wasn't strictly true. Amongst some of the engagements I booked for Ruby there was an occasion when I had to telephone the agent concerned to tell him that Ruby was 'not well enough to appear.'

A short while later, I thought all my prayers had been answered when Ruby came to me and said: "You'll be pleased to know that I am going to contact the A.A.".

My elation was short lived when she added she was going to stay in London with Winnie to find a branch there. Immediately I thought that 'if it's just for tramps and vagabonds' why the change of heart? I was naturally pleased with the news, but would have preferred to personally take Ruby myself. To my great joy she agreed so I made a few calls and soon was able to contact the Director of Alcoholism for Wellingborough Council, a Mr. Edwards. He was himself a 'dry' alcoholic. I started by asking for his assurance that there would be 100% confidentiality. He gave his word that both he and his staff were sworn to secrecy. It was only with this assurance that I told him about Ruby. I underlined that because my wife was a celebrity and was very much in the public eye, she was finding it extremely difficult to reveal her secrets. He naturally understood the difficulty and explained the normal practice within A.A., that of using a bogus name.

"From this moment on," he explained, "your wife will be known and referred to as 'Pat' to hide her identity".

He asked 'Pat' to come to his office for a meeting. An appointment was made and I drove Ruby to Wellingborough to meet Mr. Edwards. We were ushered into his office by his secretary and he soon told us that the four walls were completely gossip proof. His conversation started by telling us that the majority of 'sufferers' who came to see him were referred to him by their doctors. The biggest percentage of them came through his office door alone, without a partner, without a friend, without money and many without a home.

"You 'Pat', are extremely lucky. You walked through my door with a husband, with a home and with two loveable children!"

He went on to ask Ruby some very probing and pertinent questions that visibly touched a nerve. At the end of his interview of assessment he turned to a graph on the wall and pinpointed where he had calculated 'Pat' had descended. I could see that Ruby was uncomfortable with his findings.

Mr Edwards suggested that Ruby should consider attending a specialised clinic, the Graylingwell Hospital near Chichester, West Sussex. It was part of a National Health scheme to combat the ever-growing numbers of people with alcoholism. The British Medical Council had at long last recognised that alcoholism was a genuine illness, which required specialised treatment. Several units had been set up around the country specifically to tackle this immense problem. A colleague of Mr. Edwards ran this unit, which took only 14 patients at a time and was secure with complete anonymity. Once he had established 'Pat' was willing to go to Graylingwell he arrange her admission in one week's time for a stay of one month. However, she would have to take a medical report from her own G.P.

I was extremely grateful to Mr. Edwards for his prompt action. As we left his office and I could see Ruby had been quite unsettled by Mr. Edward's assessment and the impeding commitment. I began to wonder whether Ruby really intended to go through with this treatment, which she knew would be very strict. Would she be strong enough to overcome her craving? Could our marriage be saved? I prayed she would be able to overcome all the difficulties that she would have to encounter, for her sake, for my sake and for the sake of our children. To my relief, Ruby let me drive her to see the family G.P. to collect the medical report to take to the Graylingwell Hospital.

Freddie Clayton had already enlightened me about this course of treatment. He emphasised that no doctor can prescribe a pill, a potion, an injection or any other form of medication that could in any way cure a problem drinker. Any practitioner who claimed he could was not telling

RUBY—My Precious Gem!

the truth and if he actually charged a fee for making this claim, he, or she, was a charlatan. Freddie himself had been a patient in several clinics over the years and he had been given a special drug. He explained that after taking this drug, followed by alcohol, the patient would be overtaken with a feeling of nausea and that his head was swelling. Despite taking the medication Freddie managed to drink through it! He went on to tell me that the National Health Service special units had, at that time, quite a good record of success. They used the group method of rehabilitation making me feel optimistic about Ruby's chances of success. By using this method of working with fellow sufferers, each was able to help each other gain strength and understanding about their illness. By working through this intensive programme, over a four-week period, most would at least have a good chance of coming to terms with their illness ONE DAY AT A TIME.

When we arrived at the G.P.'s surgery, Ruby decided she wanted to go in to see him alone. This surprised me but I agreed. All she required was a medical report to take to Chichester so I foolishly stayed in the waiting room! Some time passed before she came out and, without speaking, we left for the car park. I soon discovered that she had not got the required medical report. I asked her… why?

Ruby then told me that she had explained the whole situation to her doctor. He was totally amazed at her request: "What ever do you want to go to these people for? That's for social drop-outs and the like. It's not for you! It could tarnish your image and also your career if it got out".

I couldn't believe what I was hearing. He had gone on to say that she should not consider going for this treatment but he had a friend, a Harley Street specialist, whose programme would be a much more civilised way for someone in her position. He promised to make the necessary arrangements. Now, I was not only astonished by the doctor's reactions but was very angry. My mind went straight back to what Freddie Clayton had told us. From that very moment her GP had brought about an irreversible change in Ruby's life which was to have devastating results. He had effectively destroyed my world, our children's world and the rest of our lives together. I couldn't wait to make an appointment to see this man who had turned my world upside down. On arrival I questioned him in detail about his attitude towards Ruby's problem. He repeated his claim that the treatment on offer was linked closely to AA and was not for someone in Ruby's position. I pointed out that I was desperate to get help for my wife. In my sheer desperation I had even written to Marjory Proops, an agony aunt, asking for her help and guidance. He dismissed my plight with a hurtful reply: "Well, of course, you are a publicity hunter, aren't you?" How I stopped myself from going over the top of his desk to get at him I will never know. The conversation ended with him saying that as Ruby's doctor he would make whatever arrangement he considered best for her. Later, I did get a reply from Marjory Proops telling me that she sympathised with my predicament and added that in her opinion my wife desperately needed help because, in her opinion, she had set herself on a course of self destruction.

Chapter 20
♪ 'Doctor, I'm in Trouble!' ♪

I managed to persuade Ruby to return to see Mr. Edwards, the Director of Alcoholism at Wellingborough Council. However, the damage had already been done! He was bitterly disappointed with the actions of her G.P. but explained, without the medical report, there would be no possibility of admission at Graylingwell Hospital. He did however succeed in getting 'Pat' to agree to contact A.A. and gave her all the necessary details, but the seeds of doubt had been sown in her mind already. Although she attended one or two meetings, I could see that she was only half hearted in her attitude. She did not intend to follow it through. Perhaps the stigma had rubbed off onto her too. The fact that one of these meetings was held in a dimly lit church room and devoid of a friendly atmosphere, must have contributed towards putting Ruby off the treatment.

The G.P. made an appointment for Ruby to see his friend Dr. Robert A'Brook in Harley Street and, as a result, she was admitted to his private clinic in Northampton. I wasn't once invited to speak with him. She stayed in a brand new, plush clinic for a two-week period. I was completely mystified by the fact that I was never consulted. Surely the doctor would want to talk to me about Ruby's addiction. A man with his credentials must know that the problem drinker is, to say the least, economical with the truth. He was supposedly a specialist and therefore should be familiar with the problem of alcoholism and should surely have asked me some questions. I saw him once, as he passed me by whilst on his rounds, and he appeared to be quite aggressive towards me, something I could not under stand. I visited Ruby in the clinic and enquired about the type of treatment the doctor had prescribed but apparently only mild sedatives had been given. I gathered that Ruby had told the doctor that there was a lot of stress at home pointing the blame in my direction. During the stay the nursing staff noticed a small wound on her forearm that looked inflamed and was tender to touch. I never found out what reason Ruby gave when an x-ray examination discovered a small piece of glass which was duly removed. The truth was that she had smashed a window in the house whilst unfortunately under the influence of alcohol. I was still not asked how it got there!

After the two-week stay I picked her up from the hospital to take her home hoping that there might be some kind of improvement. The very next day Ruby was intoxicated! A bill came through the post from Dr. A'Brook's office for £500, a very sizeable sum of money at that time. Now I fully understood what Freddie Clayton meant!

By now we had reached a very disturbing stage and it still gives me great pain to describe just how much suffering Ruby was inflicting on herself. The personality changes were horrendous and affected the whole family. Ruby went through phases of being a Jekyll and Hyde. She was great when sober but became a totally different person when under the influence. That lovely lady was no longer the gentle, vulnerable, delicate, feminine, adorable Ruby once she had consumed alcohol, Even small amounts would change her into a violent person capable of viscous physical attacks. She would thump, bite, kick, scream and smash anything within reach and I was invariably on the receiving end of these outbursts. These distressing scenes could go on for hours on end and if I was in the firing line, the only way I could fend off the blows aimed at me was to bear hug her and hold her arms to her sides.

More often than not the two children were asleep in their rooms when these attacks happened. However, on one such occasion, Ruby was in full cry and I was trying to fend off the blows reigning in on me. I finished up hugging her and pinning her arms down and I eventually finished up holding her down on the bed. Julie, our daughter walked into the room, saw me holding her mother down and shouted: "Leave mummy alone!"

RUBY—My Precious Gem!

That went through me like a knife! How could I explain to our child that it was not her mother who was being attacked but me. After seeing the way I was holding Ruby down, how could I expect her to believe me? The next day I tried to explain what had taken place but I knew that she didn't accept my story of events and I don't think she ever did.

Regrettably, it was not just me that came in for abuse when Ruby was in full cry. Quite a number of my possessions did too. I had a very attractive glass cabinet bought originally for my mother when I had started to earn my own money. It stood about five feet tall and had three or four glass shelves upon which were some decorative glasses and two cut glass decanters. The cabinet and all the contents came back into my possession after my mother passed away and I cherished them. In a particularly dramatic scene, in the early hours of the morning, Ruby went into a spate of violence and the cabinet was sent flying and everything was completely smashed to pieces. Then she turned her attention to me and blows came raining in at an alarming rate. I tried to restrain her but she managed to break loose, opened the window and screamed: "You're a murderer, Bernie Burgess!" As fast as I closed one window she opened another screaming and shouting out into the night. Even though this horrifying scene was taking place in a wing of the house, I feared for the children sleeping in another part of the cottage. I wrestled her away from the window and eventually we ended up on the floor. As I held her down she was kicking, biting, scratching and even spitting at me. Her screaming and hysteria had got to stop so I slapped her round the face, hoping that it would stop this frightening outburst. It was the only time I was unable to keep my self-restraint and I have lived with remorse about this incident ever since. The fracas continued until Ruby succumbed to sheer exhaustion.

I later discovered that as a result of a telephone call to her mother (or was it the other way around?) she went to see her doctor the next day about the bruise on her face. Perhaps with future legal action in mind, he made out a report in which he stated that I had punched Ruby and must have been wearing a ring on my hand. Obviously he had heard only one side of the story which was most definitely not correct in any of its detail. He never bothered to enquire about my side of the story and completely accepted Ruby's version of events as the truth. This proved quite conclusively to me that he knew nothing about alcoholism and its symptoms.

I was in a terrible predicament. I could never reveal the truth to anyone about Ruby's drinking which brought about her duel personality. Everybody knew her as a sweet, unassuming, adorable lady with a placid temperament. How could I tell them about the ongoing series of violent scenes when under the influence? Even if I did, I felt nobody would believe me. Besides, I was desperate to keep the true situation away from the media knowing that, if the newspapers had got hold of the story, then her career would be finished. I desperately yearned for this nightmare to come to an end and to have my lovable Ruby back once more. I was suffering with her and could see no solution to this terrible predicament.

A new body of people was set up by the National Health Service to deal explicitly with patients' complaints about GPs. Its title was 'The Family Practitioners' Authority.' I made it my business to find out more about them and where they could be found. I then wrote them a complaint, in detail, about this G.P. who had so devastatingly shattered my life, those of our children and had condemned Ruby to turmoil and misery for the rest of her life. As expected, despite their brief, there was a conspicuous closing of ranks, in their letter of reply.

I was told that my complaint was meaningless unless my wife endorsed it. If she was happy with the GPs recommendations then nothing could be done. The letter writer did at least say that he sympathised with my problem but, as the doctor had refused to recognise AA and the work they did, then no further action could be taken. It was apparent that I was wasting my time and efforts.

I felt that Freddie Clayton would find this ludicrous situation very interesting so I rang him with the story. He recognised it as a familiar story. Most doctors, at that time, had precious little knowledge on the subject of alcoholism and its devastating effects on the entire family. Not many GPs appreciated the work and support that AA carried out amongst the sufferers. The age old stigma was still very much in existence. Fortunately, with the passage of time, attitudes have changed and the AA has gradually become accepted by doctors and the medical profession in general. Sadly the change of heart came too late for me.

RUBY—My Precious Gem!

From then on the door had been well and truly slammed in my face and all hopes of getting help for Ruby had been effectively destroyed. To this day I still live with some big burning questions: What would have happened if my lovely wife had demanded the medical report, gone to Chichester and completed the programme? Could she have become 'dry' and perhaps still be alive today? After all, her sister Lilian had sought the help of AA in Canada and is, hopefully, still alive and 'dry'. Ruby could have been spared years of turmoil and alcohol damage and still be at my side. I should still have a happy and contented wife and family laughing and singing together as we once did.

The all too familiar pattern continued. One evening, returning home from an engagement, a serious incident happened in the car. Ruby had managed to exceed the limit and her aggression bubbled to the surface. Whilst I was driving, a struggle developed and to my horror she opened the door of the car and was threatening to jump out. It was very late at night with fortunately few cars on the road. I grabbed her whilst braking. She snatched away and a beautiful gown that she was still wearing was irreparably torn. A similar scene took place when she was returning with a driving pianist. He too had to wrestle to keep the car under control and Ruby in her seat.

The combined worry of Ruby's illness, and the effect that it was having on the two children, brought about an enormous amount of mental and physical strain on me. I was on the verge of a breakdown.

Chapter 21
♪ 'After You're Gone!' ♪

Ruby was still receiving persistent telephone calls from Winnie in London and also continuing to seek 'solace' across the village green with Jean and Peter Barbour. Frequently there would be serious incidences. On one frantic night I had to chase after Ruby, in her dressing gown, and bring her back home. She had been drinking and was on her way back, across the village green, in an attempt to get more. On another occasion, when I returned from taking the children to my sister's home to avoid them losing precious sleep, I discovered that Ruby had attempted to set fire to some papers on my desk and had then smashed the typewriter. There could have been some kind of hidden message in her actions. Perhaps she resented my work!

Sleeping tablets again became a concern. I knew there were some in the house. The bottle had been taken out of the medicine cabinet and several were missing. I found her attempting to lie down on the settee and realised that something was wrong as her speech was slurred and she was drowsy. It was late at night but I decided that a doctor was needed. Luckily, the junior doctor in the village practice lived next door so I rang him. I apologised for the late hour but asked him to attend Ruby. I was very grateful when he came almost immediately.

Contrary to his senior partner's attitude, he was prepared to listen to me and was sympathetic. Studying the bottle's size, and the date that it was prescribed, he roughly calculated how many tablets should have been in the bottle. His judgement was that there was no real cause for alarm and no need to take her to the hospital. By giving her black coffee and keeping

RUBY—My Precious Gem!

her walking around the house, for as long as I possibly could, the effects would gradually wear off. He even stayed with me for about an hour so that the two of us could support her, one either side, going round from one room to another. Eventually he considered that it was safe for him to leave saying that I should continue for as long as I could and then let her sleep off the effects. I kept the walking and the coffee going as long as I could stay awake then managed to get her to bed. Sleep overcame me and I slumped down beside Ruby and took the opportunity to cuddle up to her for a few hours whilst peace lasted. I longed for this nightmare to end and a return to normality in all our lives.

The following day I spoke with the same doctor and he enlightened me about the sleeping tablets episode. He told me that Ruby was inclined to be manic-depressive and, like others in a similar situation, would invariably leave a clue as to what they had done. Usually, there was a note prominently displayed giving a clear indication of their intentions.

Yet another attempt was made to go to the Barbours' house. I didn't want her to go seeking more alcohol so I stood with my back to the kitchen door, barring her way. In her rage she let fly with her fists whilst screaming at me to let her go out but I stood firm. At the height of this disturbance, Peter Barbour arrived and tried to gain entry to the kitchen by pushing the back door, which was at my back. I had no idea who was there but I allowed the door to open and he burst in and exclaimed: "don't you know that everyone in the village can hear you beating your wife?"

All my pent up feelings came to the surface. I was furious and I ejected him from the house. As well as being angry with his wild and inaccurate remark, I now had some idea of what Ruby must have been telling the Barbours about our situation. Quite naturally they must have believed the stories and then supplying her with more drink. They had no idea of the true situation. Why should they believe otherwise. As it was coming from gentle Ruby, it must be true!

By now Ruby had started making trips to Torquay to see Lamar sometimes taking the children with her. During one period of heavy drinking she rang Lamar from the bedroom telephone. She was hysterical and sobbing convulsively but blurted out that she loved him. I was devastated, yet at the same time, I tried to convince myself that it was the drink that was talking. It couldn't be my Ruby saying that to someone else!

A short while later, in 1974, a large envelope arrived for me bearing legal documents. Ruby had filed for divorce. This was the second time I had received documents of this nature. A few months earlier the letter was from a solicitor in London. Winnie had been stoking the fire and goading Ruby to act. For some inexplicable reason, Ruby didn't follow it through on that occasion but just allowed it to fizzle out. This time it was for real. I had no alternative other than to defend myself by engaging a solicitor to represent me. Ruby's file was based on my 'unreasonable behaviour' then it was changed. It crossed my mind that perhaps her solicitor had put that reason forward but maybe Ruby's conscience wouldn't allow her to take that line. The legal minds got together and came up with an alternative suggestion that I file for the divorce, instead of Ruby, on the grounds that the marriage had 'broken down irretrievably'. My life was now in ruins. After thinking that I had found the answer by eliminating the stresses for Ruby and providing an alternative income I had now lost. I had not only lost the general managership of the cabaret restaurant, although that was of little importance, but also my wife. There was the possibility that I would also lose the children and my home if the judgement went against me.

More indignation was to come my way. Despite the fact that initial divorce papers had been exchanged an embarrassing scene was played out at Rectory Cottage. A host of people arrived at the house including Ruby and Lamar along with members of her family. It was as though they were holding a party. The drink flowed, in front of the children, and to my horror foul language was being freely used. I am by no means a prude, I served two years National Service and became familiar with all the barrack room expletives, but for this bad language to be voiced in my home and in front of my children was objectionable. I wanted them all to leave but I had already found out to my cost that you cannot reason with a bottle. I had to bite the bullet and keep the children out of harm's way.

The divorce came to court but thankfully I didn't have to appear. My solicitor, who was a family friend, had prior talks with both parties beforehand, and had warned Ruby that it was possible that she might not get

RUBY—My Precious Gem!

custody of the children, presumably because of her touring and her lifestyle. The wrangling seemed to be going on forever. I started to lose patience with it all! I asked my solicitor to finalise everything as quickly as possible as I didn't want to have to go through a long drawn-out messy divorce. Ruby had already left our home in 1974 to go to Lamar in Torquay leaving me with the children. Julie was just 14 years old, a very difficult age for a young girl to be without her mother. Tim was only 9 years old. Both were far too young to understand everything that had been going on, besides, I did everything that I could to protect them from all the upheaval. Fortunately they saw very little of the problems, when the storms were gathering I drove them across town to sleep at my sister's house and collected them for school the following morning.

In 1976 the case was settled. Everything was to be divided equally. I was to stay in the matrimonial home and I gained custody of the children. I had been led to believe that in most divorce cases the wife is more likely to get custody. However, the judge found in my favour which meant that Julie and Tim could continue their schooling from home. I would be required to put the house on the market when Tim reached the age of 17 or if I chose to re-marry, which ever came sooner, then there would be a division of proceeds. There was also the matter of R&B Burgess Properties Limited and the houses we had purchased for an investment. However, I did not want to contest that especially as Ruby had left Rectory Cottage to me, albeit temporarily. I was completely devastated, Ruby had made her final exit and would not be coming back. Now I was alone with two children to raise, a home to run and a business to handle. I was wafer thin and frequently gushed with floods of tears which I struggled to keep the children from seeing.

I knew that losing their mother was going to be a traumatic experience for Tim and Julie. I tried to soften the immediate impact by asking my two sisters, Jean and Pat, to take them on holiday to Majorca. Even so I knew that I could not possibly heal their wounds entirely. For legal purposes my solicitor had made the children wards of court. He felt that he had to do this because of pressure being placed on both children by Winnie and the Murray family. When Julie was around 14 or 15, and still a juvenile, she left the cottage for Torquay one day. There was no way that she could have undertaken that long journey without collusion from someone. I was so angry and drove straight to Torquay to bring her back. When I got to

Lamar's harbour-side flat I found the entrance door and the door to his flat both open. I walked straight in and confronted Ruby and Ray but they did not put up any opposition because they were aware that I was the custodian. Legally they were totally in the wrong. Julie came home with me. In a former biography, Julie was quoted as saying she 'escaped' and had to use a ladder to get out of her bedroom window. This was pure melodrama, because the ladder, so dramatically referred to, was just some steps on the side of a bunk-bed, all of four feet tall! Her bedroom was on ground level so it would have been possible for Julie to get out without the aid of steps. The outcome was that Julie was either caught up in a thrilling adventure as seen in Hollywood films or she was being greatly influenced by others who were eager to lure her away from me. Winnie once had the audacity to say to me: "We've got Julie, now we'll get Tim!" This woman was capable of many wicked things.

The two years between 1974 and 1976 and waiting for the divorce to become finalised, were extremely difficult times for all three of us. I hated being on my own and with all the household chores to do as well as running the office and tending to all the children's needs, it became a heavy strain on me. I had been through hell for far too many years and I had become threadbare. After leaving the cabaret restaurant, I had very little travelling to do so was able to be on hand for the children at all times. Combining the revenue from booking entertainment via my agency office and with the commissions earned from the artistes that I continued to handle, I had a sizeable income and we could live very well. I was only required to make one journey each week to the Cabaret Restaurant and that was for the band call (artiste's band rehearsal) normally on Sunday afternoons or should an emergency crop up.

Julie, as a young teenager, started to become very rebellious. Being tugged in all directions didn't help one bit, as she was being torn between me, Winnie in London and Ruby in Torquay. She had been present too many times when Winnie had been heavily criticising me and even by Ruby when she was under the influence. Quite a lot of the vitriolic nonsense must have sunk in and taken effect.

Finally she went missing from home for a second time. I was away on business for a couple of hours, leaving her at 16 to take care of Tim, who was 11 years old. When I arrived back home Julie was nowhere to be found

RUBY—My Precious Gem!

and I was bewildered. Not only had she left home but she had left her brother unattended. She had left me a note (I still have that note) and I didn't know which way to turn or what to do. I was the legal guardian and therefore responsible for her welfare so I had to find her quickly. I felt I had to report her missing. I made very extensive enquiries without a hint of success. I knew that she wouldn't risk going to Torquay again so it was my guess that she must have gone to London. I felt sure that Winnie wouldn't risk breaking the Ward of Court Order a second time or would she? I decided to ask my sister to look after Tim whilst I set off to London in search of Julie.

To this day I feel sure that Julie had no idea of the amount of anguish that I had to endure through this terrifying ordeal. I picked up a feint trail which appeared to be connected to friends that Julie had met whilst she was in Torquay. I followed it. Then I had the strangest of feelings! Each time I started to get close to finding her she was moved on to another place. Again I got a whiff of collusion. I stayed walking the streets of London for two whole days and nights without rest. I had one more lead that needed to be investigated but I had to return to Northampton to attend to Tim. Someone had told me that the Salvation Army undertook searches for missing persons so I contacted them for help but they could only offer limited assistance until Julie reached the age of 17 years, so I passed the lead on to the missing persons department of the police service. Several days later I received a message that Julie had been found. I was in Wolverhampton at the time, a hundred and twenty miles from London. The message went on to say that, for her own safety, they would have to take her into protective custody to await my arrival. Again someone was trying to influence my daughter against me by saying that I had given instructions to have Julie 'arrested', a statement that was clearly untrue and meant to severely undermine our relationship.

I took off from Wolverhampton to drive to London at great speed and found the police station where Julie was being temporarily housed. There was no sign of Julie! The duty sergeant told me that Winnie, her grandmother, had picked her up. I should have guessed. I telephoned her to say that I would come straight over to pick up Julie. The obvious questions remain unanswered to this day. Who arranged Julie's departures? Was she picked up by car? If she travelled by train or bus, where did the money come from? How did she find her way around the big city?

At school, Julie was getting herself into all kinds of trouble. First she was chastised when it was discovered that quite a few of the girls had been trying to create tattoos by using a pin and some ink, a very silly and highly dangerous fad. I find it difficult to understand why these fads, or fashions, become so vitally important to the younger generation. It is obvious that there is playground pressure that states 'if you don't do it you are not one of us.' It dictates that everyone must follow suit, whether it be tattoos, unkempt frayed jeans, or shirts worn outside trousers by boys as well as girls. Individuality is a forgotten word. She was then brought home from school in disgrace. She had been found with a click of other girls – DRINKING ALCOHOL. One was the daughter of the local village 'pub' licensee, hence the availability of drink. It was all the more embarrassing for me because the teacher, who had delivered her to our house, was a family friend.

Looking back at my tolerance level towards bad behaviour and, having been through endless nightmares and countless sleepless nights, I had become far less tolerant so consequently we clashed quite a few times. The reverse was also true on Julie's part. She had been almost brainwashed against me as her quotes in Ruby's biography bears out. She referred to my apparent insistence that 'silence had to be maintained at the meal table' and that I had 'Victorian methods of discipline'. Those accusations had been attributed to Big Dan, not me. He was the one that insisted on silence at meal times. I most certainly didn't, so how did Julie get that story? Despite it all, I tried very hard to please her. I had wanted her to grow up in a happy, stable home but because that wasn't to be, I bought things to please her. Apart from the lovely suits I also purchased the latest quadraphonic sound system and set it all up in her bedroom. Perhaps that could be seen as trying to do what I had criticised Winnie of doing, trying to buy love with gifts. At the same time, I hoped to instil a sense of responsibility into her by suggesting that she found a job with a view to paying back a part of the cost. That was perhaps asking too much, so I paid for it in full.

Winnie's accusation that I preferred Tim to Julie was a monstrous statement for her to implant into Julie's mind. I can honestly say that I loved my children equally, and tried to ensure that what I did for one I would do for the other. In the days when Tim was embarking upon a career in show business, I took him to a recording studio in Ringwood,

RUBY—My Precious Gem!

Hampshire to make a professional demonstration disc to enable him to submit it to major record companies. It was quite an expensive project, some £500 and, at the time, a sizable sum of money. To make quite sure that I evened things up, I offered the same arrangement for Julie. She had a very good singing voice and had taken part in the making of one of Ruby's records 'Ways and Means'. I negotiated for the use of a concert room in Northampton so that Julie could rehearse with some of my backing tapes. It was then my intention to take her to the same recording studio in Hampshire to make a similar demonstration disc. Julie had the concert room to herself, in case she was self conscious. She tried but felt that she didn't really want to do it. To avoid her missing out I deposited £500 into a savings account for her.

I now reflect back to the hours that I spent with Julie as a child. I played various games with her, such as her riding on my foot when I crossed my legs and, quoting from a film that I had also seen as a lad "Ride like the wind child", pretending she was riding a horse. I sang the alphabet with her learning it well and long before her playmates knew it. I can still remember a beautiful song that I sang to Julie when she was very tiny:

You're the end of the rainbow, my pot of gold,
You're Daddy's little girl, to have and to hold,
A precious gem is what you are,
You're Daddy's bright and shining star'
You're the spirit of Christmas, my star on the tree,
You're the Easter bunny to your Mummy and me,
You're sugar, you're spice, you're everything nice,
And you're Daddy's little girl.

I converted an outbuilding at Rectory Cottage into a playroom with all the toys she could possibly need, neatly housed and displayed, mostly for her and her playmate Sally to use. They tired of it after a couple of days and it became redundant. She loved horses, possibly from riding on my foot, so I took her to regular riding lessons. I later paid for a course of tennis lessons in the hope that she might enjoy the game. It was a waste of money. During other moments of precious parent/child play I would relate stories that might have fascinated her like the story of 'The Ballet of the Red Shoes', a story that excited me in my younger days.

When Julie reached the age of 17, she was no longer a juvenile and decided that she wanted to return to London. I could no longer stop her from going although I still felt the need to see that she was coming to no harm. I decided to go to see where she was living and what it was like. It was a house converted into flats with four doorbells on the side of the entrance. There were no names on the bells that I could recognise so I remained outside until someone arrived with a key. I enquired as to whether Julie was at home. He showed me the way to her flat when I told him I was her father. After a few seconds the door opened a mere six inches and Julie peered around the edge, looked me straight in the eyes and said … "Yes?" It stunned me! She looked straight at me but it was as if I was a complete stranger.

Shortly after that hurtful incident Julie moved from London to Torquay and became a 'Blue Coat' at Pontins Holiday Camp. It meant that she was close to the harbour-side flat where Ruby was living with Lamar. Whilst she was on a day off from her duties she arranged to meet both Ruby and Ray in an hotel on the quay. The drink was flowing and a heated argument broke out in front of Julie. Ruby left the bar to go to the ladies room. Julie became concerned when her mother had not return for a good 10 minutes so decided to go in search for her. She discovered that the door was still locked and got no answer from her knocking. The management were alerted and arrived to gain entry. Ruby still had a mouthful of pills—sleeping pills. She was rushed to hospital and a stomach pump was used to clear her stomach. When I heard the news I found it deeply disturbing but then I wondered—who is taking the blame for her drinking now? Would Winnie now turn her attention to Lamar? Would they reflect that perhaps I was not to blame for it after all?

After two years of being a single parent and raising a young son, I decided to join a group of single parents who called themselves 'Gingerbread'. I hated being on my own and dreaded the thought of staying that way for the rest of my life. My own father suffered that fate, and I knew what misery it caused him. By being with other parents who were in a similar position, at least gave me the means of conversation and to socialise. I desperately needed company.

Chapter 22

♪ 'The Second Time Around' ♪

Life was not easy as a single parent, but I knew that I had to be both mother and father to Tim. I tried to encourage him in whatever activities he appeared to enjoy. The local butcher in Wootton, David Hillier, was the leader of a branch of the Boys Brigade in the village and Tim decided to join, which pleased me enormously. He did well and seemed to take great pride in his unit. They had a band and I was more than surprised when Tim came home with a bugle and wanted to practice to be eligible. I was elated when he learned how and what to play so very easily and was soon taking part in their Sunday morning marches. Looking spick and span in his uniform, I felt ten feet tall as he paraded around the village in the front row of the buglers. I know that his mother would have been as proud as I was.

Cricket was my favourite sport. As a young boy in my home town of Oxford my mother would take me to see football and cricket matches as she came from a sporting family. I had a ritual for after school hours. My mother would prepare me some sandwiches and lemonade, it was made from powder in those days. I took them to school so that I could scamper down the main Banbury Road to the University Parks, some distance away, to watch the last hour of cricket before stumps were drawn. The Oxford University team played against all the County Cricket teams in those days so I was privileged to see some of the star players of that era. We had four lawns at Rectory Cottage, all of different sizes and the largest one was just right for a knock-about game of cricket. I was delighted when Tim showed an interest and it gave me great pleasure teaching him how to hold a bat, make his stance and perform some of the basic strokes. Together, with a couple of his school pals, we would play 'three times and out' which translated means that you had to be 'out' three times before you handed the bat over to the next man. I do confess to cheating, just a little. Although I only bowled underarm, Tim could never read my leg breaks. They kept him really guessing. I thoroughly enjoyed those halcyon days teaching Tim to play cricket. He quickly showed an interest for the game. He joined the cricket team of the Boys Brigade and thrilled me when he told me he was in the Roade School cricket team as well. On summer evenings he would sometimes play two matches, one for the school followed by a Boys Brigade match. His school, Roade Comprehensive School, could boast of some very fine cricketers, one of whom played eventually for England – David Capel. I remember being a spectator at a school match against Wellingborough when Tim and David Capel were 'in' together. To my delight Tim scored the winning runs. He soon became one of the star players in the school team and was chosen for a trial for the under 16s for Northamptonshire—the county team. He passed his 'audition' and then could proudly wear the county sweater with the county badge emblazoned on his chest. I was a very proud father. He was chosen to go on a short tour with the under 16s team playing against other county teams. I have kept a record of his performances and a large photograph of him in his Northamptonshire cricket whites showing a straight bat stance. It's displayed proudly in my apartment right now!

During the early days of single parenthood I began to receive telephone calls from Ruby, sadly in various degrees of intoxication. It was heartbreaking. In one of these calls she confessed to me that she had made a big mistake and echoed Big Dan's saying "I've made my bed, now I must lie on it!"

I was still a comparatively young man when my wife left me and just 48 when I became a divorcee two years later. There had to be a life out there somewhere for me and I had to find it. I needed to put the past behind me. It wasn't going to be easy as I still loved my wife and knew in my heart that she still loved me.

Mark, one of Tim's school pals, started joining in with our lawn cricket. He lived with his mother next door to the Barbours and were obviously a single parent family. He told me that his mother didn't get home from work until 5.30pm so he was alone until she arrived which enabled him to

RUBY—My Precious Gem!

join us. I soon wanted to hear how his mother had become a single parent? Mark's normal routine was to join his mother as she walked passed Rectory Cottage on her way home. One day I asked Mark to bring his mother into the garden to have tea with us, but she was a sun worshipper and wanted to get a little sun bathing in before sunset. A few days later she did accept my invitation and I left the boys playing cricket whilst we had tea. She introduced herself as Jane and after a few of these teatime chats, opened up to tell me that she was in fact the battered wife of a violent alcoholic husband. Small world!

She had left the matrimonial home with Mark, her youngest son. Needless to say I had every sympathy for her. Her life had become a living hell and for a very long time she was too frightened to leave her home for fear that her husband would find her and take revenge. Eventually, she plucked up enough courage to go to see a solicitor who took out a restraining order and with the help of other relatives she moved out. Sadly she was only able to take one of her five children with her to where she had found accommodation. All that she could find was a bedroom in her friend's house with a shared use of a kitchen and bathroom. We became very good friends and fortunately for me, after time, a relationship started to blossom and I began to shed my desperate loneliness. As our friendship progressed we discussed her cramped living conditions. She was sharing the one bedroom with her nine-year-old son, which gave her no privacy —not the best of situations.

We socialised as one family and went everywhere together. I had great sympathy for Mark. He was separated from his brothers and sister, although he had no feelings at all for his father. I had to tread very carefully with Mark because I was in danger of alienating him by becoming close to his mother. She was all that he had left in the world. The young lad must have felt it possible that I could take his mother away from him. Eventually, the situation that we were in just didn't make sense. I was living in a four-bedroomed house and Jane shared one bedroom with her young son. I suggested that we join forces and become one unit so Jane and Mark came to live with Tim and myself. It was better for all of us. I had someone in the house with whom I could share everything and Jane no longer had the discomfort of sharing a room with Mark. The two boys became like brothers. We were a happy family of four once again.

Bernie Burgess & Frank Bowles

It wasn't long before Ruby heard the news about my new relationship and the fact that Jane had moved into Rectory Cottage. Consequently telephone calls started to come in at all hours of the day and night especially late at night. To a degree I could understood her concern, but felt she should accept that we had both moved in with partners. Whenever Jane picked up the 'phone, Ruby would ask to speak to her 'husband' although we had been divorced for over two years. Shortly after the start of these telephone calls Ruby travelled to Wootton and stayed with Jean and Peter Barbour across the green from the cottage. With the help of a little 'Dutch courage' she came to call but we happened to be out. Not to be denied, she smashed the bathroom window and entered the house. The window was very small so I could not imagine how a delicate feminine creature, such as Ruby, could enter through the broken pane. She went from room to room leaving caustic notes wherever she went including one on Jane's pillow. Apart from everything else this was not conducive to the start of my new relationship. Apparently, according to all the newspaper reports, her new life with Ray was supposedly very happy.

Ruby's agency office was long since off the scene and, as I was no longer doing Ruby's bookings, she needed another agent/manager. Lamar was no agent and had never been associated with the booking of artistes. Lee Stevens, another Danny LaRue type of artiste, contacted Ruby and took control of her datebook and continued for a number of years. Astonishingly, in a radio interview, after Ruby's demise, he had the audacity to criticise her with a number of detrimental remarks about her professionalism and her appearance. It would have been more fitting for him, who was supposedly looking after her welfare, to have shown a little compassion for a fallen star who had scaled the heights in show business, heights that he could never hope to attain himself. If he stood on tiptoe he couldn't even have reached her ankles! I'm so very grateful that I never met the man.

Cabaret venues were now becoming few in number and artistes were turning to the cruise ships for engagements. Financially they offered very little by way of salary but artistes were allowed free travel and accommodation for themselves and a partner. They were not called upon to do too many performances during the cruise so overall it was a very pleasant way to work. Ruby undertook several cruises including the QE2 and The Black Watch. Lamar, who was no longer working, accompanied Ruby.

RUBY—My Precious Gem!

The recording scene had also changed quite dramatically, in a very short space of time, and was completely dominated by youth. Ballad singers and sentimental songs were eased out of the picture. The 'beat' scene had arrived in a big way. Ruby's voice was the kind that could have easily made the transition to country music, but no one thought about her trying. Another factor was that Ruby was from Ireland and country music is extremely popular with Irish folk worldwide, This was a source that might have proved to be very productive.

After leaving Columbia Records, Ruby joined the Philips/Fontana label and A&R man Terry Brown came very close to achieving a hit single for Ruby with a song called 'Sooner or Later' which had a decidedly country feel in its arrangement. Two albums were made during her stay with the new label. Terry was in tune with Ruby and tried a few different techniques in a 'state of the art' studio that was new to Ruby. For example, if 'mood' was required during the take of a sad song, then he would arrange the studio lighting to provide a 'mood' atmosphere. Neither Ruby nor myself had experienced this technique before although I daresay it became part of the normal procedure in ensuing years. In later years I picked up the story that Ruby had been given an award by BASCA for her services to music. She received the award from Don Black, a very successful song writer who had a long term link-up with Matt Monro, the most famous of all his hits must be 'Born Free'.

Whilst still living in Wootton our new family knitted well together and I felt that Tim had got the much needed stability he required. Jane and I tried hard to ensure that we treated the two boys both fairly. I had a good income and Jane had a secure job so we were able to buy things for the boys to enjoy. We bought each of them a bicycle and a tape recorder, although their choice of music was not exactly easy on my ears! Hard rock to me could be summed up in one single word – DIN! I encouraged the two lads to use earphones but they had no intention of using them so deafening music continued to pervade the entire house. My inability to be able to accept the offending level of decibels caused one or two hiccups along the way. It was difficult for the two growing lads to understand that, after years of stress and strain, noise was the last thing I needed. I was completely threadbare and screaming, whining guitars and interminable heavy drum beats were not therapeutic in any way. Like it or not, I had to accept their music. They were young and perhaps one day, I hoped soon, they might progress to a better level of 'proper' music!

Telephone calls from Torquay were frequent and continued to be an ongoing worry. Naturally, Jane wanted me to call a halt to them being made but I tried to explain to her that, in reality, they were a cry for help. Short of leaving the 'phone permanently off the hook there was nothing that I could do about it. Knowing Jane's feelings, I should have put the 'phone down when I established who was calling but I couldn't bring myself to do that.

Ruby made another heartbreaking visit whilst Jane was at work. She arrived once again via the Barbours' home just across the green. She had obviously accepted their hospitality and apparently, as usual, heated words were exchanged. Ruby was only semi-coherent. What she said didn't make much sense. Then, out of the blue, she asked me to kiss her. My mind went into a spin. Here was I in a new relationship with another partner, having stepped out of a complete nightmare, yet she wanted a kiss! I was deeply perplexed. I was still very much in love with Ruby but how could I lead her to believe that our relationship was still alive? Then there was Jane to consider. Could I betray her trust and shatter her life again? With immense pangs of remorse I declined to kiss her. I instantly realised that rejection was the last thing that I wanted to inflict on a very sick Ruby. In all honesty, I lived to regret refusing that kiss, even though I knew it was the right decision.

RUBY—My Precious Gem!

The time came around for me to place Rectory Cottage on the market as required by the conditions of the divorce. The property market at this time was very slow and a good price did not seem likely. I was placed under immense pressure by the solicitors to sell quickly, irrespective of the amount. Ruby was no doubt strongly influenced by Lamar, so there was an insistence that I accepted the first offer that came along. The urgency seemed very odd to me. There could not be a shortage of money in the Property Company's bank account. I had not contested the company, or its finances, during the divorce.

I resisted their unrelenting pressure and began to improve the chances of a better offer by decorating and renovating the cottage for both our sakes. I worked hard to make the house attractive for prospective buyers. We had bought Rectory Cottage twenty years earlier so improvements needed to be made in any case to make a good sale. I considered that it was in both our interests to get the highest possible price without rushing it.

Although I say it myself, I made our home look a million dollars. I updated the kitchen, an essential for any female looking over a property with a view to purchase. When we obtained a good price and the sale was completed, the new owners wanted to move in within four weeks. I made their deadline by holding a hurried furniture sale and by moving in with one of Jane's sons until we could find somewhere else to live.

I managed to arrive at an amicable agreement with Ruby regarding the sale of the furniture but I was forced to accept ridiculously low prices. The possessions and items that I took with me had to be shared out amongst Jane's family and friends until we bought our own home together. Both Tim and Julie had flown the nest by this time so we needed to buy a smaller property for just the two of us. I had loved living at Rectory Cottage. It was heartbreaking to walk away from it. I remembered so well the many happy times spent there, but it was now time to move on and make a new life – hopefully!

Chapter 23
♪ 'Over The Sea To Skye' ♪

Having sold the cottage and most of the furniture, the division of proceeds took place. I was quite happy that I had withstood the pressure of "take the first offer" and gained a reasonable price. Jane and I had to endure a rather cramped few weeks with one of her sons and his wife and although it was quite a difficult period, the fact that the son allowed us into his home was very much appreciated.

We gazed into many estate agents' windows looking for property. Financially, I had to scale down quite substantially so we were looking in the first time buyers' bracket which narrowed the search considerably. I was window shopping on my own one afternoon, whilst Jane was at work, when I came across a very interesting property that had particular appeal. At Wootton I had encouraged Jane to follow a hobby, that of growing fuchsias, and I had constructed a polythene greenhouse for that purpose. The property that I stumbled across was a very small semi-detached, two-bedroomed, house in a quiet cul-de-sac. It wasn't great to look at but it had almost two acres of land at the rear. I went to view and was completely fascinated by the possibilities it offered for Jane's fuchsias. I rang her and said that I had found a property in Sywell, on the outskirts of Northampton. She was not very impressed to begin with until I told her about the two acres of land at the rear. We bought it! Jane had all the room in the world to grow thousands of fuchsia and in fact started a small business which we called 'Blooming Things'. Once again I worked night and day to create a lovely home out of a very ordinary house. I gutted the

RUBY—My Precious Gem!

inside, modernised the kitchen and bathroom, installed central heating and an open fireplace for log burning. There was no shortage of those in the back garden!

The previous owners had two enormous rows of outbuildings running down the middle of the land. Apparently they had a contract with a cosmetics company and also cages for breeding rabbits of all things! We declined the chance of continuing as the thought of such an operation nauseated the both of us so I couldn't wait to demolish them. The open fireplace had a good christening with all the debris that resulted! We were there for approximately four years during which time my agency/management business declined dramatically with the arrival of the Disco. My income plummeted and I feared for the future.

One of the artistes that I represented for a while, Dave Sheriff, had developed a good career for himself in country music and had gone to live near Inverness in Scotland. When speaking to him about my future he suggested that it might be a good idea to buy a croft as they were very reasonably priced in Scotland. At first I didn't take his suggestion too seriously but on second thoughts it seemed to offer a possible financial solution. I thought back to the time when I had taken Jane and the two boys on a camping holiday to the Highlands. Jane's father had served in the Royal Navy during World War ll and was stationed on the Isle of Skye. As we toured around the Highlands Jane requested that we go to the isle. She would love to be able to trace the croft-house that her father had been allocated as naval married quarters. When he had settled in, he sent for his wife and baby Jane so she had many childhood memories of her younger days playing with the lambs on Skye. I made for the ferry, drove the car onto the ferryboat and we were on our way 'over the sea to Skye!' I fell in love with the 'Misty Isle' straight away and vowed that if ever I had the opportunity to opt out of show business, this is where I'd love to settle.

My friend Dave was right, there were crofts to be purchased at reasonable prices. After three journeys, up and down from Northampton to Skye, some 560 or so miles each way, we eventually found a suitable property, a 'cotter', or small croft, in a tiny township called Kilbride near Broadford. Loch Slappin that opened out into the sea, was a mere 300 yards from the house. We had a magnificent view of a mountain called Blaven, which was part of the breathtaking Cuillin range made famous by the Scottish entertainer Sir Harry Lauder with his famous song 'The Far Cuillins.'

Wildlife was in abundance and the bird population included species such as Buzzards, Oyster Catchers, Curlew and the magnificent Golden Eagle. The house was on a feu, which can be compared to a building plot, and with it came the lease on four and a half acres of land—absolute bliss! As an only child Jane would roam alone in the countryside surrounding the village of Wootton studying the wild life and flowers, so Kilbride's acreage and the surrounding mountains were going to be paradise for her. We bought it! Financially, I could afford to buy the croft and place the balance into Income Bonds thereby bringing in a monthly income. I was still a long way from drawing an old age pension but we could live on the interest and be comfortable. I had a vision of spending many years on this idyllic island and being able to walk off into the sunset, hand in hand, with a happy ending—Hollywood style! It was not to be.

In the meantime Ruby continued with her engagements and completed a summer season in Blackpool with George Roper on the Central Pier. In 1985, she was honoured by being asked to appear in a Royal Celebration Show titled 'Forty Years of Peace' in the West End of London. I was delighted for her. Included in the 50s line-up were such stars as Anne Shelton, Lonnie Donegan, The Beverley Sisters, Lita Rosa, Dennis Lotis, Craig Douglas, Bryan Johnson, Pearl Carr and Teddy Johnson. It was televised by London Weekend Television and produced by David Bell on Sunday 5th May. The following

Ruby with Sandy Powell

RUBY—My Precious Gem!

summer Ruby was Special Guest Star in a production at Swansons Hotel in Jersey, the Channel Islands with the grand old man of comedy Sandy ("Can you hear me mother?") Powell.

Ruby then teamed up with other 50s singing stars—Ronnie Hilton, Joan Regan and Clinton Ford. They joined forces in a 'Stars of the Fifties' Roadshow and toured quite extensively throughout the British Isles.

Presumably through Tim, Ruby got to know my address and telephone number on Skye. Predictably the 'phone calls started once more and Jane was again, quite rightly, upset by them. I had been separated from Ruby since 1974 and my divorce was finalised two years later and here we were in 1988 still receiving dramatic and upsetting calls from my ex-wife some 14 years later! I could understand Jane's concern. To add to it Ruby still insisted in asking to "speak to my husband".

Ruby with Joan Regan

I had to explain to Jane again that there was no way I could stop the calls. I had no idea when Ruby would call and I couldn't possibly leave the 'phone off the hook indefinitely. Then I received a very frightening call. She'd had a blazing row with Ray. Between sobs and long passages of unintelligible talk I gathered that things had got out of hand. She had gone to the kitchen drawer and had taken out a knife. Ray immediately made a grab for it but held the blade. Ruby withdrew the knife and, in so doing, badly cut Ray's hand. She didn't know what to do. What could I possibly do some 700 miles away? It was obviously another cry for help but I was powerless. I established that the cut was serious but not dangerous and suggested calling for a doctor or getting him to hospital. With Jane standing by my side I knew that I should put the telephone down. However, I felt strongly that I would be deserting her in her time of need. She could have dialled 999 but she had needed to call me. Somehow I managed to cut the call short, and feeling consumed with guilt, I replaced the telephone. I had sewn the seeds that would eventually bring about a termination of my new life.

Before departing for Skye, Tim had made a decision to make show business his career. I considered it my duty to warn him about the frailty of the profession and that it was no bed of roses. I made great efforts to give him a start, but with the memories of 'Big' Dan and how he treated his daughter still in my mind, I was anxious to impress on Tim that I had no desire at all of becoming his agent or his manager. I was prepared to point him in the right direction enabling him to walk through the minefield and to open a few closed doors for him, thus putting his feet firmly on the first rung of the ladder.

Before leaving Northampton for Skye I had featured him in a show of mine that I had booked into a local venue in Northampton. I paid for his musician friends, who were familiar with his repertoire, to come from Torquay to Northampton to accompany him. Then I contacted EMI and spoke to a powerful contact man Vic Lanza and persuaded him to travel to Northampton to see Tim's performance. I did everything I could to make sure that Tim was presented well by means of the stage setting and lighting. I compered the show myself and gave Tim as big a build up as possible. He took to the stage with all the confidence in the world. The audience were familiar with my shows and I had schooled them personally on how to receive 'live' acts. I must say, they responded magnificently. Tim 'did a storm' and I could not have been more pleased with his performance. Vic Lanza certainly liked what he saw and heard and told Tim so. He proceeded to enquire whether Tim wrote his own material. At that time Tim had only just started song writing and had not enough numbers ready to record. I knew what was coming next—"when you have sufficient material of your own, contact me and I will see you again."

Television was my next target. I had a friend who was on the road with me when we were both young men touring as stage managers. Bill Hetterley was with George and Alfred Black Productions and I was with

RUBY—My Precious Gem!

Sam Newsome Productions. Bill made his way into television and became a producer with several major TV companies. I contacted him via London Weekend. I told him all about Tim and he agreed to come and see him, again in Northampton. Despite having to travel from the south coast through gale force winds, he made it through some really rough weather to catch Tim's act. Once again I pulled out all the stops to present Tim and to my delight Bill told me he was very impressed. We had a long conversation back stage and he voiced his opinions. He pointed to the fact that 'live' spots in major television shows for entertainers had become few and far between and that in any case a single performance was no longer sufficient to turn a budding talent into a star. New Faces on the other hand was compelling viewing for agents and managers and was just right for up and coming artistes. How did Tim feel about appearing on that show? He added that he should not fear the infamous, outspoken controversial lady on the panel of judges, Nina Myskow, because he was good looking, sang in tune and was well turned out. She couldn't fault him, in fact, she'd fall for him.

Tim decided that he would go along with Bill's suggestion. I was very confident that he would do well on the programme. I had personally been in many contests as a judge and knew the sort of things that would score good points. His voice was great, his overall presentation could not be faulted, his choice of material was right for both him and the viewing audience. He was also confident in himself. I'd give him 10 out of 10 without hesitation! Me biased? – Never!

Both Jane and I travelled down from Skye to attend the show in Birmingham. It was good to meet up with Marti Caine again. She had appeared for me at the Cabaret Restaurant in Solihull on numerous occasions. She was a very fine commere and undertook that duty for me by doing what is known in the business as 'spot and commere'. When I walked into the auditorium at rehearsal I immediately saw Marti and she came to greet me just like old times. We chatted about the times that I booked her at The New Cresta Club, Solihull. In her early days Marti's material tended to be rather risqué and she recalled my reaction to it at the time. I asked her to delete certain parts from her act, much to her surprise. When Tim came to join us, she related the incident to him and revealed that she had to fill in so many holes in her script after my deletions!

"It was like doing a whole new act, but I certainly learned from it Tim," she told him. "So take heed of what your father tells you".

We had a wonderful seat in the orchestra stalls and Jane and I sat together with our fingers tightly crossed. I looked up into the box to see who the members of the panel were. The fearsome Nina was not on the programme for this particular edition of 'New Faces'. A female presenter from Central Television, Anna Soubray, has replaced her. Paul Jones (the lead singer with Manfred Mann before becoming a successful singer in his own right) was the second in the trio followed by, and to my pleasant surprise, Stan Dallas from The Dallas Boys. Stan and the boys were great rivals to The Jones Boys in the hey-day of theatre and cabaret. He was currently attached to International Artistes, an Agency/Management office. The three of them made a very formidable panel indeed.

We settled back in our seats filled with excitement and I was mentally transported back in years as the orchestra struck up, the house lights dimmed, and on walked the star presenter of 'New Faces' Marti Caine. It immediately came to my mind that Marti herself had shot to fame via this same television show. She was superb, and her banter with the controversial Nina throughout the series injected the right amount of controversy to stimulate the popularity of the 'New Faces'.

When it was Tim's turn to perform I had butterflies in my stomach and wondered whether his nerves would be visible. Not at all! He had to descend a flight of stairs and sit down at the halfway point on stage. That manoeuvre for a newcomer, whilst singing, is no easy task. Tim waltzed through it with surprising ease and strode down stage with the confidence of an experienced television performer. I swelled with pride. My boy was going to be okay. He sang a Barry Manilow song called 'Weekend in New England', a song that he had sung many times in his cabaret act. I suggested that he chose it for the show because he was familiar with the song and could perform it with feeling. The audience loved it, Jane and I loved it, and so did the panel. Marti turned to each of them in turn asking for their verdict on Tim's performance. To my great relief he had won them over, all three of them. Stan's closing remark, after a glowing appraisal of Tim's performance was "…certainly star potential!"

RUBY—My Precious Gem!

All artistes had given their best and it came to the part of the show that Eric Morecambe always described as—"all down for the — who's best". As each artiste re-entered for the finale, the electronic meter showed the individual scores. We held our breath for the verdict. GREAT! My lad had won. Tim was the winner. Subsequently he went on to appear in the final. Twelve superb finalists were on the show and Tim gave an immaculate performance with a song called 'She Believes In Me." He came fifth out of twelve, a great achievement for a newcomer. These television performances proved to be a great asset to Tim's future career. They were invaluable experience, which gave him a terrific boost in obtaining engagements.

Soon after this episode, I drove down from Skye to visit Tim in Torquay. Because of the huge amount of mileage that Tim was doing in his cabaret work he clocked up many thousands of miles, consequently his car was under great strain and had to be serviced regularly. When I arrived he was just about to return his mother's car. He'd borrowed it whilst his car was in the repair shop. Ruby's flat was about two miles away from his so he asked me to follow him in my car so that he could return the car to her. I was very reluctant, saying that I would come with him into town but I couldn't go with him to her apartment. He pressed me but I explained that I had lived through a nightmare for many years with a combination of family feuding and Ruby's problem. Although I had survived it had left its wounds. I feared stepping back in time. He took the keys back to Ruby and on his return he pleaded with me: "She wants to see you for old times sake. She just wants to say 'hello', that's all" and without waiting for confirmation he turned on his heels and went back to the apartment. When he came back with Ruby on his arm, I couldn't believe what I was seeing. Her familiar hesitant step had changed dramatically. She was unsteady on her feet and clung to Tim's arm for support. I felt deeply upset as she approached my car. I got out and greeted her then helped her get into my car and I sat beside her. Her voice had changed too and as we spoke I noticed an occasional tremor of her head. I desperately wanted to take her in my arms, cuddle her head as if to make her better.

Tim suggested that we find somewhere nice to have a coffee and reminisce. He told me there was a nice coffee shop in the new shopping precinct just over the road. It turned out to be the old Pavilion Theatre, the same theatre that we had appeared in together in that record breaking Cinderella pantomime in 1961/2.

Bernie Burgess & Frank Bowles

How could anyone imagine my feelings as I took a tottering, ailing lady, for whom I had always had so much feeling, back in time? The auditorium had been transformed into a shopping mall with beautiful shops and a sweeping staircase leading up to where the balcony used to be, now a cafeteria, bar and coffee shop. Tim found us a secluded table and made an excuse that he had to shop for something and left his mother and father alone together. We both realised that we were sitting in the theatre where Ruby played Cinderella so successfully all those years ago. If only her fairy godmother could magically reappear and wave her magic wand to transport us back through the years to … 'living happily ever after!' Nostalgia dominated our conversation with an abundance of "do you remember when ….?" We even managed to make each other laugh. Tim returned to take his mother back to her apartment. He had a show to do and had to hurry. As Tim walked Ruby back across the road I didn't want to watch that very sad sight but I couldn't stop myself. I had a big lump in my throat and a very heavy heart as I watched them disappear!

Chapter 24

♪ 'Every Time We Say Goodbye' ♪

My dream of being able to spend the rest of my life on the idyllic 'Misty Isle' began to disintegrate. In the ensuing telephone calls a decidedly different picture emerged. Jane started answering the telephone when I wasn't around and I then discovered that the cunning side of Ruby's problem had come into being again. She was heavily criticising me to Jane. To my utter amazement Jane started taking her side. This was the beginning of the end of my relationship with Jane and the island. The details of the melt down is of no concern to this story other that to say that Jane used my own money to engage a solicitor and proceeded to 'take me to the cleaners.' I had to part with 50% of my finances. I came home to a note on the table. She had left me along with my means of surviving on Skye. I managed to struggle on for nearly a year on my own but my remaining resources simply couldn't sustain me. Besides, life on Skye without a partner is totally different. From being a paradise for two it became more like enforced solitary confinement. I had learned a bitter lesson. Trust had lost its meaning for me. All my hard labour had come to nothing and I was forced to sell up and rebuild the bridges that I had burned six years previously. I will never forget Skye. When it isn't raining and the 'midges' are not biting, it's a magical place, and when the sun shines, it's paradise.

I had to sell everything, lock, stock and barrel to move on yet again. I had to literally wrench myself away to return to Northampton. My ever dependable sister Jean, bless her, came to my rescue by offering me her third bedroom until I could find yet another new home. I'd had my fill of renovating houses, only to have to give them all up and leave them behind. This time I was keen to buy a new place. Within a month I found what I considered to be an excellent home. It was within a mile of my sister, who by now had become slightly disabled and needed help from time to time. Being so close by was a bonus to both of us. The new house had all the amenities on hand, a huge shopping mall, doctors' surgery, a dentist, and a post office. I shopped for furniture, a task that isn't the same when there is no partner to help you choose. There was no decorating to be done, no back breaking DIY and a garden with very little maintenance needed. I moved in straight away, settling in quickly and started to renew my old acquaintances. Senior citizenship arrived two days after Jane's departure so I was now drawing my old age pension. I was faced with the fact that there was every possibility that I would have to live a life of loneliness for the rest of my days. Not a happy thought!

Tim kept me in touch with news about Ruby, his mother. He persisted in trying to stop her drinking, despite the fact that I had warned him that he didn't stand an earthly chance of achieving his aim. He could do nothing that I hadn't already tried hard to bring about over many years. I emphasised the inescapable fact that the only person who could stop her drinking was herself. Tim was now experiencing some of the heartache that I had suffered whilst trying to achieve the impossible. He was fighting a losing battle.

He experienced a few embarrassing moments when Ruby would turn up at a venue where he was performing and would become very troublesome. These occasions became unsettling for the lad. He found it difficult to handle, as I had done at the New Crest Cabaret Restaurant. During my chat with Ruby at the coffee shop in Torquay I dared to delicately suggest that she must stop drinking and her unforgettable reply was: "well,… it's too late for me now anyway!" How I wished that Dr. Toseland, the GP in Northampton, who was responsible for scuppering her specialised treatment all those years ago, had heard that devastating remark.

Despite Ruby's statement to me that she would never re-marry, Ray eventually persuaded her that they should tie the knot "for financial and tax reasons". As far as Ruby was concerned, the very mention of the word 'tax' was reason enough to agree to anything. They married in 1993, the

RUBY—My Precious Gem!

same year that Jane had walked out on me. Soon after their marriage, Tim rang me to say that all was not well with his mother's health. He told me that her world was shrinking daily and that she was withdrawing into herself and becoming more like a recluse.

Tim had never seen eye to eye with Ray, and gradually it became open warfare. It occurred to me that perhaps Tim was blaming Ray for his mother's condition. It was still difficult for Tim to understand that Ruby's illness was self-inflicted. Ray, the heavy drinker, was always prepared to drink alongside Ruby, a recipe for disaster. He was considered to be the epitome of a big 'boozer'. The difference was that he didn't go through the personality change, whereas Ruby did. It became a vicious circle. At that time he could see no reason to curtail her drinking. He enjoyed their drinking sessions.

"I was no good for her, I enjoyed a drink too much myself" was his open confession in a television interview. He was to eventually realise the error in his thinking and the fact that there really was a problem, a big problem, but by then it was all too late. Ray's own health had also been on the decline. For years he had been warned to stop drinking and smoking but he totally ignored all the warnings. I heard that he had diabetes, another very good reason for him to give up these bad habits.

Eventually a call came from Tim that I didn't want to receive. Ruby had been taken into hospital with a liver disorder. Now it was really very serious. Without waiting to hear the details, I drove straight to the Torbay Hospital where Ruby had been admitted. I was anxious to avoid any confrontation with Ray. Due to the fact that he could no longer drive Ruby's car made his visits to Ruby few and far between. On the other hand, they had an on-going arrangement with a local driver that, providing he drove Ruby and Ray to wherever they needed to go at any time, he could use the car as his own. In truth Ray should have been able to visit on a regular basis, even if the driver was not available. The hospital was only a mile or two from the flat and, as this was an urgent situation, why not call for a taxi? That is not what happened!

The drive from my home to Torquay could take as long as five hours but I confess to doing that journey in four. I went to her bedside, joining both Tim and Julie, who had arrived from London. I was eager to have a word with the consultant in charge so, using the excuse that I needed to visit the little boys' room, I went in search of information. The consultant happened to be at the end of the ward so I approached him and asked for the latest details on Ruby's condition. He asked if I was a relative and after explaining who I was, he opened up to me. The news shook me to my foundations. He told me that Ruby had not only progressed from having cirrhosis of the liver to fibrosis of the liver but now a more sinister presence had been found in the form of a cancerous growth. I gathered that Tim and Julie had already been told the terrible news. Julie, having noticed the devastating effect on me, had left her mother's bedside to console me. The consultant went on to say that he had placed Ruby on a form of morphine. I questioned whether a patient could be taken off the drug once they were prescribed it. He tried to assure me that it was possible but he didn't convince me. I then asked for the prognosis and my devastation was complete.

"A matter of months rather than years," he confessed. To add to her misery Ruby also had a cataract which was badly restricting her eyesight. My shock was such that I omitted to enquire whether Ruby had been told about her condition. I don't think she was ever told and hoped that she never was. I stayed in Torquay with Tim and Julie at Tim's apartment, visiting Ruby regularly until she was discharged. There was nothing more that we could do. She went back to her apartment with Ray, who was ailing himself. How on earth would they cope? I crawled all the way back to Northampton, choked with emotion and hardly able to see the road in front of me through the uncontrollable tears.

It was shortly after this time that Ruby summoned up enough strength to fly to Canada, with Ray, to see her sister Lilian, who had somehow struggled to hold on to her sobriety. How Ruby ever managed to undertake such an arduous journey is a complete mystery to me, knowing how desperately ill she was.

The domestic situation in their lives was getting very serious. Ruby had been sent home from the hospital and needed care and attention. Ray meanwhile was reaching the stage where he was not capable of looking after himself so the chances of Ruby being nursed were zero. The GP, who lived some 200 yards away stepped in and arranged for Ruby to be admitted to a nursing home. The diplomatic doctor convinced Ruby that she

RUBY—My Precious Gem!

was going into the home for a period of rest and it was only a temporary measure. Once I knew where she was going, I motored back to Torquay to help her 'settle in'. She was not confined to bed so it was possible for her to walk around as she wished. Tim and I made sure that she had everything that she could possibly need. I found that she was particularly fond of 'snowballs,' a coconut covered marshmallow-type of cake. I shopped around until I found some, keeping her well supplied.

Tim made arrangements for me to sleep at his flat allowing me to stay most of the day with Ruby. I spent valuable time with her but had to repeatedly return to Northampton. In my absence Ray turned up at the nursing home inebriated and, unbeknown to the matron, persuaded Ruby to walk to a local public house. The matron's orders were that Ruby must not, under any circumstances, have access to alcohol. When she learned of the escapade she made her feelings clearly known to Ray and forbade him to do such a stupid thing again. He came to the nursing home on another occasion, in the same drunken state, but this time he didn't take Ruby out. However, the matron discovered that he had brought in a bottle and was convinced it contained alcohol. She also discovered that Ray deprived Ruby of money which meant that Ruby had no means of buying things that she needed. She frequently found Ruby crying and established that it was Ray who was upsetting her. From that moment on he was banned from entering the home.

The upsets continued via the telephone and the matron threatened to stop his incoming calls. He then made arrangements for a friend to drive to the front door of the home and telephoned Ruby to come to the front door. He wanted her at home desperately. Ray had apparently told Ruby that he was unable to manage on his own. Unbelievably, Ruby was talked into going to his assistance. Knowing that he needed to have special food for his condition she felt that it was her duty to help him. She managed to get to the entrance of the home unnoticed and was driven to their flat. The plan was soon wrecked! Ruby had not taken her medication, Pro-morphine, with her. She was in desperate pain during the night and was forced to take a taxi back to the nursing home at the crack of dawn. She almost had to crawl in through the front door. Such was the mentality of the man to pressurise a desperately sick woman and to risk her life in that way.

From that moment on he was not allowed to contact Ruby in any way. Ruby was extremely distressed by his entire behaviour. I learned that her life with him had deteriorated over a long period of time. Tim was infuriated by the whole affair and tried to comfort his mother. After discussions with Tim she asked him to contact her solicitor. She wanted a divorce. What a nightmare scenario! With Tim's help she made it to the solicitor's office on a couple of occasions. She was adamant that she wanted a divorce. On my next visit she told me of her intentions. I could see that she was in no condition to be able to stand up to litigation. Due to this, I gently suggested that she could perhaps ask for a legal separation as an alternative. She could have a legal restraint placed on him which would bar Ray from seeing her or coming anywhere near her. However, she was adamant. She wanted a divorce and continued to push for it.

To help her through the day, Ruby wanted her painting equipment. Tim managed to get it despite Ray's annoyance. He succeeded and he set up the facility for Ruby to paint. With the aid of a huge magnifying glass to combat the cataract condition, Ruby was able to see quite well. She then persuaded Tim to take her to the hairdressers and even to the opticians. He was so pleased to be able to help his mother by giving her some small quality of life.

In the meantime I was allowed to take Ruby out for an hour or two, depending on how she felt. I would take her in my car to Babbacombe and park near the cliff tops. We could look down to the sea and we would talk about the business and the 'good old days'. My love and affection for her had never really left me but now it grew stronger and stronger. To see her without the curse of drink was a miracle. I would try to get her to eat something before taking her back to the nursing home in the hope that it might keep up her strength. Each time I left to return to Northampton she would ask when I would be back and I would joke with her by saying "when I have saved up enough pennies!" This was a line we used with the children when they were small. Each time I arrived home there would be a message on my answerphone. It was from Ruby asking: "have you saved up enough pennies yet?" My visits to Torquay became a regular trip, only a few days apart. I wanted to spend as much time with her as I could. When at home I would telephone her twice a day, the second time would coincide with her preparing to curl up to sleep.

RUBY—My Precious Gem!

We spent many happy hours on the cliff top at Babbacombe enjoying one another's company. Ruby wondered if she could come to see my new home. Would I take her? I agreed that I would as soon as she was strong enough to make the journey. I knew exactly what was on her mind. She wanted us to be back together again. Here we were, at the beginning of the end, wanting to be together and having the old feelings for each other. They turned out to be very precious moments for both of us. We were alone together, at long last, at peace with the world and desperately wanting time to stand still. Regrettably time passed all too quickly and soon we would be rudely interrupted by her need to return to the nursing home for more medication. I will always be eternally grateful that I was given the chance to see flashes of the real Ruby, my Ruby, even though it was for only a brief period of time.

In the nursing home Ruby had made friends with Claire, a very elderly lady in her nineties, who was a resident. This very frail lady was confined to her room and consequently was anxious to have someone to come and have a chat. The matron was most considerate and changed Ruby's room so that she could make her way next door to see Claire regularly. They had long chats over cups of tea which helped to keep their minds off their immense problems. I also got to know Claire during my visits. She was a very gentle lady with a pleasing smile and a witty sense of humour. It was gratifying to know that they both had company.

My recollections of the next period of time are extremely vivid but I will relate only what is necessary for the story.

Although I had been told that it would only be 'months rather than years' I was still totally unprepared for what was to come. I had just returned home from another visit to Torquay when I had a frantic telephone call from Tim. Ruby had been taken from the nursing home to hospital and was in emergency. Apparently something had happened to Ruby during the night and Claire had witnessed it all. Ruby had managed to get to Claire's room but she was fast asleep. Ruby woke her up trying to make herself understood but she was incoherent and unable to make sense. According to Claire it was total gibberish but had the presence to ring the night bell. Fortunately the matron herself was on duty and hurried to Claire's room. An ambulance was called and rushed Ruby to the

Torbay Hospital. Tim was called out and he dashed to be with his mother but on his arrival Ruby was not capable of making herself understood. The telephone call that I received from Tim was made from the ward. I immediately left for the south again. The frantic journey seemed interminable but in the middle of the night at least there was only light traffic. On arrival I was met by both Tim and Julie, who had arrived from London. I went to Ruby's bedside to find her conscious but unable to talk. There was no consultant around at the time and the night sister was unable to tell me very much. A duty doctor had examined Ruby and the consultant in charge of her case would see her the moment he arrived. I was desperate with worry. I wanted every single doctor in the world to come right now to attend to her. However, in my heart I knew that there was probably nothing they could now do for her. I was demented with sorrow but realised that the children wanted my support right now. On the contrary, they could plainly see that it was me who required their support.

The three of us alternated a vigil at her bedside for five days. The children eventually had to get some sleep back at Tim's flat whilst I stayed with Ruby. The nursing staff arranged for me to have a bed in an adjoining room so that I could get some rest. Sleep eluded me completely. After two days Ray appeared in the ward and, much to my dismay, had been drinking heavily. I could smell it on him. I sat by the side of Ruby's bed, holding her hand. I acknowledged Ray but he didn't reply. He just went straight to the head of the bed, looked down at Ruby and said: "Never mind love, you'll be out of here in a couple of days!"

He then turned to me, shrugged his shoulders and LEFT. His visit didn't last more than 30 seconds. I simply couldn't believe what I had just heard or what I had just seen. He didn't ever come back!

There can be nothing more soul-destroying than to watch a loved one, who is terminally ill, gradually drift away. You are powerless to help. As the last few hours passed by my mind filled with 'if onlys!' IF ONLY we'd been allowed to have a marriage. IF ONLY her parents had not been so vindictive and overpowering. IF ONLY her dictatorial father and scheming, manipulative mother had given us a chance. IF ONLY her confidence had not been so devastatingly destroyed by that farming couple in her childhood. IF ONLY the doctor at home in Northampton had allowed Ruby to

RUBY—My Precious Gem!

attend the specialised clinic. IF ONLY we could turn the clock back and live a life of love together with two wonderful children. IF ONLY the world had more genuine, gentle human beings like my Ruby.

Then I was cruelly jolted back to reality!

For what was to be the last time, Tim and Julie returned to the hospital ward to relieve me. I had witnessed dramatic changes to Ruby in their absence and my attitude was beginning to change. Now, I didn't want the situation to continue. I wanted the end to come quickly. What she was going through was indescribable. She really didn't deserve this suffering.

The children insisted that I went into the next room to get some rest. I reluctantly left her room, although I didn't want to let go of her hand. I had just got into bed when Tim knocked on the door: "I think that you had better come back to her, Dad"

I went straight back to her bedside and the attending night nurse told me that the end was near. I sat holding her hand, as she slipped slowly away from me. The time was 1.20am on 17th December 1996. My entire world had come tumbling down. I was totally devastated.

The children and I sat consoling one another for quite a long time, then I realised there were things to be done. Ray, as her husband, had to be notified immediately despite the fact that he had walked out of the hospital never to return. Tim went to the telephone to call him but was greeted by the answerphone. We called repeatedly but without success. I found myself taking charge and planning what should now happen as though I were her current husband. Before we left we requested that the night sister called Ray's number until she could give him the news. We had done all that we could. It was now turned 3am and we had to get some sleep if possible. We then had to start on the unpleasantries that needed to be done in these circumstances. The necessary certificate had to be collected and taken to an appointed undertaker along with other duties.

Ruby's passing was soon big news throughout the media and, true to form, the usual press manipulation of facts was soon in evidence. Far from being kind to her memory they latched on to the alcoholism and couldn't resist the cruel 'before and after' photographs. They got hold of a collection of distorted facts, some downright lies and a few cheap innuendoes. This was a girl who had become a bright shining star and had created history in the world of music and entertainment and had brought so much happiness to millions of people. They had hardly a good word to say about her. For both the children and myself to read such 'gutter press' rubbish was, to say the least, very distressing, most distasteful and also degrading. Her memory was sacred to each of us and we found it difficult to believe how some of the reports had to be so disparaging.

Chapter 25
♪ 'PS—I Love You' ♪

Back in Tim's flat we attempted to get some sleep, but the need to make a start on the unpleasant tasks lying before us took precedence. Lengthy discussions took place and it was decided that because Ray had not been seen or heard of since leaving the hospital three days before, we should go ahead with certain arrangements as Ruby's family and next of kin. The priority was to collect the death certificate from the hospital and appoint an undertaker who could then attend to arrangements for a chapel of rest. At 9am Tim volunteered to drive to the hospital to collect the document. He was told on arrival that the death certificate had not been made out but would be ready later on in the morning. He returned at 11am only to be told that a solicitor's letter had been delivered, by hand, on behalf of Mr. Ray Lamar. It stipulated that under no circumstances should the document be released to anyone other than Ruby's husband. I immediately withdrew realising that Ray fully intended to take charge of all the arrangements. I wouldn't and couldn't argue with that. The three of us backed right off and waited to find out what the arrangements were going to be especially who the undertaker was and when and where the funeral would take place.

    The tragedy and trauma of this time was exacerbated by Ray's total disregard for Ruby's welfare. I returned to Northampton and the anxious waiting went on and on and still no word from Ray. Eventually, I made enquiries which revealed that Ray had not collected the certificate for over a week after Ruby's passing. This meant that no undertaker had been appointed and consequently no chapel of rest had been arranged. He had callously left Ruby in the hospital mortuary all that time, a very distressing situation for the three of us. His uncaring and total disregard for our feelings was beyond comprehension.

The funeral was delayed until well into the New Year and during that time Ray was completely impassive to the feelings of other people. The family was not contacted nor did we receive any notification regarding the funeral so I had to make my own enquiries. I managed to trace the funeral directors and they in turn gave me all the necessary details of when and where the funeral would take place. We all waited for the sad day, with me in Northampton, Julie in London and Tim in Torquay. Being local Tim kept me informed of what was happening. He confirmed the funeral arrangements and had called other friends and colleagues concerning the details. Marie, Ruby's best friend in Belfast, was the first priority. Tim told her that I would pick her up from any airport in the UK and take her on to Torquay.

It was a horrible experience being totally ignored and kept in the dark by Lamar. Meanwhile the media, especially the newspapers, were having a field day. Some even stated that, due to the total disharmony between the two parties, there would be 'a police presence at the funeral to counter any trouble that may arise.' I found this to be thoroughly outrageous. As if a member of the family, or any descent person, would deliberately create a disturbance at a ceremony where someone they loved was being laid to rest. How can members of the press justify this type of sensationalism by inserting such controversy? They are tampering with personal family emotions by inventing such a story and trying to create readers interest purely to sell newspapers. Yes, obviously bad feelings did exist, but it was private and personal and the media should have respected that. It saddened me very much and added further to my grief.

The day of the funeral arrived and I arranged to pick up Marie at Birmingham Airport. We then drove straight to Torquay. Ray had appointed a female minister to carry out the service at a church not too far from their harbour-side apartment. He chose the hymns and the recorded music, which included some of Ruby's own songs. Naturally 'Softly, Softly' was part of the service, so too was 'Danny Boy'. The church was crowded, so much so that the overflow extended to the pavements outside. Throughout the service my brain was numb and I was completely unaware of anyone amongst the congregation. As a family we were situated next to

RUBY—My Precious Gem!

the aisle and therefore in close proximity to the casket. At the end of the service, when the pall-bearers began the exit from the church, I had an overwhelming urge to reach out and touch the casket. I wanted desperately to be in personal contact. I succeeded!

After the service the procession made its way to the crematorium for a brief ceremony. I had no idea who was there and then it was all over. The curtains were drawn for the very last time on my dear Ruby. She had made her final exit. There was a kind of reception somewhere in Torquay but all I wanted to do was to say goodbye to Tim and Julie, pick up Marie and drive her back to Birmingham and from there to go home. Before departing Julie told me that the nursing staff at the hospital had handed over Ruby's rings. Julie considered that, as I had bought them for Ruby and placed then on her hand they should be returned to me. I thanked her profusely but then we decided to give one to Marie. We felt that it was a kind of thank you for all the things that she had done for Ruby throughout her life. I kept the engagement ring and it is still one of many treasured possessions.

A full six months elapsed before I made yet another disturbing discovery. Ray had not paid the funeral director's or the florist's bills. As a consequence, the funeral director had refused to release the urn containing the ashes until he had been paid. For six whole months the ashes remained in the hands of the funeral director and had not been properly interred. In my mind Ruby had not yet been laid to rest. I was deeply sickened by the thought. Once more I set off for Torquay to try to resolve the sorry matter. There was more to come. Apart from the unpaid bills, no plot had been purchased for the interment of the ashes, and no inscribed stone of remembrance. This was the final indignation.

I was fortunate enough to track down a very close friend of ours, Melissa, a very kind and caring lady. We had met her many years ago when travelling with David Whitfield. She owned a jewellery shop in St. Marychurch and throughout Ruby's illness had visited her on numerous occasions, for which I will always be eternally grateful. I felt sure that she would know where I had to go to resolve all these problems. Thankfully she kindly offered to accompany me around the area on my tour of sadness to pay off all the unpaid bills. Our first call was the funeral director. He then released the ashes and added his apologies for any distress his action may have caused. Our next call was to the stonemason's office to purchase a memorial stone with gold-leaf inscription and then on to the crematorium to purchase a plot of land for the interment. At the office of the crematorium a major problem stood in our way. No interment could take place without the death certificate This document was held by Ray and we instantly concluded that he would not be agreeable to releasing that to me. It meant that I could not purchase the plot without it. Melissa came up with a possible solution. As she knew Ray, she would suggest that if the funeral business was upsetting him she, Melissa, would relieve him of all the financial responsibilities and settle the debts outstanding. She set off for Ray's flat with my gratitude. Fortunately he agreed but, with one condition, no other name must appear on the stone, only Ruby's. This appeared to be a strong hint that he knew that I was behind the scheme. We now had the means to purchase the plot of land but there now appeared another obstacle. As I was not a resident of Torbay the plot would cost double! Thankfully Melissa solved that hiccup too. She suggested that as a resident of the area she could have the deeds to the plot placed in her name. She then paid for the plot of land herself. A wonderful gesture. Her generosity, for which I was immensely grateful, solved the last of the difficulties. I thanked her profusely at that sad time in my life and I do so again now. Thank you, Melissa.

Before leaving the area, I returned to the stonemason's office to discuss the inscription on the stone. Strangely, he was aware of the problem between Ray Lamar and my family. I explained about Ray's stipulation in connection with the names on the stone. He understood my dilemma and then came up with a solution. He would arrange the wording in such a way as to leave a space at the bottom of the stone in case other names needed to be added in the future when the problem might be resolved. I readily accepted his idea and placed an order for the stone, the plinth and the gold-leaf inscription. I carefully chose fitting words which I hoped would please not only our children, family and friends but all Ruby's devoted fans.

It later came to light that some of her fans considered that I might not want to disclose the whereabouts of Ruby's resting place. On the contrary. I am thrilled and delighted for them to know where our dear Ruby is resting. I hope many of them will choose to visit the site in the Torbay Crematorium and feel as close to her as I do whenever I visit.

RUBY—My Precious Gem!

Finally, everything had been taken care of and I could breathe a sigh of relief. The love of my life, RUBY – MY PRECIOUS GEM, my gentle Ruby, now rests peacefully in the tranquillity of the Torbay Crematorium. Her grave is there for the world to see with the words I carefully chose:

DEAR RUBY—SLEEP 'SOFTLY SOFTLY' IN PEACE — 'EVERMORE'

Here are my final thoughts about my life with, my love for, and my marriage to darling Ruby. They say that time is a great healer but I sometimes wonder whether the time will ever come when I feel healed of the great sorrow that took root in my heart when I lost the great love of my life. After struggling for far too many years with her problem, Ruby managed to find sobriety for only a very brief period before the end of her life. During that time she told her great friend Marie — "If it hadn't been for my family, I would still have been married to Bernie now."

During our early days of courtship, and throughout our marriage, Ruby and I frequently exchanged a line that meant so much to both of us. It always followed those three famous words "I Love You" and that line was – "…No Matter What!"

Shortly after we married, Ruby bought a gold bracelet for me and had it inscribed with these words:

To Bernie " - - -, No Matter What!" No other words were ever needed.

Life can be so cruel at times. My home was robbed and the bracelet was stolen by a drug-addicted burglar, presumably to be either sold or melted down to provide cash for his addiction. I would love to be still wearing that bracelet. It meant the world to me.

Throughout all the good times and the bad, all the peaceful times and the turbulent ones, I always knew in my heart that we both meant those precious words. I had promised to take Ruby to see my new home. Sadly she never made it but I knew precisely what she was thinking, what was in her mind and in her heart.

Ruby Darling - " - - - , NO MATTER WHAT!"

I will always be eternally grateful that Ruby made an 'entrance' into my life. She came and she sang and danced on my stage, she lit up my life with her love. The breeze of her entrance was like a breath of fresh air. The breeze of her passing … BLEW MY CANDLE OUT.

Chapter 26
♪ 'I Remember You!' ♪

Frank Bowles (co-author) recounted many treasured show business memories when he began collaborating with Bernie Burgess to tell the definitive story of Ruby Murray.

"I was on the scene when Ruby had already made her mark but enjoyed the halcyon days of Frank Ifield, the Beatles, Cliff and the Shadows. I always remember an old friend Dorothy Squires saying to me: "how can those four ****** (the Beatles) have so many hits with the rubbish they write." Within a few months Dorothy was recording cover versions of at least two of their songs! That's show business!

Ruby just breezed through her performances like a breath of fresh air. Her songs were simple, easy to whistle and catchy. Her stage presence appeared to always be a terrible ordeal but the public loved her and so did her fellow artistes.

Toni Dalli (I wrote his biography—'I….Who Had Nothing!') worked with her at Great Yarmouth in 1977 and was full of praise for her 'no nonsense' performances.

'She got on with her act, appeared to be full of nerves, but soon won over the audience. She was a real pro!'

I never met Ruby but, through Bernie, I feel a certain friendship towards her. Her voice will still be heard for many years to come. It was unique and belonged to an era never to be forgotten. It's over 50 years from the day Ruby hit the headlines. Belfast is still proud of her achievements and is about to honour her with a plaque on the wall of Ulster Hall. I hope many folk, including the youngsters who never had the pleasure of seeing Ruby perform, will find this biography interesting enough to want to listen to some of her recordings.

Thank you Bernie for allowing me into your world and by publishing this book you are sharing your memories with all those who admired her."

Many folk however, did have the privilege to have known Ruby Murray during her lifetime. She always treated other people with great respect and had a knack of taking an interest in their welfare and their achievements. Coming herself from a working-class background, Ruby had no airs and graces and was deeply appreciative of all her fans and her fellow performers. They weren't all 'stars' either! She established long friendships with many artistes who helped make up the bills during her long career at the top.

One of her closest and dearest friends was musician Marie Cunningham who accompanied Ruby throughout the world.

Marie had this to say about Ruby and their friendship in the Tinderbox Theatre Company's programme notes taken from 'The Life of Ruby Murray' a play by Marie Jones first performed in the year 2000.

Marie Cunningham

"I met Ruby Murray in 1952 when we were both appearing in a show in Bundoran, Co. Donegal. We stayed in 'digs' together and we had a big treat on pay-day. We bought a large tin of peaches and a carton of cream and ate them in our room!

When the season ended, I returned to work in the Gramophone Shop in Belfast for Mervyn Solomon. His brother Philip was, at that time, organising a show to tour the South of Ireland and then England. Philip asked me if I could find a female singer to be in the show. I immediately thought of Ruby and went to her home in Benburb Street and arranged for her to join the company.

Whilst playing in the Metropolitan Theatre in London, Ruby was seen

RUBY—My Precious Gem!

by Richard Afton, a TV producer, who engaged her to appear in a show called 'Quite Contrary'. Keith Devon, from the Bernard Delfont agency spotted her, as did Norrie Paramor and Ray Martin who signed her up to Columbia Records.

She went on to star at the London Palladium for over seven months alongside Norman Wisdom and, during this period, had five hits in the top 20 at the same time – an all-time record.

I moved to London to work with Ruby in 1954/55 having kept in touch with her during her rise to fame. As well as touring all over England and Scotland, we were lucky enough to have the opportunity to travel to several exotic locations over the years including Libya, Cyprus, Malta, France, America, Canada and Rhodesia – now Zimbabwe. We were fortunate to take afternoon tea with the then Prime Minister, Ian Smith.

When I married Frank Murphy in 1956, the Irish tenor who had also appeared in shows with us, Ruby was a guest and it seemed that all Belfast turned out to see her. Donegal Street was a sea of faces. She was so popular.

Over the years Ruby and I never lost touch. Whenever she visited Belfast, she stayed at my home and we would reminisce long into the night about past events and our involvement.

We had many wonderful years of priceless friendship and I miss her a great deal. I am delighted to be able to say that Ruby Murray was my best friend."

....

The following programme notes from the same publication were written by John Bennett, a broadcaster with BBC Radio Ulster.

"Ruby Murray's chart career lasted almost five years but the niche she carved in the memories and the hearts of her fans is still current. From 'Heartbeat' in December 1954 to 'Goodbye Jimmy Goodbye' in October 1959 Ruby's songs were amongst the first to break the stranglehold the

Americans had previously exercised on the 'Top Twenty' as it came to be known. When the New Musical Express Chart began in 1952 (as a Top Twelve) Al Martino was the Ricky Martin of his day with a song called 'Here in My Heart' which stayed at No. 1 for nine weeks.

In 1953, whilst Mount Everest was being conquered and Queen Elizabeth was being crowned, the Americans again dominated. Only two British singers reached the pinnacle of pop: dark-haired Lita Rosa was enquiring 'How Much is that Doggy in the Window?' and David Whitfield implored an unidentified listener to 'Answer Me!'

The following year only two home-grown musicians graced the No. 1 spot and they were both instrumentalists. Eddie Calvert trumpeted 'Oh! Mein Papa' to sales exceeding three million and Winifred Atwell wheeled out her other piano and said 'Let's Have Another Party!'

Ruby began an onslaught on the statistics in December 1954 when 'Heartbeat' ascended the rungs and reached No. 3 staying in the charts for four months. Nowadays, a stay at the top for more than a fortnight may be considered phenomenal but 50 years ago there was no Internet, no Top of the Pops, no Virgin, EMI or any other musical superstores. In 1955, even though Bill Haley moved all the goalposts with 'Rock Around the Clock,' it was the Belfast girl who rocked the musical establishment with half a dozen hits including her No. 1 'Softly! Softly!'

1955 was the year that balladeers began to make an impact. Tony Bennett's 'Stranger in Paradise' reached No. 2 while the British warblers Dickie Valentine and Jimmy Young were successful with cover versions of American hits. The girl with a smile in her voice, Alma Cogan, grinned her way to No. 2 with 'Dreamboat.'

The following year, while Alma Cogan had just one hit 'You Are My Dreamboat,' the Americans were reclaiming their chart territory. Kay Starr, Pat Boone, Tennessee Ernie Ford, Johnnie Ray and Doris Day were the big names while at home Ronnie Hilton was beginning his success with 'No Other Love.' The big surprise was Anne Shelton's return to the Hit Parade.

A very popular big-band singer from the 40's, her style had gone out

RUBY—My Precious Gem!

of fashion in the 50's but when Britain and France went to war over Suez, Anne swiftly recorded 'Lay Down Your Arms.' She hoped it would be adopted as a marching song for the troops and she might end up as the 50's Vera Lynn! The song climbed to No. 7 but the war, and Anne's popular appeal, didn't last as long as was predicted.

Ruby's final sojourn in the charts was in 1959 with 'Goodbye Jimmy Goodbye.' The hits that year were eclectic with little or no discernible theme or trend.

From Elvis to Russ Conway, The Platters to Cliff Richard, Buddy Holly to Bobby Darin it seemed that the impact of television had, at last, exposed the record-buying public to an ever increasing range of musical styles."

....

Other programme notes were written by Eddie McIlwaine, the former Entertainment Correspondent of the Belfast Telegraph.

"On the Donegal Road in Belfast they called Ruby Murray the Duchess of Windsor! The village people in this warm-hearted corner of the city loved her unreservedly. She was the Duchess way back in the early 60's and just down the road at Windsor Park, Lindfield's Tommy Dickson was the Duke. But even with that grand title the singer with a sob in her throat from Benburb Street never lost the common touch. One day she could be dining with Ian Smith, the Prime Minister of Rhodesia, the next she was rushing home to Belfast to worship at Richview Presbyterian Church where she used to sing in the choir.

I first met Ruby when she was a teenager in ankle socks singing nice Irish ballads in St. Mary's Hall. We kind of grew up together and I was one of the first to congratulate her when she became an overnight sensation in black and white on the BBC Television's 'Quite Contrary Show.' You couldn't have missed her. There was only one channel in those days!

Bernie Burgess & Frank Bowles

I was up in the grand circle when she starred at the famous London Palladium with Norman Wisdom. I watched in awe that night as she melted a hard-hearted audience with that celebrated husky voice that became a trademark for a generation along with the intimate 'Softly! Softly!' which was her first big hit and her theme song down 40 magical years. She appeared in movies and toured the world. I was jealous when Frank Sinatra came to her stage door in New York to say that she was his favourite girl singer.

Ruby of course made it clear that she preferred the words I was always writing about her and made sure that our long friendship remained intact. She was ever shy and retiring and never made the mistake of believing her own publicity even when it was written by me!

At the height of her career Ruby, slightly bewildered by the fame, had five chart-toppers in the UK Top Twenty at the same time. Even after her time as a high-flying pop star was over, Miss Murray remained a favourite with fans across the British Isles who had a deep and abiding love for the lady who had a fund of great stories and was indeed a legend.

Her friend and pianist Marie Cunningham told me: 'I tried again and again to get her to write a book but she was always reluctant. She was convinced that committing her thoughts to paper would betray confidences and spoil the memories.'

She leaves one indelible memory with me. Ruby was in my party one night in the old Strathearn Hotel near Holywood when the lights went out in a storm. Suddenly she started to sing 'Softly! Softly!' by the light of a flickering candle. It was a cherished and homely incident to look back on after her own candle burned out prematurely four years ago when she was only 61 years old."

....

RUBY—My Precious Gem!

LETTERS FROM SOME OF RUBY'S MANY FANS, most of whom are ardent contributors to the Ruby Murray website—www.rubymurray.org

Bernie Burgess has kept in touch will several ardent Ruby Murray fans via the website and he invited them to write about their memories and their love for her as a singer and a person. We reproduce several letters received recently to illustrate Ruby's affect on her fans even ten years after her death.

WHATEVER THE WEATHER!

There are so many lovely memories of Ruby, it would be impossible to write them all down but I think one of my happiest and treasured memories of her would be the very first time I got to meet her in person.

I stood at the entrance to the North Pier, Blackpool on a very wet and windy night in September 1957. I was the only one there, may I add! The theatre where Ruby was appearing happened to be way down at the end of the pier. She had to walk the whole length so I waited in the rain and sure enough she eventually came out onto the promenade. She had Bernie (her husband of only a few weeks) with her. Bernie was a member of The Jones Boys who were starring in the same show.

She stood and talked with me even though the weather was so awful. Many artistes would have just probably said a quick "hello" and scurried off, but not Ruby and Bernie. They chatted and signed the programme and Ruby said wherever she was appearing in the future, I was always welcome to come round and say 'hello' to her.

Ruby was always so natural and kind, remaining so throughout her life. For me, one of the most memorable things over the years is the fact that I was proud and privileged to have known her. A truly lovely person and a great STAR.

David Frankish - (Devoted Fan and Ruby Murray Fan Club Secretary 1965- 1973)

....

"THE TELEPHONE NUMBER"

Dear Bernie,

I hope all is well with you. Thanks for your email and for giving me and many other fans the opportunity of putting forward a story about a meeting with Ruby.

I hope you like mine.

At fourteen years of age I had never taken much interest in music. Then suddenly I heard this voice coming from the radio and I was hooked. Ruby Murray had entered my life.

RUBY—My Precious Gem!

I was one of many fans who immediately fell in love with her looks and her voice. Over the next few years I saw Ruby on stage in summer season shows and pantomime but had never met her. I was now in my twenties and Ruby was visiting my home town to appear in a club. This was going to be my chance to meet her. At the club the tables had been arranged around the floor and Ruby was to perform her songs on the dance floor, not a stage. I booked a really good seat so that I would get a good view of Ruby singing. Suddenly she was in the room with Bernie by her side. Without hesitation, I left my seat. I had an LP in my hand and found myself asking for her autograph.

"Oh! This is my latest LP," she said in such a friendly manner.

We talked for a moment then she signed my record. The organisers of the show then approached Ruby.

"Let's talk again," she said. "I will give you my home telephone number."

She then wrote it down on the LP cover (0604 61259.) The show was wonderful. I knew all the songs and as Ruby sang I mimed along with her (I'm no singer.) She kept smiling at me. I knew where she would sing high then go low and even where she would take her intakes of breath. After the show I went to her and said " You sang beautifully."

She answered " Sure, you didn't do too badly yourself!"

As I turned to go she said, "Don't forget to phone me!"

That night I could have walked on water. Ruby Murray had given me her home telephone number.

Did I use it?

Of course I did and when she was home she always talked to me telling me where she was travelling to and where she was appearing.

The LP is a treasured possession as, not only does it give me Ruby's love, but also her telephone number. An American friend, who is also a big Ruby Murray fan, recently suggested that I should use the telephone number as part of my lottery ticket. If it comes up Bernie, I will let you know! My story shows that Ruby did have time for her fans and really earned her title as 'The Girl Next Door.' She was a real trouper and was so approachable.

Writing this letter has brought back many happy memories and I promise to let you have one or two more as soon as possible.

Best wishes,

Graham Bunn.

....

FALLING IN LOVE!

Hi Bernie,

I first saw Ruby on Quite Contrary and, being a young lad of about 14, I immediately fell in love with this beautiful young lady. Every week I would tune in to the BBC and watch the show. I was well and truly hooked.

My first live show to see Ruby was around 1955 at the Hulme Hippodrome in Manchester. I was taken by a friend of the family, who use to live in the next street to Ruby. She was on stage for over an hour and at the end she finished with 'Softly, Softly.' The audience went wild! I had never seen anything like it before. Ruby then went on to repeat it twice more. After the show we went to the stage door and Ruby came out to talk to all her fans and then signed autographs.

After that I went to as many shows as I could including the London Palladium where she was appearing with Norman Wisdom. Again I met her and Norman and had a good chat. After that came many summer seasons, including Blackpool, Margate, Weymouth, Great Yarmouth, Llandudno, Liverpool and Chester. I could go on all day. I was also at the

RUBY—My Precious Gem!

show on the night Ruby got married to Bernie and, if I remember rightly, she sang 'Mr. Wonderful' with a sparkle in her eyes. I had been to the show a week before but this night was special and the audience knew it. As I come from Wigan, Blackpool was only 36 miles away so I got to see Ruby many times and met a lot of other artistes who where in the shows with her.

Hope this will do, Bernie. I could go on all day talking about Ruby,

Regards,

John Kendall.

....

FORWARD YOUNG MAN!

I became a fan of Ruby's when I was just 14 years old and she appeared on BBC's Quite Contrary show in 1954. By the end of the year, when Heartbeat reached the charts, I had acquired an old clockwork gramophone and was able to buy and play her first hit. In March 1955, she made a personal appearance at my local record shop, and I decided to go there to see her, and to buy a copy of 'Softly, Softly'. I queued for ages outside the shop and, as I neared the door, I could see that Ruby was sitting at a low desk on the left hand side of the shop. The queue made its way in on the right hand side to the back counter, where the record that you wanted Ruby to sign could be bought. I purchased 'Softly, Softly' and a shop assistant stuck a small yellow sticker on the record before handing it to me to turn left and to continue in the queue to where Ruby was sitting. When my turn came, she took the record without really looking up, and put her signature on the yellow label. I said very quietly in my best schoolboy voice "Thank you Miss Murray" and was rewarded with her looking up at me with her beautiful blue eyes straight into mine! She replied with something like "You're welcome" and gave me a big smile. I was transfixed to the spot! Well, I would have been, but another assistant, obviously with his eye on the huge queue outside, took my arm and led me towards the door. When I related this story to my father, the way he rolled his eyes upwards said it all! I still have that 78 rpm record.

Bernie Burgess & Frank Bowles

On another occasion I met Ruby when she made a personal appearance at the Radio and TV Exhibition at Olympia in London. I knew the day and time she was going to be there, and made sure I was in the right area well before time. I was standing at the front of the waiting crowd when she appeared at a high desk on a platform, and being only 15 at the time and not very tall, I was pushed forward in the surge and jammed up against the desk. She was signing autographs and suddenly looked down at me and asked if I was all right. When I thanked her and replied that I was enjoying every moment of it, she said "Well, I'm rather glad I'm not down there in all that crush!" I quickly retorted "I wish you were!"

I suddenly realised the implications of what that meant, and being very shy, I blushed a bright red. I need not have worried. Ruby gave me the loveliest smile and a little chuckle as she too enjoyed the innocent remark.

Gerald Lawrence.

Sandy Everitt, Bernie Burgess, Rosemary Lawrence, Gerald Lawrence and Brian Henson

RUBY—My Precious Gem!

SCRAPBOOKS OF MEMORIES!

Hi Bernie,

The first time I heard of Ruby Murray was when I was 13 and in my pyjamas! My mother called me from the bedroom to listen to this lovely girl singing on television. It was a grainy old black and white set and the programme was 'Quite Contrary.' We watched enthralled as Ruby "bravely" delivered her song. This nervous-looking girl was like nobody we had ever heard before, so natural and with a unique singing voice. From then on 'Quite Contrary' became a regular viewing date.

It was obvious that millions of other people were also entranced by 'this girl next door' image that Ruby portrayed as she became a star overnight. I started a scrapbook and collected every item about her. My friends at school were instructed, under pain of death, to search their daily papers for articles and every day there was some new snippet for the book.

My mother loaned me the money to buy an old wind-up gramophone which I paid for in weekly instalments from my pocket money and started my gramophone collection. I did extra chores to earn the money for the records.

Out of the blue came a message from my aunt in Chesterfield that Ruby was appearing at the local theatre. We had to go! We bounced along in a rickety old bus for the 80-mile trip. The theatre was packed and after the show we joined what seemed to be hundreds of clamouring fans outside the stage door hoping for a glimpse of Ruby. I hadn't counted on my mother's determination to get more than a glimpse. This diminutive five foot nothing lady dragged me through the crowd and banged on the door. It opened and my mother gave a very convincing story of having travelled half way across the country and we were led up some stairs and waited. Suddenly there she was! I can't remember the conversation because I burst into tears!

As I got older I went to several venues where Ruby was appearing and regularly joined the fans that went backstage for a chat. She knew us all and always made time to pose for photos and sign autographs.

In adult life, our meetings were less frequent and the furore of her stardom had lessened but we continued to bump into each other around the country. Usually my mum would come too. We would chat about old times and spend some time together. Ruby painted for relaxation in the dressing room and she gave me an oil painting, which I still have. Every Christmas I received a card, usually a photo of one of her paintings. Occasionally I would pick up the phone to hear her husky tones singing 'Softly, Softly'.

The scrapbook I started developed into four, crammed with every aspect of her life and she borrowed them for reference when her story was being written. I made her promise to send them back, and she did, two years later!

Now, heading for my dotage, I have extreme pleasure in meeting other remaining fans and, in particular Bernie, to share memories of a wonderful, warm lady with a rare gift of a voice which gave pleasure to millions.

Sandy Everitt

....

AN IRISH LEGEND!

Hi Bernie,

My name is Martin Foster and I am 30 years old. I live in Manchester but I am of Irish stock, my parents coming from Co Mayo. I grew up on stories and songs of the "auld country" and this instilled in me a love of all things Irish, in particular Irish music and song.

By chance, when visiting an obscure record shop in 1991, I came across an LP of Ruby Murray entitled 'Your Favourite Colleen'. From that day on I became hooked and I have since built up a collection of Ruby's records. I am proud to say that I now have every recording that she ever made.

RUBY—My Precious Gem!

As well as collecting Ruby's records, I have also built up a collection of some of her contemporaries such as Bridie Gallagher, Eileen Donaghy, Teresa Duffy, Carmel Quinn and many more. However, I have a special affection for Ruby as to me, her unique voice, perfect phrasing and the quality of her singing as well as her genuine sincerity have always hit home.

Ruby has done much to preserve our Irish musical heritage and to promote Irish music to a wider audience. She was a great ambassador for both Northern and Southern Ireland and a credit to her country and the music industry of the 1950's and 60's.

Martin Foster.

....

THOUGHT I WAS HER RELATION!

I was 19 and doing my National service in the RAF. One evening when watching TV in the NAAFI, Ruby appeared on screen in the BBC Quite Contrary Show. I wrote to her that evening, care of the BBC, saying how much I had enjoyed her performance and that I thought she would become a big star.

Imagine my surprise, when, just a few days later, I received a handwritten reply from Ruby together with a signed photograph giving me her uncle's address in London where I could contact her. We corresponded regularly from then on.

I subsequently had the pleasure of being in Ruby's company on approximately fifteen occasions, all around the time when she was at the pinnacle of her career. Some of the venues were Leeds, Sheffield, Liverpool, Great Yarmouth, Brighton and Blackpool.

At various times she introduced me to her mother, Tommy Cooper and even a certain young fellow called Bernie somebody or other! She also introduced me to the Irish singer Ronnie Carroll telling him that I was her very first fan outside Ireland.

I was once in a queue outside the Sheffield Empire, where Ruby was appearing, when this car pulled up alongside me. Ruby stepped out dressed in a stunning fur coat, made a beeline for me and asked why I was going to see the show again as I had seen her so many times already! She said I should have come backstage to see her.

My very best memory was of being backstage with her on the North Pier, Blackpool when she asked if I would like to watch her performance from the wings.

This she arranged. I watched her act whilst stood just a few yards away from her. I will always remember that the Jones Boys were behind the stage backdrop cheering her on! One of the Vernon Girls, who were appearing in the show, said she thought I was related to Ruby as we seemed on such friendly terms.

Many, many happy memories of a very special and most sincere friend....

Don Wearmouth.

....

PRESS RELEASE – BELFAST TELEGRAPH – FRIDAY, 19th AUGUST 1955

RUBY MURRAY STEALS THE SHOW!

London critics hail her performance at the Palladium. London newspaper critics today give unstinted praise to Ruby Murray for her debut last night at the London Palladium.

The Daily Telegraph says: "Ruby Murray, with her attractive adenoidal voice and impeccable technique, was an interesting newcomer. But it was a mistake to make her the centre of an elaborate artificial setting. She should sing sad Cinderella songs alone and in rags."

RUBY—My Precious Gem!

The Daily Mail says: "Miss Murray was a revelation. Here was an artless little Irish girl of 20 nobody knew at all a year ago welcomed as warmly as any sleek, seasoned Hollywood star could wish and owing it all to TV.

For her £500 a week she gave us an 18-minute act of five mainly sugar songs sung in a nasal, plaintive voice with an abject droop of the head. The more sugary her songs the more the audience loved them.

For 'Softly! Softly!' the producer Dick Hurran, never one to stint, considered the sentiments important enough to demand harps, a choir and a corps de ballet!"

The Daily Express says: "Ruby Murray, a 20-year-old lass from Belfast was the hit of the show. She is the record singer who is simple and terribly sincere. She has no tricks. She needs none! Last night she was cheered and was too shy and inexperienced to know what to do about it.

Her success comes with songs such as 'Heartbeat' 'Let Me Go Lover' and 'Softly! Softly!' As she paused between numbers she nervously clutched the back seam of her lilac sequinned gown. Afterwards she said: 'I was so terribly frightened. I did not know what to do when they kept applauding and my agent had to push me forward to bow!'

She took the show right away from its star Norman Wisdom, who appears like a little peanut in his too-tight suit.

Says John Balfour in the Daily Sketch: "When the show ended there were bobby-soxers outside the stage door shouting 'We want Ruby!' It scared her to death. Her manager had to push her onto the stage. At the show's end Norman Wisdom brought her forward and she could only tremble and open her mouth. She could not say a word! There were 18 bouquets in her dressing room along with 200 telegrams from people in Ulster, from the Royal Enniskillen Fusiliers, who have adopted her, and even from Belfast Prison.

She has a nice, sweet singing voice of the Vera Lynn style and she clearly deserves the £500 a week she is being paid for appearing in 'Painting the Town.'

Bernie Burgess & Frank Bowles

Finally, from the New Chronicle:

"Ruby Murray sings broken-hearted songs with a broken-hearted smile!"

RUBY—My Precious Gem!

Bernie Burgess & Frank Bowles

AUTHORS' FOOTNOTE

Arguably Ruby's best-loved song 'Softly! Softly!' was played and heard in every corner of the Western World in 1955. A simple, easy-to-remember melody was garnished with words equally uncomplicated and unpretentious.

We reproduce them here to allow you, the reader, to understand how romance and love could be exchanged though simple words coupled with a melodious song in this era.

SOFTLY! SOFTLY!

Softly, softly come to me
Touch my lips so tenderly
Softly, softly turn the key
And open up my heart

Handle me with gentleness and say you'll leave me never
In the warmth of your caress my love will live for ever and ever

So softly, softly come to me
Touch my lips so tenderly
Softly, softly turn the key
And open up my heart.

Duncan/Paul/Roberts © 1955

The UK was still recovering from WW2, rationing had only just finished and television was still in its infancy. Ruby's appearance on BBC TV's 'Quite Contrary' along with her EMI recording contract and clever song selection was the stepping stone she needed to become a star for many years to come.

RUBY—My Precious Gem!
PLAQUE TO RUBY

On 29th March 2006 a commemorative plaque was erected outside the famous Ulster Hall in Belfast in recognition of Ruby's contribution to music, recording and entertainment.

Wallace Brown, The Lord Mayor of Belfast, along with her first husband Bernie Burgess, jointly unveiled the plaque surrounded by friends and family of the local girl who went on to great stardom.

Amongst the large crowd that attended the ceremony were many of her old fans from across the water in the UK along with her two children Tim and Julie. The date coincided with Ruby's birthday and Tim and Julie sang a duet of several of Ruby's hits including "Softly, Softly' which delighted those present.

Ruby's name is now preserved for posterity on the front of the Ulster Hall, a fitting venue as Ruby made her debut there at the age of just 12 years old!

Ruby passed away in 1996, but her name and her music lives on!

Bernie Burgess & Frank Bowles

INDEX—NAMES OF PEOPLE

ABBOTT, Russ, 117
AFTON, Richard, 24, 32, 33, 179
ALCOCK, Reverend, 61, 62
BAKER, Hylda, 53
BAKER, Joe, 143
BALL, Lucille, 13
BARBOUR, Peter & Sue, 20, 117, 120, 137, 167, 168 179
BASSEY, Dame Shirley, 101
BELL, David, 185
BENNETT, John, 210
BENNETT, Tony, 211
BEVERLEY SISTERS, 185
BLACK ABBOTTS (The), 117
BLACK, George & Alfred, 187
BLAIR, Tony, 7
BOONE, Pat, 211
BOWLES, Frank, i, 208
BRAUN, Eric, 117
BRENNAN, Walter, 125
BREWER, Teresa, 35
BROWN, Terry, 126, 153
BUNN, Graham, 217
BURDEN, Billy, 155
BURGESS, Julie, 89, 91-97, 99, 108, 117, 119, 120, 128, 129, 130, 132, 134, 135, 142-147, 163, 170-175, 182, 194, 195, 199, 203, 204
BURGESS, Tim, 128,129, 131, 132, 134, 142, 147, 170-189, 190-198, 199-203
Burleson, Timothy, i
BURNETT, Paul, 48, 71, 92, 97, 107, 125
BURNETT, Paul Jnr., 125
CADEN, Father, 7
CAINE, Marti, 188, 189
CALVERT, Eddie, 7, 211
CAPEL, David, 177
CARIOLI, Charlie & Paul, 53
CARON, Jessie, 120
CARROLL, Ronnie, 27, 43, 222
CASTLE, Roy, 80, 102
CHURCH, Joe, 52

CLAYTON, Freddie, 156, 157, 159, 160, 163, 165
COGAN, Alma, 119, 211
COLE, Nat 'King', 27
COLLIS, Ronnie, 82
CONWAY, Russ, 212
COOPER, Gary, 127
COOPER, Tommy, 36, 47, 74, 222
CREIGHTON, Jack, 43
CRITCHLEY, Denis, 116
CROCKETT, Don, 120, 145
CUNNINGHAM, Marie, 20, 30, 44, 92, 209, 213
DALLI, Toni, 143, 208
DARIN, Bobby, 36, 90, 212
DAY, Doris, 40, 211
DELFONT, Bernard, 46, 53, 105, 106, 139, 149, 155, 210
DELRINA, Neil & Pat, 47
DESMOND, Frankie, 120
DEVON, Keith, 5, 105, 108, 109, 110, 112, 139, 220
DODD, Ken, 109
DONEGAN, Lonnie, 74, 185
DOONICAN, Val, 7, 72
DOUGLAS, Craig, 185
DRAKE, Charlie, 53
EATON, Shirley, 49
EDMUNDSON & ELLIOTT, 134
EVERITT, Sandy, 219, 221
FARLEY, Eric, 102
FISHER, Carl, 31
FLYNN, Errol, 116
FORD, Clinton, 156
FORSYTH, Bruce, 120
FOSTER, Martin, 221
FOUR FRESHMEN (The), 57
FOUR RAMBLERS (The), 7
FRANCIS, Bob, 145
FRANKISH, David, i, 215
FRINTON, Freddie, 72, 80
GOODWRIGHT, Peter, 116, 117
GORSHIN, Frank, 147
GRAHAM, Jim, 24

RUBY—My Precious Gem!

GREEN, Bertie, 141
HACKETT, Johnny, 134
HAGAN, Patrick, 27
HALEY, Bill, 149, 211
HARRIS, Keith, 117
HARRIS, Ronnie, 46
HART, Anne, 66
HAYNES, Arthur, 72, 80
HEDLEY WARD TRIO (The), 74
HELLIWELL, Arthur, 46
HENSON, Brian, ii, 219
HETTERLEY, Bill, 187
HILL, Benny, 93
HILL, Jimmy, 29
HILL, Vince, 134
HILLIER, David, 176
HILTON, Ronnie, 186, 211
HOLIDAY, Michael, 53
HOLLOWAY, Guy & Pat, 83
HOLLY, Buddy, 212
HOWERD, Frankie, 46
HURRAN, Dick, 224
IFIELD, Frank, 208
JEWELL, Jimmy, 72
JOHNSON, Bryan, 185
JOHNSON, Teddy, 74, 185
JONES BOYS (The), 36, 47, 48, 52, 62, 64, 66, 68, 71, 72, 74, 76, 80, 107, 125, 139, 180, 214, 223
KARLOFF, Boris, 125
KENDALL, John, 218
KING, Dave, 53
KIRKWOOD, Sam, 24
KLISSER, Michael, 97
LACEY, Daphne, 116
LACEY, George, 116
LAINE, Frankie, 30, 31
LAMAR, Ray, 40, 47, 154, 155, 168, 169, 170, 175, 179, 182
LANZA, Vic, 187
LARGE, Eddie, 148
LAUDER, Sir Harry, 185
LAWRENCE, Gerald, 2, 187
LITTLE, Syd, 148
LOCKE, Joseph, 27
LOCKY, Tommy, 45
LOGAN, Johnnie, 27
LORRE, Peter, 125
LOTIS, Dennis, 185
LUCAN, Arthur, 83
LYNN, Dame Vera, 212, 224
MADONNA, 213
MAN 'Mountain' BENNY, 145
MANDELA, Nelson, 100
MARSH, Billy, 105
MARTIN, Dean, 342
MARTIN, Ray, 34, 210
MARTIN, Ricky, 211
MARTINO, Al, 211
MAXIM, Ernest, 47, 48, 49
McDONALD, Ray, 53
McGUIRE SISTERS (The), 101
McILWAINE, Eddie, 212
McSHANE, Kitty, 83
MELISSA, 204
MILLS, Freddie, 87, 88
MILLS, Nat & Bobby, 116
MILLS, Sir John, 36, 46
MITCHUM, Robert, 124
MONRO, Matt, 120, 180
MORECAMBE, Eric, 189
MORGAN, Tommy, 28, 29
MORRIS, Ken, 91
MORTON FRASER Harmonica Gang (The), 47
MUNRO, Alex, 116
MURPHY, Frank, 30, 210
MYSKOW, Nina, 188
NEWSOME, Sam, 187
NIXON, David, 152
NOLAN SISTERS (The), 27
O'CONNOR, Des, 120
O'CONNOR, Donald, 53
O'TOOLE, Peter, 127
OSMONDS (The), 147
PADLEY, John, 62
PAGE, Patti, 73
PARAMOR, Norrie, 36, 40, 89, 90, 210
PARNELL, Val, 38
PLATT, Ken, 47, 152
PLATTERS (The), 212
POLLOCK, Tina, 15
POWELL, Sandy, 185
PRINCE, Bill, 99

PURCHES, Danny, 43
QUEEN ELIZABETH, 39, 211
QUINN, Anthony, 127
RAE, Lynnette, 8, 72
RAY, Johnnie, 211
REGAN, Joan, 5, 6, 32, 37, 186,
RICHARD, Sir Cliff, 212
RIMMER, Shane, 44
ROACH, Hal, 82
ROBERTS, Paddy, 34
ROBINSON, Edward G., 113
ROGERS, Ted, 110, 112, 117
ROPER, George, 185
ROSA, Lita, 35, 185, 211
ROY, Derek, 107
RYAN, Peggy, 53
SANDERS, Geoff, i, 80, 83, 96, 102
SAVAGE, Joan, 91
SECOMBE, Sir Harry, 91
SHADOWS (The), 130, 208
SHAUN, Dev, 143
SHAW, Chris, 148
SHELTON, Anne, 185, 211
SHERIFF, Dave, 184
SINATRA, Frank, 40, 57, 213
SKUES, Keith, 124
SMITH, Ian, 148, 210, 212
SOLOMON, Mervyn & Philip, 209
SQUIRES, Dorothy, 41, 208
STARR, Freddie, 145
STARR, Kay, 211
STEEL, Tommy, 119
STENNETT, Stan, 74
STEVENS, Lee, 179
TAYLOR, Maurice, 48-51
THOMPSON, Renee & Wally, 59, 60, 61, 62, 63, 66
THREE DEUCES (The), 44
TORME, Mel, 2, 53
TORNADOS (The), 143
VALENTINE, Dickie, 211
VAUGHAN, Frankie, 41
VERNON GIRLS (The), 47, 223
WALL, Max, 155
WARRIS, Ben, 72
WEARMOUTH, Don, 223
WHEELER, Jimmy, 7, 53
WHITFIELD, David, 145, 204, 211
WILDE, Marty, 68
WILLIAMS, Llewellyn, 115
WISDOM, Norman, 38, 210, 213, 217, 224
WORTH, Harry, 89, 105
YOUNG, Jimmy, 211

To order further copies of this book
Ruby—My Precious Gem!

Please send a cheque,
made out to:

FRANK BOWLES:
Los Limones 12
Urb. El Faro
Mijas-Costa 29649
(Malaga)
SPAIN

PRICE:
UK & Ireland: £13.45
Spain: €20.00
Rest of Europe: €25.00

Printed in the United Kingdom
by Lightning Source UK Ltd.
115067UKS00001B/400-450